SERG
BULGAKOV

SERGII BULGAKOV

Towards a Russian Political Theology

Texts edited and introduced
by
ROWAN WILLIAMS

T&T CLARK
EDINBURGH

T&T CLARK LTD
59 GEORGE STREET
EDINBURGH EH2 2LQ
SCOTLAND

Copyright © T&T Clark Ltd, 1999

All rights reserved. No part of this publication may be reproduced, stored in a retrieval system, or transmitted, in any form or by any means, electronic, mechanical, photocopying, recording or otherwise, without the prior permission of T&T Clark Ltd.

First published 1999

ISBN 0 567 08650 X HB
ISBN 0 567 08685 2 PB

British Library Cataloguing-in-Publication Data
A catalogue record for this book is available from the British Library

Typeset by Fakenham Photosetting Limited, Fakenham, Norfolk
Printed and bound in Great Britain by Bookcraft Ltd, Avon

Contents

Preface	vii
General Introduction	1
Sources for Texts in this Volume	21
1. 'The Economic Ideal' (1903)	23
2. 'Heroism and the Spiritual Struggle' (1909)	55
3. *The Unfading Light* (1917)	113
4. *The Lamb of God: On the Divine Humanity* (1933)	163
5. 'The Soul of Socialism' (1932–3)	229
6. *Social Teaching in Modern Russian Orthodox Theology* (1934) and 'The Spirit of Prophecy' (1939)	269
Appendix: Bulgakov and Anti-Semitism	293
Figures in Russian History or Literature Referred to by Bulgakov	304
Some Background Reading	306
Index	309

In loving memory of
Nicolas
and Militsa
Zernov

With the saints give rest, O Christ,
to the souls of your servants

Preface

Like many a labour of love, this collection of texts has been a long time in preparation, constantly pushed away from the desk by more urgent commissions. It is now over ten years since the idea of a critical anthology of extracts from Bulgakov was first discussed with a publisher. During that decade, the level of scholarly interest in Russian religious thought has risen in an extraordinary way, and the publication of primary texts, biographical studies and learned monographs increases weekly. I hope that this volume may at least contribute to the deepening of interest among those unfamiliar with Russian, or with the general cultural and religious tradition from which Bulgakov draws. He deserves fuller and closer attention than he has on the whole received in the past half-century or so.

During his lifetime (he died in 1944), those who were aware of him were also, for the most part, dimly aware of his standing among Russian intellectuals. A promising Marxist academic who abandoned 'scientific socialism' for a kind of Christian political radicalism in the dying days of the Russian Empire, a hyperactive editor of and contributor to journals, ordained priest as the old Russia was finally being dismantled; persecuted and exiled, creating a new life as teacher and spiritual director in Paris, at the heart of the Russian émigré community – it would be hard to overlook or to patronise such a man. But the inaccessibility of so much of his major work and the unfamiliarity of his idiom meant that he was increasingly relegated to slightly puzzled footnotes; and the climate of Russian Orthodox theology in the next generation was not sympathetic to his more speculative vein.

This book attempts an introduction to his life and thought, in the hope of stimulating further and better research and of inspiring exploration of his ideas. He was a vastly prolific

Preface

author, and I have found it impossible to provide in one volume anything like a comprehensive selection from the whole course of his career. An earlier anthology solved the problem by rationing very severely the length of the extracts reproduced and generally avoiding the longer works. This has its uses, but fails to give much sense of how Bulgakov manages a sustained argument. I have preferred to make use of longer extracts, but have restricted myself to earlier works, mostly before 1930, with the aim of building up a picture of how Bulgakov's religious worldview gradually took shape. The details of how this was worked out in his doctrine of Christ, the Spirit and the Church would provide material for at least a further volume. Each extract has been provided with a full introduction to set it in the context of Bulgakov's intellectual and spiritual evolution. I can claim little originality here, but have tried to bring together material that is otherwise scattered and difficult to find: a surprising number of those who have written about Bulgakov seem to have done so in relative ignorance of each other, and I have often found that the narrative of one discussion needs supplementing, sometimes in quite important particulars, from another apparently unknown to the first. There are gaps in all the published records known to me – notably in the details of Bulgakov's career between 1912 and 1917 – which I have not attempted to fill. The work of those who have quarried unpublished archives suggests that there is actually little evidence as yet identified. In short, an adequate and comprehensive intellectual biography remains to be written; this is not it, but may perhaps in certain respects ease the path of whoever undertakes it.

The bulk of the material included in the extracts has not appeared in English. A brief portion of text 1 was included in the earlier anthology mentioned above (some five pages of English). Two English versions of text 2 have appeared, and I have compared my translation with them and occasionally corrected it – though there are other places where I should want to retain and defend my own rendering. Text 3 has never appeared in any form in English. For text 4, I have made extensive use of the French translation, correcting it on occasions from the Russian original. Text 5 is a translation made from the German version, the original Russian being

Preface

unavailable to me at the time. Texts 6 and 7 were originally published in English. Transliteration of Russian follows the British Library conventions for the most part, but there is no way of standardising the transliteration of names without seeming artificial. I have used what I think are the spellings in commonest use, although this entails a few glaring inconsistencies (as with 'Soloviev' and 'Fyodorov'). A brief who's who of Russian names mentioned by Bulgakov that may be unfamiliar to foreign readers is included in the volume. On the whole I have not included Bulgakov's footnotes to the texts translated: they are mostly to do with technicalities or allusions to contemporary discussions that would themselves need further annotation.

My first real introduction to Bulgakov came from the late Nicolas Zernov, in a talk given in Cambridge in 1970. To me as to generations of British enthusiasts for the Russian Christian world, Nicolas was an unfailingly generous friend, a source of advice and information of a unique kind. Even more importantly, he and his wife Militsa were able to testify to Bulgakov's stature as pastor and spiritual director; through them, I came to feel that I knew him a little as a human being and gained some sense of the extraordinary personal impact he made on younger intellectuals of the emigration. There could be no hesitation in dedicating this book to the memory of Nicolas and Militsa, with prayer and gratitude. Others who have assisted include Dr E. R. Moberly, who passed on to me copies of Bulgakov's works signed by the author and originally presented to family friends; Dr Philip Walters, with whom I enjoyed conversations about Bulgakov many years ago, when we were both writing doctoral theses on the Russian religious renaissance, at a time when no one else seemed to be interested; Dr Katya Andreyev, who helped me untangle some of Bulgakov's more convoluted pieces of Russian prose; and those who are bringing Bulgakov's legacy to life in Russia today, especially Aleksei Chernyakov and Arkady Shufrin. My wife and family have been patient and encouraging as always, though even their patience has been outstripped by that of Stratford Caldecott at T&T Clark, who initially encouraged the preparation of this book and has waited a long time for it. May it mark the beginning of a fresh appropriation of Bulgakov's

Preface

remarkable heritage among Christians and others – in the English-speaking world.

Newport,
Feast of All Saints, 1997

General Introduction

Russia at the end of the twentieth century is a baffling and in many ways troubling spectacle: the collapse of communism has left not only a vacuum in public vision and ideology but a very visible and tangible breakdown in social order and the provision of social goods. The government struggles for moral credibility and stability, and claims from the old left and the new right to provide a more plausible style of leadership are heard more and more loudly; while the Orthodox Church is finding (at best) very limited success in coming to terms with a new situation in which there is enormous interest in faith and spirituality, and great receptivity to the Christian contribution to education and public welfare. The ecclesiastical leadership, formed largely during the years of repression, has found it hard to respond to challenges and opportunities for which nothing in the old regime could have prepared it. Yet there are signs of extraordinary intellectual and spiritual vitality in Russian Christianity, and friends of the Russian Church in other places can only pray that this vitality will outweigh the forces of reaction and defensiveness in the long term.[1]

Friends of the Russian Church may well have been praying similar prayers a hundred years ago; and the social and political situation in Russia was at least as troubling and baffling. The moral credibility and practical stability of the Russian state apparatus were fragile, even though they were reinforced by a

---

[1] The polarisation in Russian Christianity is represented by the resurgence of old-style Russian anti-Semitism in some Orthodox circles on the one hand (see the articles on this in *Religion, State and Society* (the journal of Keston College, 20:1 (1992)), and the work of the St Petersburg School of Religion and Philosophy on the other (see, for example, their publication *Patrologiya, filosofiya, germenevtika* (*Patrology, Philosophy, Hermeneutics*, St Petersburg 1992). Recent (autumn 1997) controversy over legislation in Russia against religious minorities has aroused much anxiety inside and outside Russia.

good deal of savagery in the courts and an oppressive system of surveillance. Anti-Semitism was widespread and violent – then, as now, an index of social panic. The Church was governed by a clumsy and unedifying bureaucracy, controlled ultimately by a lay civil servant (who happened to be, at this period, a formidable conservative ideologue[2]); its educational institutions left much to be desired and its episcopal leadership was for the most part uninspiring. Yet the end of the nineteenth and the beginning of the twentieth century saw an unprecedented growth in the liveliness and creativity of religious thought in the Russian Empire, moving in tandem with the development of the variegated cultural renaissance usually described as the 'Silver Age' of the Russian arts.[3] The material presented and discussed in the following pages has its roots in this renaissance; and if it has anything to say to Russia and indeed to Europe in our own day, this will have a good deal to do with the shared background of puzzles over political legitimacy and turbulent cultural experimentation – in which there is a growing suspicion that a Christian and theological perspective might not be so much of an irrelevance as was formerly assumed.

Sergei[4] Nikolaevich Bulgakov was, as the most recent and valuable study of his early career[5] makes abundantly plain, a significant figure of the Silver Age, and many, then and later, saw his mental and spiritual evolution as paradigmatic of a whole generation – even though few followed his exact path. It is certainly striking when Russians today speak, as a good many do, of finding Bulgakov's story a foreshadowing of their

---

[2] Konstantin Pobedonostsev (1827–1907), notoriously an opponent of any constitutional reform. He held the crucially important office of Procurator of the Holy Synod (i.e. the effective overseer of the ruling committee of bishops) for twenty-five years. It should be noted, though, that he supported various intra-ecclesial attempts to improve the education and performance of the clergy.

[3] There is a general survey in John Bowlt, *The Silver Age: Russian Art of the Early Twentieth Century and the 'World of Art' Groups* (Newtonville, Mass., 1979). In relation to Bulgakov, see now Catherine Evtuhov, *The Cross and the Sickle: Sergei Bulgakov and the Fate of Russian Religious Philosophy* (Ithaca, NY and London, 1997), pp. 1–17.

[4] Baptised Sergei, he followed the normal Russian custom of adopting the more archaic spelling (Sergii) on his ordination (similarly 'Ivan' would become 'Ioann', and so on).

[5] Evtuhov, *The Cross and the Sickle*.

own intellectual journeyings.[6] Initially, of course, he was typical of the large numbers of educated young Russians who turned away from Orthodox Christianity in the later nineteenth century. He came from a priestly family (the 'levitical' succession went back to the sixteenth century; the ultimate origins of the line were traced through a medieval Tatar convert who entered the service of the Muscovite princes[7]), which he describes vividly in the autobiographical notes he wrote in the late thirties. It is not a happy picture: his father, Nikolai had been a good seminary student, but his intelligence found little outlet except in crude and unsympathetic sarcasm;[8] his mother appears an obsessional character, uniting weakness of character with domestic despotism.[9] Nikolai Bulgakov was chaplain to the cemetery in Livny, an undistinguished provincial town in south-central Russia (rather more than halfway between Moscow and Kharkov, in the Orel administrative district which Sergei was briefly to represent in the Second Duma in 1907); the family was not desperately poor, but there was little that could be counted as luxury in the household and nothing of a cultural life. The family's economic security cannot have been helped by Nikolai's problems with alcohol and his wife's irresponsibility with money.[10] The overall impression is of dour anxiety, and, although Sergei was later to dedicate a major theological work to the memory of his

---

[6] Apart from personal conversations with young Russians in the late eighties, I might take in evidence the interest shown in Bulgakov by the leading figures of the St Petersburg School of Religion and Philosophy; see A. M. Choufrine, 'Sergei Bulgakov: His Life and His Reflections on it: A Case Study for the Churching of the Russian Intelligentsia', in Natalia A. Pecherskaya (ed.), *The Emancipation of Russian Christianity* (Lampeter, 1995), pp. 1–16.
[7] Bulgakov's *Avtobiograficheskiya zametki* (*Autobiographical Fragments*), posthumously edited by Lev Zander (Paris, 1946), refers (pp. 18–19) to the family background, attributing to 'Tatar blood' a family tendency to sullenness. Makarii Bulgakov, author of a widely used nineteenth-century theological textbook, and a senior ecclesiastic of his day, was a relative, though not a close one. The family connection with the novelist Mikhail Bulgakov is obscure, though it is intriguing to see themes in Mikhail's work reflecting certain theological ideas (about language and about the weakness of Christ incarnate) discernible in Sergii.
[8] *Avtobiograficheskiya zametki*, pp. 18–19.
[9] Ibid., pp. 17, 19–20.
[10] Ibid., pp. 17, 19.

parents,[11] there is not much to suggest that he recognised any great spiritual debt to them.

Yet, as he insists in his autobiography,[12] the churchly atmosphere of his upbringing never really left him, even though he became an atheist as a teenager. He had entered the seminary at Orel in 1885, but left three years later to transfer to a secular high school; the Orthodox faith had ceased to make sense to him. In a telling phrase, he speaks of the poetry of childhood being displaced by the prose of the seminary;[13] and the religious apologetic of the seminary seemed lame and vacuous in the face of the critical questions that were beginning to arise in his mind. The ex-seminarist who has lost his faith is something of a cliché in nineteenth-century literature,[14] and this fact illustrates something of the meagreness of the intellectual and spiritual diet provided in seminary education at a period of enormous upheaval in the world of ideas. Bulgakov is certainly a prototypical Russian *intelligent* in this disaffection from the seminary, and the theology he later discovered and made his own owed nothing to the textbook divinity of these early teenage years. Yet the 'poetry' of the Church haunted him, and he says that faith never completely died in his heart: his conversion to atheism evidently left something of his emotions and imagination untouched.[15]

This conversion brought with it – as for so many of his contemporaries – the immediate espousal of a social and political programme, a commitment to revolutionary reconstruction in Russian society. During his studies at Moscow University (1890–4), he specialised in economics and law, in the hope of contributing to the reform of Russia, and nailed his colours firmly to the Marxist mast (he published in 1895 a review of the third volume of *Das Kapital*[16]). His graduate work, however, was leading him in potentially contradictory directions. While he defended an uncompromising determinism

---

[11] *Svet nevechernii* (1917) is dedicated to the memory of Archpriest Nikolai Vasilievich Bulgakov and Aleksandra Kosminichna, née Azbukina.
[12] *Avtobiograficheskiya zametki*, p. 25.
[13] Ibid., p. 26.
[14] Dostoevsky provides a classic example in the figure of Rakitin in *The Brothers Karamazov*.
[15] *Avtobiograficheskiya zametki*, p. 26.
[16] In *Russkaia mysl'* (*Russian Thought*), (1895), pp. 1–20.

in human history, prescribed by economic laws as unified and inflexible as the laws of nature,[17] his more narrowly conceived writing on economics was already suggesting lines other than strictly Marxist ones: the inflexible laws appeared not to apply all that inflexibly to the Russian situation. When he finally completed what was to have been his doctoral dissertation, on capitalism and agriculture, in 1900, he must have known that he had moved quite decisively away from Marxist orthodoxy.[18] The 1890s had been marked by intense debate among Russian radicals and others as to how the future of Russian agrarian policy should evolve; land reform was a major issue for many beyond the strict Marxist camp, and the terrible famine of 1891 had given the whole issue of agrarian reform some urgency.[19] Reformists on the left, and some conservative populists as well, looked to the peasant commune, suitably reformed and organised, as the basis for some kind of agrarian democracy. But Lenin and Plekhanov insisted on the absolutely orthodox Marxist view that capitalist patterns of ownership were bound to develop in agricultural life, so that there would be a growing polarisation between the landowner and the landless worker, analogous to the industrial situation of the labourer 'selling' his productive power to the controllers of industrial capital.[20] The peasant proprietor would soon be an historical memory, and the commune of peasant farmers owning their own land was a useless anachronism. Plekhanov in particular ruled out any constructive political involvement on the part of peasant proprietors.[21] Yet the facts of economic life in rural Russia were not so straightforward. When Bulgakov turned his attention to this issue, he must have known that he was sailing into turbulent

[17] See the article 'O zakonomernosti sotsial'nykh yavlenii' ('On the Law-governed Character of Social Phenomena'), *Voprosy filosofii i psikhologii* (*Questions of Philosophy and Psychology*), 35 (1896), pp. 575–611, reprinted in the collection *Ot marksizma k idealizmu* (*From Marxism to Idealism*, St Petersburg, 1903).
[18] Evtuhov, *The Cross and the Sickle*, pp. 33–7, gives an excellent summary of the dissertation and its background.
[19] On the general context, see Donald Treadgold, *Lenin and His Rivals. The Struggle for Russia's Future, 1898–1906* (London, 1955), pp. 8–12, 42–6; this book provides what is still an authoritative overview of the different approaches to the agrarian problem in Russia at the turn of the century.
[20] Ibid., pp. 44–5.
[21] Ibid., pp. 45, 47–51, detailing the increasingly vitriolic attacks on the political capacity of peasant proprietors.

waters; and indeed, his conclusions were in effect that Lenin and Plekhanov were dramatically wrong in their analysis and prediction – though it is Marx, not his Russian disciples, who is the target of Bulgakov's direct polemic. The thesis embodied very extensive research on the agrarian situation in Western Europe and the United States, as well as detailed discussion of the Russian situation and of the theoretical structures being used to interpret it. In the course of this research, Bulgakov had travelled widely in Europe, meeting prominent socialist thinkers and activists in Germany and Austria; his encounters with English theory and practice represented the beginning of a long-lasting fascination with British politics and culture – including, in due course, British theology.[22]

But, although the thesis secured academic employment for him, it did not win him a doctorate, nor was it regarded as a very satisfactory work, failing, as it did, to present any coherent proposals as an alternative to the Marxist–Leninist models and prescriptions. Its importance is not in being a decisive or effective intervention in the agrarian debate, but in its sharpening-up of the tensions in Bulgakov's intellectual position. The years following its publication saw the rapid unravelling of his Marxist commitments and his return to a recognisably religious, though not at first strictly Orthodox, perspective on cultural, ethical and social questions. This development is detailed further in the introductions to the first and second texts in this book. But it is worth noting the rapidity with which Bulgakov became involved also with prominent radicals and with the public debate over Russia's political future. While it is in one sense correct to say that Bulgakov 'was not a political person', he was involved very closely with serious political figures like Struve; and in 1903 he was among those who established the broad-based 'Union of Liberation', a coalition of non-revolutionary reformists.[23] *Osvobozhdenie* (*Liberation*),

---

[22] He was intrigued by Carlyle and Ruskin; later on, he read works of British biblical scholarship such as Sanday and Headlam's commentary on the Epistle to the Romans.
[23] Treadgold, *Lenin and His Rivals*, pp. 117–19; Evtuhov, *The Cross and the Sickle*, ch. 5. Rather suprisingly, there is no mention of the Union in Christopher Read's *Religion, Revolution and the Russian Intelligentsia, 1900–1912* (London, 1979).

the journal of this group, published in 1905 the manifesto of the 'Christian Brotherhood of Struggle' (see below, pp. 56–7), in which Bulgakov was heavily involved, and he was instrumental in shaping the agrarian policy which the Union of Liberation favoured.[24] The movement provided the ground upon which the 'Kadet' (Constitutional Democratic) party was eventually established as a left–liberal grouping; initially, Bulgakov supported the Kadets, but his own views were taking him further and further from the original Liberationist coalition, and the general secularism of the Kadet left prompted a new departure, with Bulgakov's attempts to establish a Christian Socialist group in 1906 and 1907.

His disillusion with political activism of a straightforward kind was acute by the end of 1907, after his brief period as a deputy in the representative assembly, the Second Duma, of 1907 (see below, pp. 58–60). But this did not signal an abandonment of reflection on socio-political issues, as the following pages will make clear. Bulgakov was apolitical in the sense that he had little sense of political strategy and little taste, energy or gift for the bread-and-butter business of planning and negotiating. Yet the direction of his thought could well be read as a systematic attempt to work out the basis on which political action and policy could be seen as philosophically – and, eventually, theologically – legitimate. It is worth noting too that in the first decade of the century he seems to have spent more time on issues that could properly be called political than on wider cultural matters, despite his intense interest in the latter.[25] While he is quite rightly considered in relation to the other major intellectual figures of the 'Silver Age', it is not at all clear how much he was really in step with the turbulent movements around him in the world of aesthetics (and in this he stands somewhat in contrast to his friend and mentor Florensky[26]).

[24] Evtuhov, *The Cross and the Sickle*, p. 93; as might be expected from Bulgakov's dissertation, he favours a controlled redistribution of land, breaking down enormous concentrations of property in favour of the peasant proprietor.
[25] As evidenced in the essays he published on Dostoevsky, Tolstoy and Soloviev in the first decade of the century.
[26] On Florensky, see below, pp. 56–7, 113, 117–20; his major theological work, *Stolp i utverzhdenie istiny* (*The Pillar and Ground of Truth*, Moscow, 1914), shows in its literary style a good deal of Symbolist influence, and its colossal load of annotations and appendices make it clear that he is engaging with contemporary

When he does write about aesthetic subjects, he is often fairly conservative in his taste.[27] One area where Silver Age speculations may have left their mark, however, is in his thinking about language, as revealed in his involvement in a little-known controversy early in the second decade of the century, when he was already beginning his work in religious philosophy. The controversy, which was quite sharp at the time, was provoked by certain ideas current in the Russian monasteries of Mount Athos; it provides important evidence for Bulgakov's familiarity with the Byzantine theological tradition, but also suggests that he was attempting to make theological and philosophical use of some of the concepts current in the aesthetics of the Silver Age writers, and particularly the Symbolists.[28]

The details of the controversy are not directly relevant; it is enough to note that the monastic teaching in question consciously based itself upon the teachings of the great fourteenth-century theologian and mystic Gregory Palamas (a figure somewhat overlooked in Orthodox theology between the sixteenth and the twentieth centuries[29]), in claiming that the invocation of the name of Jesus in prayer effected the presence of the divine Person, since the active reality of the Person subsists in the name. The first full statement of this came from a Russian monk, Ilarion, in 1907 (his book was several times reprinted in

---

aesthetics very directly. On his aesthetic theory, see Victor Bychkov, *The Aesthetic Face of Being. Art in the Theology of Pavel Florensky* (Crestwood, NY, 1993).

[27] His favoured literary sources are unmistakably 'classical' in Russian terms, and he seems to have had little sympathy for new movements in the visual arts, judging from remarks in *Svet nevechernii* and in his 1915 essay on Picasso (below, p. 129).

[28] On the controversy, see Evtuhov, *The Cross and the Sickle*, ch. 11 – a very good survey, though occasionally shaky on theological detail. A fuller account of the course of the dispute, with some important primary documentation in Greek, is the work of Constantine Papoulides, *Oi Rōsoi onomatolatriai tou Agiou Orous* (*The Russian Name-worshippers of the Holy Mountain*, Thessaloniki, 1977).

[29] The basic introductory study of Palamas remains John Meyendorff, *A Study of Gregory Palamas* (London, 1964). On the appropriation of Palamas between the Middle Ages and the twentieth century, there is an excellent overview in Reinhard Flogaus, *Theosis bei Palamas und Luther: Ein Beitrag zum ökumenischen Gespräch* (Göttingen, 1997); pp. 54–67. pp. 66–7 deal briefly with the Athonite controversy.

GENERAL INTRODUCTION

the years immediately following);[30] and the initial reception from the Russian hierarchy was cautiously positive.[31] Criticism of the 'name-worshippers'[32] in the Athonite houses and beyond, however, prompted another monk, Antonii (Bulatovich), to publish a more extreme statement of Ilarion's position in 1913.[33] The controversy reached such a pitch of violence that no fewer than 833 Russian monks were forcibly removed from Mount Athos by the Russian Navy in 1913. The Synod of the Russian Church condemned the 'name-worshippers', and a bitter controversy developed in the pages of various Russian theological reviews, a controversy still alive in 1917 at the time of the abortive Council which intended to reform the Russian Church.

The debate within Russia engaged some of the foremost figures of the Church. The 'name-worshippers' were attacked with characteristic ferocity by the formidable conservative theologian Antonii Khrapovitsky, at that time Archbishop of Volhynia and later to become Metropolitan of Kiev,[34] and by S. V. Troitsky, a senior seminary academic.[35] But they were defended by a curious mixture of left and right: Florensky, already celebrated as an innovative and somewhat controversial theologian, with a history of sympathy towards reformist politics, wrote a foreword to Bulatovich's book; Evgenii Trubetskoi, another thinker clearly identified with reformist views,

---

[30] Skhimonakh Ilarion, *Na gorakh Kavkaza* (*In the Mountains of the Caucasus*, Batalpashinsk, 1907); Ilarion had been a monk on Athos and had become a hermit in the Caucasus.
[31] A statement in May 1913 from the Synod declared that Ilarion's book was spiritually helpful.
[32] In Russian, *Imyaslavtsy*, literally 'glorifiers of the Name'.
[33] *Apologiya very vo Imya Bozhie i vo Imya Iisus* (*An Apologia for Belief in the Name of God and the Name of Jesus*, Moscow, 1913); much the same material is in *I doxa tou Theou einai o Iēsous* (*The Glory of God is Jesus*, Thessaloniki, 1913), reprinted in its entirety in Papoulides, *Oi Rōsoi onomatolatríai*.
[34] He was later to become the head of the Synod of Russian Bishops outside Russia after the Revolution, a resolutely traditionalist, anti-ecumenical group which continued to resist any suggestion of rapprochement with the Patriarchate of Moscow.
[35] Author of several articles debating the patristic foundations for the Athonite claims, and two books on the controversy.

wrote a supportive article;[36] but the cause was also defended by appealing to the memory of Ioann Sergiev, 'Father Ioann of Kronstadt', who had died in 1908.[37] Sergiev (who is now a canonised saint of the Russian Orthodox Church) had been a powerful spiritual influence for many years, with a widespread reputation as a healer and wonder-worker; but he was also a man of forthright conservative opinions on national matters. His support for Ilarion, and his general sympathy towards the Palamite tradition, certainly gave a weight to the Athonite theology that it might otherwise have lacked in the eyes of the devout and unacademic Orthodox public. Thus, while it is broadly true that the supporters of the 'name-worshippers' tended to represent more radical trends in the Russian Church, this cannot be read as a simple case of liberal or democratic ideals being opposed to hierarchical tyranny.[38] It is more that Sergiev and Florensky alike objected to the (paradoxically) modernising, subjectivising flavour of the theology of the seminaries (as they interpreted it) and of theologians such as Khrapovitsky. By stressing (in seminary theology) the importance of individual obedience to official decrees on matters of faith, or (in the case of Khrapovitsky) the moral importance of doctrinal orthodoxy,[39] the opponents of the cult of the divine Name showed themselves at odds with the authentic

---

[36] Florensky also published a substantial article, 'Imyaslavie kak filosofskaya predposylka' ('Name-worship as a Philosophical Premise') in a collection entitled *Materialy k sporu o pochitanii Imeni Bozhiya* (*Materials on the Controversy over the Veneration of the Name of God*, Moscow, 1913); see Bychkov, *The Aesthetic Face of Being*, p. 70. Trubetskoi's article, 'Svet Favorskii i preobrazhenie uma' ('The Light of Tabor and the Transfiguration of the Mind'), appeared in *Russkaya mysl'* in 1914.

[37] Born 1829; Ioann was unsparingly critical of attempts such as were being made by the churchmen involved in the philosophical discussion groups in Petersburg and elsewhere (see below, p. 56) to find common ground with new cultural and political movements. His spiritual autobiography, *My Life in Christ* (an abbreviated English version was published in London in 1897), became something of a popular classic.

[38] Evtuhov's otherwise admirable discussion perhaps slightly oversimplifies the 'democratic' implications of Imyaslavtsy doctrine.

[39] Khrapovitsky had published a number of monographs on the moral implications of various dogmas, as well as a major work on the freedom of the will, much influenced by Schopenhauer. His concern to display the moral dimension of dogma owes something to the perceived need to respond to the challenge of Tolstoy's critique of the Orthodox Church.

participatory and – to be guilty of an anachronism – communitarian spirituality of Byzantine and Russian, especially monastic, tradition.

It is no surprise to find Bulgakov among the defenders of the cult of the Name. He published what was for him a relatively brief article on the subject in late 1913;[40] in the years following, he continued to reflect on the questions raised. He was elected to the Council of the Russian Church that was to meet in 1917, and was nominated to the commission examining outstanding doctrinal disputes – partly, no doubt, because his essay of 1913 had defended the idea of councils representing the whole Christian community (not just bishops and clergy) as the most authentically Orthodox way of settling controversy. His own thoughts on the subject, however, were not fully elaborated in print until the publication after his death of a book on *The Philosophy of the Name* (*Filosofiya Imeni*).[41] Some of the themes had been sketched in an article in German in 1930, whose subject-matter is identical with the first chapter of the longer work.[42] It is clear that Bulgakov worked on and redrafted the material throughout his career as a theologian in exile.

Bulgakov's theology of words and names represents an intriguing and generally neglected aspect of his work. He puts forward a definition of the name as a designation of concrete or active presence, the bringing together of the abstract or ideal with the world of relations. A name is therefore never a mere label: it belongs in a relation in which some subject other than the speaker is active. Thus the name is in some sense a 'given', at least in so far as the relation in which the name arises is not simply something devised or controlled by the speaker.[43] The application to the naming of God, and to the Athonite controversy, is easy to see. To name God is to acknowledge a relation established by the active presence of God; just as the Athonite defenders of Palamas had argued, the name is a carrier of the *energeia*, the active presence of God, and is thus the

[40] 'Afonskoe delo' ('The Athos Affair'), *Russkaya mysli'* (1913), pp. 37–46.
[41] Ed. Lev Zander (Paris, 1953).
[42] 'Was ist das Wort?', *Festchrift Th. G. Masaryk zum 80 Geburtstage* (Bonn, 1930), pp. 25–46.
[43] Evtuhov, *The Cross and the Sickle*, pp. 214–15, referring to *Filosofiya imeni*.

divine essence in action in a particular context.[44] The names of God are not magic words dropped from heaven, but neither are they convenient denotations in a human conceptual system. They are spoken only in the context of the communication of God's life, and their truthfulness is to do with the way in which they are effective media of that life.

The parallels with Russian Symbolism are obvious.[45] Here too is a revolt against the notion that words are 'attached' to things out there in an atomistic and external way. Language has to be liberated from its servitude to the 'practical', the functional, so as to recover its *sacred* quality: it must once again manifest realities that we do not habitually see, the intersections of the world with the eternal. It is difficult not to imagine that Bulgakov had at least some sense of the theories of language that were around in Symbolist circles (not least because in his work on the philosophy of the name, Bulgakov borrows directly from Vyacheslav Ivanov, a leading Symbolist thinker; they had collaborated briefly on the journal, *Voprosy zhizni, Questions of Life*, in 1904–5).[46] Yet even here, we should not overestimate the degree of common ground. The Symbolists were generally hostile to social reformism as a local and practical project, being more disposed towards a somewhat elitist anarchism.[47] Bulgakov's repeated and severe strictures against 'art for art's sake' in his work between 1905 and 1917 are evidently directed against the Symbolists among others; and the sense of a clearly moral and social dimension to the artistic enterprise, while this never reduces to a sort of ethical functionalism, presupposes that art works with a coherent metaphysics and, for Bulgakov, a metaphysic in which the hidden harmonies of the world find

---

[44] See, for example, the text of Bulatovich's Greek pamphlet reprinted in Papoulides, *Oi Rōsoi onomatolatrízi* esp. pp. 130–1.
[45] Evtuhov, *The Cross and the Sickle*, pp. 210, 213.
[46] Ivanov acknowledged the importance of Florensky's influence on Symbolist theories and on the general theory of signs; see Donald Nicholl, *Triumphs of the Spirit in Russia* (London, 1997), pp. 187ff. On Florensky's possible influence on Bakhtin, see K. Clark and M. Holquist, *Mikhail Bakhtin* (Cambridge, Mass., 1984), pp. 135ff.
[47] Read, *Religion, Revolution and the Russian Intelligentsia*, pp. 24–40. See also the useful article on Symbolism by Evelyn Bristol in the *Handbook of Russian Literature*, ed. V. Terras (New Haven, 1985), pp. 460–4, and the brilliant and comprehensive study by Avril Pyman, *A History of Russian Symbolism* (Cambridge, 1994).

definition and articulation only through the Christian doctrinal system. The beauty and order of the world, the cosmos as Sophia, Holy Wisdom, was a concept as central to many Symbolists as to Bulgakov; but his interest in Sophia is controlled both by an agenda bound in to the creative labour of common human life and (consequently) to the form of the revelation of God's beauty in Christ. Bulgakov is, in other words, more than a Silver Age aesthete. This rather lengthy digression on an obscure controversy finally serves to throw into sharper relief the way in which Bulgakov remains a distinctive thinker – too political for the Symbolists, too much a contemplative and a critic for the political radicals. Even when he does show signs of being marked by Symbolist concerns, the emphasis on direct divine initiative and the saving relations established by God's *energeiai* move us away from the self-referential realm of the sacred disclosed by Symbolist art.

The Athonite controversy also shows two things of importance in Bulgakov's evolution. By 1913, he was already remarkably well attuned to the Byzantine theological tradition, significantly more so than some of his professional theological contemporaries – a point worth bearing in mind when we come across critics who emphasise his primary indebtedness to the speculative traditions of Russian religious philosophy. Furthermore, he had quite rapidly gained a secure enough position as a lay intellectual to be entrusted with important work on the Church's behalf in the period leading up to the 1917 Council. As we shall see, his ordination in 1917 was the natural conclusion of a long process; it would have come a good deal earlier, he tells us, had it not been for his uncertainties about the Church's subservient role in a political system to which he never allowed himself to become reconciled. When he eventually took up the ancestral 'levitical' role, as he calls it, it was in a church unrecognisably different from the church in which his father had been ordained; and he was to live out that vocation in a church in exile, sharing the fate of that extraordinary assortment of non-Marxist intellectuals judged by Lenin to be a threat to the new Soviet state and banished in 1922.[48]

---

[48] A fate shared by Struve, Berdyaev and other former associates of Bulgakov; also by his wife. He had married Elena Tokmakova in 1898, and the marriage

Bulgakov

Bulgakov's life in exile will not be the primary focus of this book, though I have included some material on it (see below, pp. 163ff.). Again, however, it is worth observing *both* the widespread acknowledgement of his stature and authority, within and beyond the Orthodox Church, *and* the relative lack of constructive engagement with his thought on the part of his peers. Just as in Russia he had been awkwardly positioned between two or more polemical camps, so in the world of the Russian diaspora he drifted away from the philosophical interests of Berdyaev and Frank, his old friends and collaborators, while being too far compromised with what was seen as an outworn metaphysical tradition by younger theologians like Florovsky and Lossky[49] – though Lossky continued to discuss his work seriously in unpublished lectures in the last years of his life.[50] Outside the frontiers of Russian Orthodoxy, it took a good deal of time for theologians to appreciate his significance. His earlier work remained mostly untranslated, and even when French versions of his later and magisterial dogmatic essays began to appear, their idiom was eccentric enough to deter the majority of possible commentators.[51] As we shall see (p. 172, n. 32), there were very notable exceptions – Hans Urs von Balthasar in the Roman Catholic world and Donald MacKinnon among Anglicans (thanks to the latter, Bulgakov's great work on the incarnation appeared – under its French title – on the reading list for graduate courses in dogmatic theology at Cambridge from the late sixties onwards). But the general level of discussion was low; such works as appeared in English were fairly brief and schematic, and, once again, written in an idiom

---

produced a daughter and two sons. The younger son died, aged 4, in 1909, an event that had a deep effect on Bulgakov's spiritual life; see his moving recollections of the little boy's requiem in *Svet nevechernii* pp. 12–14, and Evtuhov, *The Cross and the Sickle*, pp. 133–7. The elder son seems to have remained in the Soviet Union in 1922.

[49] See below, pp. 172–80.
[50] Lectures in November 1955 and February 1957 (transcripts in my possession by courtesy of Olivier Clément and A. M. Allchin) deal with the theme of kenosis in Bulgakov's work and with the relation of his theology to Palamism.
[51] The first volume of his major theological trilogy appeared in French in 1943, the second in 1946, both translated by Constantin Andronikof. Other works, including *Svet* and the third volume of the trilogy, had to wait until the eighties.

GENERAL INTRODUCTION

not best calculated to win serious attention from Anglican scholars.

Secondary literature on Bulgakov is thus still pretty slight. His friend Lev Zander published a summary of his system in 1948; but he would not have claimed that this was any kind of critical discussion.[52] Since then, there have been a few articles, including a particularly good study of Bulgakov's anthropology by A. Joos, published in 1972,[53] and, more recently, a couple of outstandingly helpful essays by Bernice Glatzer Rosenthal on the early Bulgakov.[54] Paul Vallière has published two studies presenting Bulgakov as representative of a 'liberal' move within Russian Orthodoxy in the pre-revolutionary period,[55] though I have some doubts as to whether a conservative–liberal typology along Western lines is at all a useful interpretative grid for reading Orthodox material. Bulgakov is emphatically a doctrinal 'traditionalist', in the sense that it would not occur to him for a moment, after his reconversion, to question the dogmatic determinations of the patristic age. There are also somewhat slighter but nonetheless significant pieces on Bulgakov's transition from Marxism to Orthodoxy by Jutta Scherer, the leading European expert on the religious study circles that flourished in Russia at the beginning of the century,[56] and by Arkady Shufrin (A. M. Choufrine),[57] a leading figure in the revival of Christian intellectual life in Russia in the late eighties and early nineties.

---

[52] Lev Zander, *Bog i mir* (*God and the World*), 2 vols. (Paris, 1948).
[53] 'L'homme et son mystère: éléments d'anthropologie dans l'oeuvre du P. Serge Boulgakov', *Irénikon*, 46 (1972), pp. 332–61.
[54] 'The Search for a Russian Orthodox Work Ethic', *Between Tsar and People*, ed. S. Kassow and E. Clowes (Princeton, 1991), pp. 57–74; 'The Nature and Function of Sophia in Sergei Bulgakov's Prerevolutionary Thought', *Russian Religious Thought*, ed. J. D. Kornblatt and R. F. Gustafson (Madison, Wisc., 1996), pp. 154–75.
[55] 'The Liberal Tradition in Russian Orthodox Theology', *The Legacy of St Vladimir*, ed. J. Breck and J. Meyendorff (Crestwood, NY, 1990), pp. 93–106; 'Sophiology as the Dialogue of Orthodoxy with Modern Civilization', Kornblatt and Gustafson (eds.), *Russian Religious Thought*, pp. 175–92.
[56] 'Du marxisme à l'idéalisme: une nouvelle lecture de Bulgakov', *Le christianisme russe entre millénarisme d'hier et soif spirituelle d'aujourd'hui*, *Cahiers du monde russe et soviétique* 29 (1988) – a special issue of CMRS to commemorate the millennium of Christianity in Russia – pp. 481–5.
[57] See above, n. 6.

15

The Appendix to this volume refers to some recent discussions of Bulgakov's attitude to Jews and Judaism.

Of longer studies there is a real shortage. Elie de Sèze wrote a Louvian licentiate thesis on Bulgakov's Christology in 1958,[58] and Philip Walters a doctorate at the London School of Economics in 1978 on the early Bulgakov.[59] Bastiaan Wielenga's immense work comparing the intellectual evolutions of Bulgakov and Lenin is an important study, deserving more notice[60] (it is another work to which Donald MacKinnon would regularly draw his students' attention). Charles Graves' Basle doctorate on Bulgakov's doctrine of the Holy Spirit is a thorough examination of the doctrinal system of Bulgakov's later work, but its critical interest is limited and much of its discussion rather naive.[61] Various aspects of Bulgakov's thought are discussed in books that deal more broadly with Russian religious or philosophical thought – Nadezhda Gorodetzky's beautiful study of the kenotic theme in Russian theology and literature,[62] Christopher Read's monograph on the different radical and religious circles of the first decade of the century,[63] and, of course, Nicolas Zernov's celebrated survey of the 'Russian religious renaissance'.[64] There are fleeting mentions in some standard works on the background to the 1917 Revolution.[65] But undoubtedly the best study to date is Catherine Evtuhov's 1997 book on Bulgakov's intellectual development up to 1917, a work that has made full use of archival material in

---

[58] *Fondements et conséquences philosophico-théologiques de l'union hypostatique d'après Serge Boulgakov* (unpublished).
[59] *The Development of the Political and Religious Philosophy of Sergii Bulgakov, 1895–1922*. The non-publication of this material is very regrettable; recent American discussion appears to know nothing of it.
[60] *Lenins Weg zur Revolution* (Munich, 1971).
[61] *The Holy Spirit in the Theology of Sergius Bulgakov* (privately printed at the World Council of Churches, Geneva, 1972).
[62] *The Humiliated Christ in Modern Russian Thought* (London, 1938); pp. 156–74 are on Bulgakov.
[63] See above, n. 23.
[64] *The Russian Religious Renaissance of the Twentieth Century* (London, 1963).
[65] As in Treadgold, *Lenin and His Rivals*, and Orlando Figes, *A People's Tragedy* (London, 1996).

Russia and elsewhere, and will be a benchmark for all future research in this field.[66] Most of Bulgakov's major works are now available in French translation, thanks to the labours over half a century of the late Constantin Andronikof;[67] some material is in German,[68] and a small selection in English (not including the longer works, especially the late doctrinal studies).[69] But it is unquestionably a good moment for further and deeper research. Not only have archival sources in Russia at last opened up more fully, and at least a fair representation of Bulgakov's chief works appeared in western-language versions; much more importantly, Bulgakov is a remarkably contemporary figure for the Western as well as the Russian intellectual scene. His is clearly a theology inextricably bound to a particular social vision; and his later work on the theology of the Christian community is marked by a careful

[66] This certainly lays the foundations for a full critical biography. But there have been other significant biographical essays, including Winston Crum, 'Sergius N. Bulgakov: From Marxism to Sophiology', *St Vladimir's Theological Quarterly*, 22 (1982), pp. 3–25, and Monakhina Yelena, 'Professor Protoierei Sergii Bulgakov', which occupies most of the 1987 issue of the Moscow theological journal *Bogoslovskie trudy* (Theological Studies); pp. 179–94 offer a very useful bibliography, though there is a slightly earlier bibliography by Kliment Naumov published by the Institut d'Etudes Slaves (Paris, 1984). These are not in fact absolutely complete, and the publication of further material since 1987 makes a fresh bibliography desirable. *Vestnik RSKhD* (*Messenger of the Russian SCM*), 170 (1994), and 174 (1997), has published extracts from Bulgakov's spiritual diary of the early twenties.
[67] See above, n. 51; the Lausanne publishing house L'Age d'Homme has included in its 'Sophia' series translations of practically all Bulgakov's longer books, as well as French versions of Florensky and Berdyaev.
[68] Portions of *Svet* appeared in *Östliches Christentum Dokumente*, ed. N. Bubnoff and Hans Ehrenberg (Munich, 1925), vol. 2, and an important essay, *Die Tragödie der Philosophie*, was published in Darmstadt in 1927; *Capita de trinitate* appeared in the *Internationale Kirchliche Zeitschrift*, 26 (1936) – a particularly useful summary of Bulgakov's trinitarian vision; and some chapters of *Filosofiya khozyaistva* were translated in the *Internationale Bibliothek für Philosophie: Periodische Sammelschrift*, 5 (1942), pp. 121–54. The collection *Sozialismus in Christentum*, incorporating some longer pieces by Bulgakov on socialism edited and translated by Hans Jürgen Ruppert, was published in Göttingen in 1977. There are also various shorter articles in German translation.
[69] Apart from short articles, and an early translation of the dialogues written in the immediate aftermath of the Revolution (see below, p. 164), the main works in English are *The Orthodox Church* (London, 1935; rev. trans. Crestwood, NY, 1988) and *The Wisdom of God: A Brief Summary of Sophiology* (London, 1937), reprinted as *Sophia, the Wisdom of God* (Hudson, NY, 1993).

17

and creative balance of the traditional and the 'charismatic' (in the broadest sense). The aphorism that 'everything is politics, but politics is not everything' encapsulates something of the vision of his early thought, especially in the transitional period when he was still finding his way back to formal Orthodoxy. His constant polemic against 'economism', the attempt to define economic goals independently of a comprehensive model of human desire and the assumption that all goals are ultimately and reductively economic, will find strong echoes in the wake of a period when the appeal to market forces as the decisive shaping power in public policy and education has left a legacy of trivialised and barbarised practice. But equally his challenges to a self-referential aestheticism, a 'post-moral' artistic idiom, will continue to pose unsettling questions to an environment obsessed with style or with the essentially abstract exploration of expressive possibilities – an environment in which what seems to matter is the artist's imposition of *will* on his or her material. Theologically, he offers some admittedly complex and none-too-accessible ways of reappropriating the classical theology of the incarnation; difficult as are his speculations in this area (though his contemporaries frequently misread what he was attempting), his version of patristic Christology has more intellectual depth and coherence than many more recent essays. And the increasingly dominant role in his thought of the governing model of kenosis, the divine self-emptying, in creation as well as incarnation, and indeed in the life of the Trinity itself, converges with some of the most searching theological work of recent years. He is not a typical representative of the Orthodox theological world; but, despite the caveats entered by many recent Orthodox theologians, he is the *kind* of theologian he is because of his Orthodox formation and commitment, and he demonstrates what is at present a vastly important fact – that theology in the Byzantine tradition is capable of engaging with modernity and post-modernity with unexpected vigour and integrity. Orthodox doubters of the precise doctrinal acceptability of his speculations about Sophia should also remember that he is one of those who – like Vladimir Lossky, his fierce critic and reluctant admirer, or Lossky's pupil Olivier Clément, or the Greeks Christos Yannaras and John Zizioulas – remind the Western theological world that Orthodox theology is not a

GENERAL INTRODUCTION

purely antiquarian pursuit, a matter of endless glossing of the Fathers, but offers some sharp critiques of Western culture as well as Western theology. As for Russia itself, Bulgakov's pertinence hardly needs emphasising: the younger generation of religious thinkers, not least those influenced by the great Alexander Men',[70] continue to find him a unique point of orientation, not least in *method*, in his willingness to allow a conversation to develop between Byzantine spirituality and the contemporary European intellect.

Research opportunities are manifold. More needs to be done on Bulgakov's use of the later Greek Fathers; on the degree to which his 'sophiology' is a transcription of Hegel, as he seems to imply at some points; on the relative importance of Hegel and Schelling to him; on the development of his thinking about the Church during the years when he was most involved in ecumenism; on his theories of language, particularly in relation to other Russian thinkers like Bakhtin and the enigmatic Losev[71] (who is currently attracting a good deal of interest); on his Mariology; and on many other subjects. But his contribution must be more than simply to provide thesis-fodder. His life and his thinking give us a sobering and challenging model for the engagement of the Christian intellectual in his or her times. If these texts provoke reflection on *that*, they will have served their purpose.

---

[70] See *Christianity for the Twenty-first Century: The Life and Work of Alexander Men*, ed. E. Roberts and A. Shukman (London, 1996).
[71] The closeness of Losev's *Filosofiya imeni* (*The Philosophy of the Name*, privately published, Moscow, 1927) to Bulgakov's speculations in this area is notable. Losev uses language manifestly resonant of the Palamite controversy, and his account of the symbolic echoes Florensky and Bulgakov.

Sources for Texts in this Volume

1. 'The Economic Ideal': 'Ob ekonomicheskom ideale', originally in *Nauchnoe slovo*, (1903), pp. 102–25; reprinted in *Ot marksizma k idealizmu* (*From Marxism to Idealism*, St Petersburg, 1903), pp. 263–87.
2. 'Heroism and the Spiritual Struggle': 'Geroizm i podvizhnichestvo', originally in *Vekhi: Sbornik statei o russkoi intelligentsii* (*Landmarks: A Collection of Essays on the Russian Intelligentsia*, Moscow, 1909); reprinted in *Dva grada* (*Two Cities*, Moscow, 1911), vol. 2, pp. 176–222.
3. *The Unfading Light*: passages from *Svet nevechernii: Sozertsaniya i umozreniya* (*The Unfading Light: Contemplations and Speculations*, Moscow, 1917).
4. *The Lamb of God: On the Divine Humanity*: passages from *Agnets Bozhii: O bogochelovechestve* (*The Lamb of God: On the Divine Humanity*, Paris, 1933).
5. 'The Soul of Socialism': 'Dusha sotsializma' ('The Soul of Socialism') *Novyi grad*, 1932: 1, pp. 49–58, 1932: 3, pp. 33–45, and 1933: 7, pp. 35–43; translation from the German version in *Sozialismus in Christentum?*, ed. and trans. Hans Jürgen Ruppert (Göttingen, 1977).
6. *Social Teaching in Modern Russian Orthodox Theology*: Published as a pamphlet by Seabury Western Theological Seminary (Chicago, 1934); also in *The Living Church*, 91 (1934), pp. 645–8.

'The Spirit of Prophecy': *Sobornost'*, n. s., 19 (1939), pp. 3–7.

I

'The Economic Ideal' (1903)

INTRODUCTION

In 1900, Bulgakov published what was to be his last major contribution to orthodox academic economics, a two-volume study of *Capitalism and Agriculture*[1] (it attracted a fair amount of attention for some years ahead; Rosa Luxembourg still thought it worth a critical discussion in 1913). A measure of scepticism about the Marxist synthesis was already apparent in this work: the applicability of strict Marxist analysis to agrarian problems was far from clear to Bulgakov, and the book signalled the beginnings of his apostasy from Marxism. It also helped to secure for him the chair of Political Economy at the Polytechnic of Kiev, which he was to hold for five years. This relatively brief period was formative for his political and philosophical evolution. The break with Marxism became decisive, though he continued, unlike some other ex-Marxists in his circle (such as Piotr Struve and Nikolai Berdyaev), to proclaim a commitment to socialism, and to speak, in a phrase echoing Soloviev, of the 'truth of socialism', *pravda sotsializma*.[2] But he also made clear, very early on in his time at Kiev, that he intended to 'revisit' the tradition of religious reflection in Russia: an open lecture on Dostoevsky in November 1901 attracted much enthusiasm, and Bulgakov became increasingly explicit about his religious commitment – though he had not as yet returned to the practice of the Orthodox faith.

[1] *Kapitalizm' i zemledelie*, 2 vols. (St Petersburg, 1900). He published a couple of shorter surveys of economic principles and theories, presumably digests of his regular lectures, in 1907 and 1913, but no further theoretical monographs – apart from the *Philosophy of Economic Activity* (*Filosofiya Khozyaistva*) in 1912, which is emphatically not an essay in orthodox economics.
[2] See Jutta Scherrer, 'Intelligentsia, réligion, révolution: premières manifestations d'un socialisme chrétien en Russie, 1905–7', pt. 1, CMRS, 17 (1976), pp. 427–66, p. 430.

The text that follows comes from this period, and is described in a note to the published version as an introductory lecture in a course entitled 'A Critical Introduction to Political Economy'. It must have occasioned some surprise among students expecting a survey of theories of production and distribution or a programmatic picture of the possibilities of economic development in Russia. It is essentially about what we might now call the ethics of development: what *human* goals are served by material economic development, and can questions of economic import be discussed without a systematic moral and philosophical foundation? These issues were to be addressed repeatedly in Bulgakov's essays over the next four or five years, and they form an important counterpoint to the evident concern in his writing at this time for the modernisation of the Russian economy.[3] In this respect, Bulgakov, on his own admission, remained faithful to his earlier Marxist agenda – as did others in what had been the Legal Marxist group.[4] While there is a quite strong commitment to industrialisation, Bulgakov's work also presses the question of how such progress is to be related to what we might call the goals of human sociality, without a sense of how material modernisation might serve personal liberty and mutual service in society.[5] It is striking that Bulgakov on occasion anticipates what has become a commonplace of more recent liberationist theologies, the recognition that spiritual maturation depends to a very significant extent on material security and emancipation: we shall see that in this lecture he speaks of freedom from poverty as 'the fundamental condition for the moral life', and assumes throughout that the capacity for human self-determination necessarily involves an element of being freed from a dependent and uncreative relation to the material environment. Here are some of the moral and political roots of his later theological work on the significance of human creativity; and it is worth noting also that, throughout his

---

[3] Cf. the introduction and several of the essays in the two volumes entitled *Dva grada* (*Two Cities*, Moscow, 1911); the piece on 'National Economy and Religious Personality' (*Narodnoe khozyaistvo i religioznaya lichnost'*) in the first volume (pp. 178–205) is particularly interesting in this connection.
[4] Jutta Scherrer, *Die Petersbürger Religiös-Philosopischen Vereinigungen* (Berlin, 1973), pp. 82–3.
[5] Cf. the conclusion of 'National Economy and Religious Personality', p. 205.

career, right up to the time of the composition of his most mature theological works, he is concerned to distinguish between Christian humility properly understood and the false humility of passivity or 'resignation'.[6]

In several respects, then, this is a revealing text, showing Bulgakov half-way to a fully explicit Orthodox Christian perspective, challenging an unthinking acceptance of the economic status quo – especially on the part of religious people – and already linking economic activity to an overarching vision of human creativity. This vision is not openly anchored in Christian theology – though we should note the critical discussion of what Bulgakov takes to be the Buddhist approach and his concern to deny an 'inaccurate' version of the teaching of the gospels that would effectively assimilate it to Buddhism (he may here have in mind some versions of Tolstoyan primitivism). He gives notice of his discontent with any economic discourse that abstracts from moral and social questions, and we find, in later essays, a consistent denunciation of the fiction that there is such a thing as *homo economicus*,[7] the economic agent isolated from all other considerations; this mythology, he believes, corrupts both Marxism and liberal capitalism. He would have agreed enthusiastically with a brilliant recent analysis of the failures of 'pure' market economics in terms of its naivety about human motivation, Will Hutton's *The State We're In*.[8] Hutton describes the 'first building block of free-market economics' as the idea that 'rational man is a trader weighing up all his options. The race to satiate those desires first is what gives economic life its vigour.'[9] Against this, he notes the indispensable role of securing mutual trust between economic agents and commitment in a workforce, which introduces the imperative for economic agents of 'caring for their reputation as

---

[6] See, for example, the comments on humility in his treatise on the Holy Spirit, *Uteshitel'* (Paris, 1936), p. 351 (*Le Paraclet*, Paris, 1946, p. 296): humility presented as a value in isolation is a covertly legalistic thing, which Christianity, properly understood, transcends.

[7] Cf. again 'National Economy and Religious Personality', as well as the celebrated piece, 'Karl Marx kak religioznyi tip', *Dva grada*, vol. 1, pp. 69–105; ET *Karl Marx as a Religious Type*, introd. Donald Treadgold (Belmont, Mass., 1979).

[8] London, 1995.

[9] Ibid., p. 248.

moral beings'.[10] As a matter of *economic* fact, there are, it seems, no purely economic processes of negotiation, no impersonal rationality in a market existing above and beyond the moral agents who operate its functions. An economic policy that assumes there are isolated economic imperatives which, in certain circumstances, override all other considerations is economically as well as morally empty. This is not far from Bulgakov's concerns in the text that follows.

A final note: some of this lecture uses as a sparring partner the work of the German economist Werner Sombart, in particular the second volume of his colossal three-volume study of modern capitalism.[11] Sombart was one of the most formidable scholars of economic history in Europe, and one of his significant contributions to the field was a demonstration of the importance in the development of capitalism of the growth during and after the eighteenth century of military demand and luxury demand, both requiring increasingly concentrated processes of production.[12] Bulgakov does not dispute the historical analysis; but he evidently reads Sombart as offering a putatively value-free picture of economic development, in which the ever-increasing scale of luxury demand guarantees economic growth. What draws Bulgakov's fire here is not so much a mythology of *homo economicus* as the spectre of an apolitical hedonism or aestheticism, the cultivation of sensibility without the development of moral imagination. In this respect, the critique of Sombart – perhaps rather unfair to a writer who does not set out to be a moralist – looks forward to the critique of aestheticism, art for art's sake, in later works, notably *The Unfading Light*.

---

[10] Ibid., p. 252.
[11] W. Sombart, *Der moderne Kapitalismus* (Leipzig, 1902).
[12] For a convenient summary, see F. L. Nussbaum, *A History of the Economic Institutions of Modern Europe: An Introduction to 'Der moderne Kapitalismus' of Werner Sombart* (New York, 1933), pp. 226–30.

The Economic Ideal

The development of scientific expertise is conditioned by two different kinds of necessity. Either it serves the interests of pure knowledge as an end in itself, or it is called forth by contingent human needs – and, as a result, though these may equally well be either material or ideal in character, it will have a goal external to itself. In the former case we have *science* in the proper sense; in the latter we have *technique*, understood in what is admittedly a loose sense, so as to include under the rubric of technology medicine, jurisprudence and scientific agronomy. Science is autonomous in its goals and its problematic; technique is entirely heteronomous. The job laid down for it is to put itself in the service of an ideal that is given from without; as a result, it presumes in advance the reality of some particular good which is presented to it as something unconditional, absolute, not open to criticism. For medicine this absolute good is human health; for technology, the augmentation of the productivity of human labour; and so forth. Nonetheless, this ideal, the given object of absolute obligation within the sphere of this or that branch of technique, proves to be only 'relatively absolute', if this expression is not too contradictory. In itself it is bound to remain at some distance from that point where human knowledge is directly fixed upon the absolute and finds its stability there. Outside the realm of the specialised discipline in question, this ideal must be the object of critical enquiry; but its very existence already presupposes the grasp of some unconditional criterion for distinguishing within its own limits between good and evil.

Political economy falls within the sphere of technique in the broad sense. It owes its development and its present existence to the practical importance which economic questions now possess in the life of civilised human beings. It emerged as the fruit of the quest of the modern mind and the modern conscience for *justice* in economic life. It was a response to the ethical not the theoretical demands of modern man. *Political economy*, in this preliminary definition, is *applied ethics*, i.e. the ethics of economic life.

Political economy is thus not autonomous but heteronomous in respect of the ideal given or prescribed for it, defined for it as a sort of axiom. At this point, however, when we have not yet actually passed over the threshold of political economy, but are still waiting at the door, we have the right and the duty to subject its ideal goals – goals which, as in every technical discipline, are only relatively absolute – to free enquiry and criticism. We can subject them to such a critical test by bringing them together with what appears to us to be the properly absolute and unconditional. As a result of such a critical examination, we acquire certain guiding principles that will help us form an opinion as to how far contemporary political economy succeeds in performing the tasks before it, and how clearly it understands these tasks. And from this point of view we can critically review both the fundamental problems and the general scope and content of modern political economy.

There are two major problems which animate political economy: the problem of the generation of wealth and the problem of its distribution – i.e. the economic question and the social question. The task of political economy is thus defined by *two* ideals, one economic, the other social. It is, above all, enquiry into these two ideals, these twin orders of absolute obligation for political economy, that should provide the subject matter for a critical introduction to political economy. Here we shall be discussing only the first sort of obligation, i.e. the question of the ideal of economic policy.

Wealth is the absolute good where political economy is concerned. It has never occurred to any economist to doubt or question this. The increase of wealth is the Law and the Prophets for political economy. But since the level of wealth is connected with the development of demand and consumption, this fundamental law could also be expressed in other terms: the increase and refinement of demand creates the conditions for a rising level of wealth. But in fact, in the subsequent development of this doctrine, economists come up against the unforeseen problem of excess production, luxury. Luxury or surplus is

The Economic Ideal

an obvious evil in the eyes of the economist, as it leads to the diminution of wealth creation and so contradicts the first commandment of the economic catechism – even though it devotedly obeys the second. Controversies about luxury and its significance thus have a particular interest in the literature of economics. Some economists begin from the assumption that luxury is useful, even necessary, because it fulfils the second commandment (e.g. Malthus's defence of agricultural overproduction, or the advocates of militarism as generating a demand for military goods, etc.); others stress the harm done by luxury, appealing to the first commandment (and from this point of view they condemn the luxury-consuming classes and the aspirations of militarism). The controversy remains unfinished and unresolved; it is obvious that the antinomy has not been removed and, consequently, that the issue cannot be settled according to purely economic criteria, within the limits of political economy alone, as if this literature for and against surplus production had never existed.

It is legitimate to pose the question of how so controversial a doctrine [as the priority of wealth creation] has acquired so uncontroversial a significance in economics, so basic an importance for its presuppositions about the meaning of the level of demand. This dogma was introduced into economics primarily as a methodological postulate, a hypothetical presumption. It is well known that, for Adam Smith, man operates in two different realms with wholly antithetical characteristics. In the realm of ethics he acts out of altruism, in the realm of economics out of egotism – what economics depicts under the slogan of 'economic man'. And once this presupposition had been introduced by Smith, it gained secure rights of citizenship in the terrain of economics through his good offices. The historico-ethical school made some feeble and fruitless theoretical attempts at protest against the ethical materialism of political economy; while on the other hand, the doctrine of economic materialism, generally in Marxian form, had already greatly sharpened the focus of this system. What had been a methodological postulate was transmuted into a fundamental thesis of the philosophy of history by way of a doctrine of the economic struggle between classes as the true ground of the entire historical process. If we leave out of account Ruskin, Tolstoy and various of the so-called utopian socialists, we can say that the question of wealth has not been understood in economics as a problem of general human import, an ethical problem. The explanation for this is certainly not to be sought in any kind of personal materialism on the part of economists, amongst whom, as we know, there are some great examples of practical idealism, but rather in the poverty of their general world-view, in their positivism, which does not provide any reason to pause for critical reflection on the threshold of the scientific enterprise, but leads immediately into its intricate byways, where there is no possibility of a wider perspective. Issues of principle are turned into questions of fact, and specialised investigations flourish in proportion to the poverty of generally shared ideas. However, in the wake of the long story of the development of economic science, a time for critical reflection must come, a time when it is possible to pose the *questio iuris*, not merely the *questio facti*.

So let us put the question concerning the 'relatively absolute' good of political economy, its economic ideal. This takes in the whole problematic of philosophy and world history: is wealth and a high level of demand and consumption a good in the light not only of political economy but also of moral philosophy? Is it not only an economically absolute good but a good in general? If so, in what sense? And if not, why not? In the first instance, political economy would have a philosophical and moral right to exist; in the second, it would all simply lead downwards into misunderstanding and error. So the issue is about the moral *raison d'être* of economics.

Such an extra-economic evaluation of wealth obviously has its place only on the basis of some general philosophical world-view; this question can be settled only by appeal to something more than political economy itself. It is to this wider appeal that we now turn.

On the question of wealth and growing consumption, human thought is divided between two extremes – Epicureanism and asceticism. We must then, above all, define how this issue relates to these twin, mutually contradictory doctrines in moral philosophy.

First, Epicureanism: the philosophical side of this doctrine is characterised by an extreme simplicity and crudity; it is normally associated with positivism or materialism, denying all absolute principles in life and all reality unknown to the senses. *Carpe diem*, do not let the possibility of any kind of sensual pleasure escape you – such is the non-moral morality of Epicureanism. It develops gradually from crude hedonism into aestheticism: the actual *scale* of possible physical consumption is too limited, and thus its *quality* must be refined, so as to get the most out of the greatest variety of delights. But this is most fully accomplished by attracting aesthetics into the service of sensuality. However, this one proposition already contains a massive contradiction, since the beautiful in its metaphysical character is inseparable from the good; aesthetics is inseparable from ethics. Yet for Epicurean aestheticism, which sets the tone for the contemporary sensibility of decadence, the aesthetic is characterised simply as such, separated from all its links with the higher activities of the spirit, and, as a result, in bondage to the lower. Epicurean aestheticism is thus the last word in the philosophy of hedonism so prevalent in our day.

Naive hedonism is always allied to a conscious or unconscious economic philosophy, in so far as wealth and high consumption or demand are ultimately taken to be the absolute good; and thus quite contrary economic tendencies are assimilated to each other. The celebrated Professor W. Sombart – one of the brightest talents among modern economists, and one who takes into his system scientific elements from Marxism and from the historical school alike – provides a fully deliberate and definitive formulation of the hedonistic doctrine. In his recent work,* Sombart quite openly expresses his view, in such a way that he furnishes us with, as it were, a clear mirror in which to see the lineaments of hedonism. We are indebted to him for his candour and clarity; and so let us look into this mirror.

What is under discussion is artistic production and the development of contemporary taste. In Sombart's view, modern Germany has achieved such advances in this respect that the first half of the nineteenth century now seems in comparison an age of archaic crudity and vulgarity. Sombart explains this difference in terms of the particular character of what constituted cultivation or education in the earlier period. He

---

* *Der moderne Kapitalismus*, vol. 2 (Leipzig, 1902).

characterises it as the age of Fichte and Schelling, Hegel and Schopenhauer, Heine and Goethe:

> It was exclusively an aesthetic-philosophical, literary, idealistic spiritual culture, non-sensual and thus non-artistic (*unsinnliche und somit unkünstlerische*), which held one thing only in esteem. Being poor in material welfare, in a stage of indigence, they made a virtue out of this poverty, building for themselves a world of ideals, and thus holding in contempt the whole sphere of sensual and bodily experience. Moderation and restraint were the order of the day; they yielded in humility to the Unseen, they sought out the embraces of shadows, the scents of celestial flowers; they lived in abstinence and mourning. Thought, ideas, learning were enthroned as absolute monarchs; art, and especially plastic art, was wholly subordinated to these ...

> It seems surprising that for this generation of writers, philosophers and aesthetes, poor in purse but rich in heart, rich in 'sentiment' but strangely poor in 'sensibility', our present understanding of material contentment and the adornment of the outer man was quite alien, either on grounds of principle or because of inadequacy of resources. Even Goethe, who belongs to the great epoch of secularity, who was no stranger to pleasure and had no shortage of the taste for luxury and splendour, even Goethe lived in a house whose furnishings would appear wretched and beggarly to our modern taste; and even Goethe could express the thought that elegant and luxurious decoration in a room is essential only for people who have no thoughts – an idea picked up by Schopenhauer.

> Not even the artists knew how magically beautiful objects could cast a spell over their surroundings; they did not understand the skill of living in beauty; they were ascetics, puritans. Either they dressed like Nazirites in coats of camel's hair, feeding on locusts and wild honey, or else they led the lives of schoolteachers or petty bureaucrats.

In our day

> the whole understanding of life is undergoing a change. It is developing away from the pre-eminence of the literary, the artistic, away from the abstract idealist sensibility. The taste for the visible products of the present concrete world is being

awakened, for the beautiful forms even of tangible material objects, for joy and delight in life. Artistic feeling is becoming the determinative principle for the whole of life, taking the artistic ideal into all its dimensions. Just as art was previously in thrall to thought, to literary fancy, so now the artistic perspective dominates over the literary as over all the regions of the spirit's life. It seems that we are in an age of cultural flowering, something which has always been artistic and non-ethical (*kulturellen Hochblüte, die stets künstlerisch und unetisch war*).

Sombart makes the following predictions for the next twenty or thirty years:

> I foresee that the coming generation, after the long centuries of privation, will at last begin to lead a new sort of life, sustained by both beauty and material sufficiency. There will be a generation capable of making a whole world of desirable and beautiful forms out of the abundance of the wealth that will flow to them in prodigal plenty, a generation of people for whom pleasure, *joie de vivre*, happen of their own accord, as the inevitable and natural concomitants of the earthly journey, people of sophisticated sensibility with an aesthetic appreciation of the world. This means that the demand for elegance and tastefulness is, quantitatively speaking, attaining proportions we cannot now figure or picture for ourselves; it is increasing beyond measure, on such a colossal scale that the 'luxury' of a Roman emperor, the splendour of Venice, the prodigal display of Versailles become as nothing in comparison with it.

Elsewhere Sombart turns his attention to

> the more costly, skilful and comfortable furnishings of restaurants and hotels, coffee-houses and taverns, trains and shipping, commercial houses and indeed all the working places of capitalist enterprise. In our times, it is the shops selling the perfumer's goods or fashionable neckwear or linen, the hairdressing salons for ladies, the barber shops, the photographic studios, and so on, that lead the way in terms of aesthetic surroundings. Working and business life nourishes itself with beauty.

Naturally, the sole index of beauty in this context is technical smoothness of fit: 'We are learning to discover the beauty that is revealed in technical accomplishment ... the style of the future lies in the machine'. Indeed, Sombart's viewpoint consistently distances itself from any real understanding of the problem of luxury.

There is no extravagance, no refinement of pleasure which cannot find sanction and thus justification in the personality of the one experiencing it. The costly pearl which Cleopatra ordered to be crushed so that its powder could be sprinkled in a cup of wine and offered to a guest is recalled in every treatise on luxury as an illustration of the 'extremes' of indulgence. But who among those who admittedly feel the fascination of exceptional personalities would want to cast them all in the mould of this great woman, or in that of Ludwig II's nocturnal expeditions or the luxury and splendour of the Sun King?

Summing up Sombart's characteristic views, we must once again note that, in this work, he is stating a *practical* position: 'we have become wealthy because all races and peoples apart from us have perished, all other parts of the world have been depopulated, all other lands and cultures laid waste' (*Der moderne Kapitalismus* I, 326–48). Such is the price of happiness for mankind, now and in the future.

But enough of this bourgeois fantasising, with its seasoning of fashionable Nietzscheanism. *There* is the perfect mirror of hedonism. In Sombart's picture, historical development moves from feral humanity (as Soloviev described it) to swinish humanity, and at the end of this sad historical path, what we meet as its self-satisfied goal of consummation is a truly Philistine figure 'not ethical but aesthetic', with the ideals of a woman of fashion! In this civilisation for hairdressers, where is there any place for bringing to birth the agonies of reflection, wrestling with the torments of conscience, the struggles [*podvigu*] of love and self-denial, the unremitting battle with self? Where in this universal restaurant can our poor spirit find room for its cosmic questions? Spirit is here surrendered without any pretence at a struggle to the claims of sensual gratification; its birthright is sold for a mess of pottage. And to compensate for the absence of ideals, we are offered the prospect of 'living in the midst of beauty'. The drowning of spirit in sensuality, life without ideals, spiritual *embourgeoisement* – this is the inevitable logic of hedonism. And this is not an individual quirk of

The Economic Ideal

Sombart's views; he simply has the merit of consistency, of providing a full and candid exposition of what constitutes the 'ideals' of hedonism and developing them to a moral *reductio ad absurdum*.

But if hedonism seeks to deliver up spirit into the bondage of matter, asceticism strives for its complete liberation from matter. For the ascetic, the body and its life are an absolute evil. Plotinus, the most forceful representative of Neoplatonism and one of the greatest philosophers of all time, was, so to speak, ashamed of living in the body, according to the report of his disciple and biographer, Porphyry, and thus refused to give any biographical information about himself and would not allow any portrait or statue of himself to be made, immortalising 'the phantom of a phantom', as he said to the artist Amelius. All pleasure is slavery for the spirit. Life is a mirage, a malign deception, an illusion. The person who can extinguish need in himself, so as to be as if dead while yet living, is liberated from cosmic evil and attains to a state of nirvana. The most consistent and definitive expression of this ascetical view of the world appeared in Buddhism. From the darkness of the ages, from the depths of the enigmatic Orient, let us summon the great shade of the Buddha and hear what was his vision of life, having so far heard only the contemporary Western European doctrine. In the *Suttanipata*, one of the canonical books of Buddhism, we read:

> Who here takes naught, long, short, small, large, good, bad,
> Nothing got given, brahman him I call.
>
> In whom no hopes are found for here or yon,
> Fetter-free, hope-free, brahman him I call ...
>
> Who pleasures here forsakes and homeless fares,
> Lust and 'life' [becoming] ended, brahman him I call ...
>
> Who for pleasure longs
> And therein hath his will,
> How happy is that man
> With all he wished for won.
>
> But when those pleasures fade,
> The wanton wight, thus steeped
> In pleasures, craving-born,
> Suffers as pierced by dart.

35

Who pleasure shuns, as one
With foot the hooded snake,
Watchful, he shall escape
The world's entanglement.

Who craves for pleasure's brood:
Fields of demesnes and gold,
Horses and cows and slaves,
Retainers, women, kin;

Him weaknesses o'erpower,
Him troubles dominate,
And on him closes ill
As sea on vessel split.

Hence, ever watchful, man
Should pleasure shun: thus rid,
Their vessels baling out,
Yon-farers cross the flood.

The man who in his care stays cleaving to't,
Clouded by many moods, in error steeped,
Is from th' aloof state surely far removed,
For hard to leave are pleasures in the world.

Who scan the past and future longingly
And yearn for pleasures now, for pleasures gone,
Tied by desire and bound by life's delights,
Are hard to free – another cannot do't! ...

Lo! in the world I see a trembling race
Caught by this craving for becoming's ways,
Poor folk lamenting at the mouth of death,
Thirsting about becoming this or that.

See how they stir about their cherished aims
Like fish in shallow pool of river-bed!
And seeing this, let him then 'mine-less' fare,
Nor form attachment for becoming's ways.

So the basic postulate of the pessimistic philosophy of asceticism is that life with all its pleasures is evil; the appropriate response is suppression and denial. The ascetical understanding of the world is to be found in a number of different philosophies and religious sects: it has been appropriated by some versions of Christianity, closer to the teachings of the Buddha than to Christ's. Based upon a one-sided and thus inaccurate interpretation of the gospel's teaching about riches, this view frequently transforms the God-given world into nothing more than the kingdom of Satan, into which no single ray of the divine light can penetrate.

Obviously the ascetical view of the world has certain consequences for history and political economy. Above all, if life is evil and its pleasures unconditionally sinful, the only escape for the fearful imagination of the ascetic will appear to be the suppression of this life in himself – suicide by degrees. Mortifying the flesh, reducing bodily needs, rejecting wealth as a seduction, as the greatest of all evils, this is the law of asceticism. Thus the norms of asceticism are diametrically opposed to the basic assumption of political economy, which rests upon the assertion of the lawfulness and desirability of maximising demand. Asceticism is the negation of political economy, economic development and material culture.

But the matter does not rest there. From the ascetic perspective, there is no such thing as history, understood as the measured development of the whole human race, as a rational and integral process. For asceticism, historical existence is not a task to be carried through, a problem to be solved by human unity and co-operation, so as to give an independent value and meaningfulness to history; it is only the manifold, multi-faceted repetition of the same sad tale of individual human life. Thus there can be only one task for humanity – the salvation of the individual soul, individual liberation from the evils of the world (though within these limits the Buddha's teaching is marked by the highest altruism), without any kind of historical engagement over and above this, without anything that survives or goes beyond the life of the individual personality. In this way, the doctrine of asceticism, which finds its purest expression in Buddhism, is necessarily anti-historical; it has room only for ethical individualism and denies the corporate moral task, the social dimension. These distinctive features of Buddhism – the rejection of economics, material culture, history and social morality – have been revived in our own times in various doctrines which have in large measure made the tenets of Buddhism their own. They may all be discerned, for example, in Tolstoy's philosophy; and the denial of history characteristic of Schopenhauer's system is strongly tinged with Buddhist colouring.

The ascetical view of the world is at no point more alien to contemporary consciousness than in this denial of history and social ethics. Contemporary man cannot learn to look at things from such a standpoint without doing moral violence to himself and cutting himself off from human society. On these points, Buddhism, leaving aside the rather special case of the Buddhist 'revival' which seems likely to spread rapidly in Western Europe in the very near future, appears as a stage in the history of thought which European man has left behind; it is no more possible to go back to this stage than it is to return to pre-Copernican astronomy. Contemporary moral thinking bases itself on a recognition of the value of history and the obligation of the historical task; it does not confine itself to the sphere of personal morality, but demands of man as a necessity that he should be aware of his ideal connection with the whole of humanity's past, present and future. In this sense even the most unassuming of men must see himself not only as a moral personality but as an historical agent: some earn the right to be known as such, but the same historical duties are laid upon all.

And so we have two contradictory and mutually exclusive views on the question of wealth. Are we to stand helplessly before this contradiction and simply opt to identify with one or other of its terms, in obedience to no more than personal whim or taste? But this would mean the complete moral bankruptcy of economic theory, once it is accepted that it owes allegiance to nothing but caprice and so can be abrogated by nothing but caprice. The poverty of both points of view appears in the ethical materialism common to both, although it seems strange to see this reproach levelled at asceticism alongside hedonism. Both views deal with material needs and material life – one could even say, more generally, with a life that has an independent and distinctive set of goals and values; and they are distinguished simply by the fact that one view accepts these goals and the other rejects them, though this rejection is only partial. Both would find quite alien the view according to which wealth and material life are not ends in themselves but only a means for the service of a higher and absolute end, so that they must be evaluated not in their own terms but on the basis of their relation to this higher end.

What, then, is the purpose and the meaning of human life overall? This is the question which unavoidably prescribes for man what is his human worth; without some kind of answer to this question, we cannot fruitfully set ourselves to any employment, whether economics, technology or medicine. For what gives life an *overall* meaning also makes sense of and fulfils any *particular* task. Now it is obvious that this question is not to be solved within the limits of economics or any other special science; on the contrary, the real solution is already given or contained in the question itself. This is why every man is revealed to be a philosopher in spite of himself, in the sense that he strives, well or badly, to resolve this philosophical problem for himself. It is clear that the answer to the question of political economy will depend on the solution provided for the philosophical problem; but it is no less clear that such a solution is to be found only outside the limits of economics as such, and that politico-economic arguments have no role to play at this level.

Can it be true, then, to say that man, and thus humanity, and thus human history, are no more than brute facts, the unforeseen product of a chain of causes with no internal necessity, only the necessity of external forces? Or does man – and historical humanity – carry in himself some absolute idea, fulfil some absolute task? Does he exist in the name and for the sake of a moral purpose rather than being just the product of a chance combination of causes? This is the basic dilemma whose resolution defines the philosophy of economics. It is clear that there is only one route out of the first point of view – Sombart's epicureanism; only one moral to be drawn – 'eat, drink and be merry'; only one ideal – a civilisation safe for hairdressers, a lady's boudoir. The second approach admits the possibility of taking quite distinct routes. One such would be the philosophy of asceticism in all its various shades and degrees. But, as we have seen, it leads into a blind alley because of the narrowness of its basic principle. At the foundation of the philosophy of asceticism lies the quite correct notion that sensual and animal life, *considered simply as a brute fact*, needs to be rejected; but it turns this rejection into a negation, instead of subordinating this brute fact to a higher ideal principle – in short, idealising or spiritualising the material fact.

Human life has no absolute meaning or value in itself alone, but only beyond and above itself; it acquires meaning and value not through some feature of its empirical or biological facticity, but as something which serves a higher ideal principle, a substantive good. Its ideal structure is thus constituted by the actuality of human spirit, which defines itself in moral terms and chooses to direct its will this way or that by free moral action. This is the proper work of the spirit; it is in this work that the purpose of human life consists, and all other goals must be considered only as means for this. It is expressed in a diversity of spiritual goods, and the union of such goods is what truly constitutes what we call the culture or the cultural achievement of any given historical epoch.

The life of a specific individual and the life of an ensemble of individuals, the life of historical humanity, have one and the same ideal structure, or more precisely, the same task to fulfil. But if this is so, what *is* the basic structure of human history? This question is most easily answered by drawing a comparison with the development of the individual. It is essentially the same questions about the good and the true, about our relation to the world and to other human beings, about human life and its purpose, and so on, that arise in our consciousness at particular stages of our life and particular moments in our spiritual development; but they arise and are resolved piecemeal, so to speak. The child's consciousness asks these questions in naive simplicity; they are sorted out with facile decisiveness in youth; but they return again in the calm spirit of maturity and the profound awareness of old age. Do we not find the same thing in history? Are not the same absolute structure of human life and the same ideal questions of the human spirit reproduced in the historical record of humanity itself, only on a far greater scale, with intensified depth and complexity? If the constitution of the spiritual life remains immutably and absolutely determined by the same spiritual questions, then, however changeable this life may be, however vulnerable to the historical development of the conditions in which it is lived, all these changing phenomena will still be different ways of meeting the same problems.

The spiritual life requires one condition, a negative condition, but invaluable and irreplaceable: *freedom*. Ethical self-determination cannot but be free, and, conversely, only free self-determination can have an ethical goal. It would be superfluous to try to demonstrate this self-evident truth. But perfect freedom belongs only to *pure* spirit, which is free from all external influence and open only to interior motivation. Man exists in *bodily* form and so is bound to the external and material world in which mechanical necessity dominates. The freedom of the human spirit is thus necessarily subject to external limitation, not to mention internal limitation as well; complete and purely spiritual freedom is an unattainable ideal for empirical man. Yet it is still his ideal! The nearer man comes to this idea and the more his spiritual life is autonomous, the more fully can he express his spiritual self, his spiritual 'I'. This contradicts Hegel's formulation of the matter: Hegel sees the structure of history simply in the development of the human spirit towards liberty and self-awareness.

The external unfreedom of human personality has two basic forms: the dependence of man upon man – i.e. political or social dependence; and the dependence of man upon nature – i.e. economic dependence. We shall restrict ourselves here to this latter area.

Man depends upon nature – nothing, perhaps, could be more trivial than this statement. But, if we reflect on it, how central a place it occupies in the explanation of human history! We are bound up with the natural order and depend upon its bodily reality. Our own bodies need nourishment, clothing, changes of place, communication with other bodies, light and warmth, and so on. Nature overall does not set out specifically to meet these needs. The accursed earth brings forth thorns and thistles, and man only gains his bread by the sweat of his brow. Nature is an alien and hostile element for us to live in, an element with which we are fated to be at war to defend our very existence. The fleshliness, the materiality of our existence is something we are aware of as a fetter and a burden, for whose sake we are obliged to bear the burden of national and individual 'economy'.

Matter is something we are aware of in its materiality through the impermeability and estrangement of human bodies.

   Yet, on the other hand, every victory over matter, every economic triumph, consists in its subordination to the goals of human spirit. The heat energy at work in an earthquake in the Andes, which seems to us simply the evil action of mindless elemental power, is the same energy that we see in the steam-engine. The destructive electrical energy in the bolt of lightning is the same thing that telephones and telegraph turn to our service. Matter ceases to be just matter for us only when the forces of nature serve our human ideas. The triumphs of technology are nothing but the spiritualising of matter, the annihilation of matter considered simply as such. The greatness of a nation's wealth, the successes of technology and industry, these are the expressions of a gradual spiritualising of matter. The impenetrability of matter, which we actually experience in our spatial division and distinction, is at least partly done away with when it is overcome by mechanical forms of transport or cloven by the 'spiritual lightning' of telephone or telegraph! And can we not now in our chemical industries extract from nature the gifts of its inner magic, which it has long hidden from us, forcing us to be slaves to its elemental and irrational processes? In striving to replace the natural with what is planned and made, i.e. the irrational with the rational, are we not binding nature by force, as it were, through the rationalism proper to us? And do we not thus bring about a 'conversion of spirit' in the natural order? Contemporary technology uses its powers to convert nature into the raw material for artistic creation, so to speak, the raw material for the incarnation of ideas in images accessible to the senses. In this sense we may speak of the aesthetic character of technology and industry. Without contemporary machinery, representing this incarnation of ideas, there would be no artistic production of this kind. Just as the raw material of a block of marble, devoid of any kind of 'ideal' content, is transformed into an artistic miracle under the sculptor's chisel, and gradually loses its materiality, its mortality, its lack of intelligibility and imperfect permeation by ideal structures, so too the forces of nature lose their materiality, i.e. their alienation from ideal reality, in the machine and become obedient servants of the idea. Surely it is this artistic aspect of contemporary machine technology that accounts for the irresistible and unique poetic charm that the picture of a train at full steam or some working piece of machinery has for us!

The tendencies of modern technology show that the prevailing relation between man and nature, the state of mutual estrangement and impermeability, is not the normal or the only possible one; that nature is capable of being penetrated by the commands of the human spirit, and that we can conceive of another kind of relation – close, intimate and harmonious between nature and man, a relation in which electricity, light and heat may become spiritual forces, in which every ground for the distinction between the external or alien and the internal, what is properly one's own, disappears. The possible victory to be won over matter, and the spiritualising of the forces of nature, constitute the great task which humanity confronts in its history, and which is being carried through with such unprecedented success in our day. Along with this, the shameful and humiliating dependence which weighs so heavily upon what we call uncivilised peoples, the dependence we know as poverty, is likewise done away with. The hungry man needs food above all else, the cold need clothing, the homeless shelter. Poverty creates the kind of suffering that degrades man and excludes the possibility of a properly human and spiritual life. Thus the battle against poverty is a battle for the rights of the human spirit. The ideal in respect of these 'lower' needs is exactly the same as the fundamental ideal of human health: we should arrive at the situation where we are not aware of them, just as the healthy man is not aware of his own body; and, conversely, when these needs are not met, then, just as with a disease in the body, there is a tendency for the felt lack to fill the entire consciousness and so to block the free activity of the spirit.

But the satisfaction of these 'lower' needs is only a minimum – unconditionally obligatory, even though by no means everywhere achieved, and yet in no way definitive for human beings. Once it has freed itself from those iron fetters, the human genius turns to the task of loosening all other bonds, struggling with matter to the utmost in the name of the spirit's freedom.

There is both a negative and a positive freedom. It is possible to be 'free' from material necessities either by not having them at all, or else by having them satisfied. So a savage is 'free' from the need for clothes since he is used to being naked, while the civilised man is 'free' because he is well clothed. Similarly, both the infant and the saint are free from sin or defilement; but the one is so because it is incapable of sin in virtue of its undeveloped consciousness and so is in a sense 'below' sin, and the other because he has overcome sin and so is 'above' it. If we want to find the characteristics of negative freedom, we could go a step further and say, for example, that the dead man is even more 'free' than the savage, since he has no needs at all. Clearly, it is not this empty freedom that is in view when people speak of the development of the human spirit towards freedom. Here freedom is understood as a positive capacity, as an expansion of wealth, and so as the expanding of potential for the manifestation and self-affirmation of the human spirit. Wealth in this sense can be defined as the indispensable condition for universal history, although it does not in itself constitute history. Savage and undeveloped peoples, living in bondage to nature, have no history; they stand outside it, and their liberation from primitive poverty is for them the beginning of history. The turn of 'higher' human needs can only come when the more basic ones have been satisfied. It is no accident that cultural flowering in the history of nations coincides with epochs of burgeoning material prosperity; and conversely, cultural decadence is accompanied by economic decline.

Once we have acknowledged, for one consideration or another, that an expansion in national wealth is a good thing, we must also acknowledge the condition necessary for this expansion. Among these necessary conditions is an expansion in need or demand, which constitutes, you might say, the reverse side of expansion in national wealth. If we are to achieve this or that conquest of nature, it is necessary for us first to feel the need of it. First, we must have a need to communicate with other people if we are to profit from the telegraph or the post; first we must have a need to know about the starry heavens if we are to make use of the telescope; first we must have a need for spiritual liberty if we are to struggle for mastery over nature. The expansion of need is a law not only for material existence but also for the spirit; indeed the development of spirit consists precisely in the expansion of its demands, in the fact that it perceives problems and tasks which it has not perceived before.

So we have arrived at the economic ideal and the fundamental law of political economy: maximise wealth, multiply demand. The question has been resolved positively in favour of recognising economics and its postulates. But in this process it has become clear that this 'absolutely relative' ideal (in the sense defined above) is not self-sufficient, not absolute in itself, as political economy takes it to be, but takes its sanctions from beyond itself, shines only with a reflected light, is admitted only as a means to a particular end. Consequently it is not autonomous but heteronomous; and in all the decisive issues of economic policy it is possible to appeal to a higher, non-economic authority, since political economy is not sufficient unto itself. This, of course, does not mean that its ideals are not fully adequate, and even autonomous within certain limits, in what may be called day-to-day economic life.

We have now come to the point where we can review the two mutually contradictory doctrines of asceticism and hedonism, and make clear what is true and what is false in both of them. These doctrines provide us with an example of what Vladimir Soloviev called 'abstract principles'. Both take up one side of the truth and divorce it from its connection with the whole; and then, with the aid of this abstract principle, they set out to evaluate the whole. Thus both are true not in what they affirm but in what they deny; they are untrue precisely in their limitedness and their abstractness. Obviously it is possible to evaluate them only from the standpoint of a doctrine which will make both their 'yes' and their 'no' appear relative and conditional, which can unite thesis and antithesis in a higher synthesis. The deep underlying sin and error of asceticism consists in its negative and reproachful attitude to human happiness. In its exclusive and in any case un-Christian gloom, it brands the world as evil; life is for it a kind of mistake, the body a vessel of the devil, and anything that satisfies the body a sin. It is necessary to grasp that this pessimism has a metaphysical or religious character if we are to replace it with any comparable point of view. In the wake of the Renaissance and all the spiritual triumphs of the modern age, we cannot return to this medieval standpoint. Obviously the deification of the human body and the world in general on account of their beauty of form, the kind of thing we find in Hellenism, ancient and modern, or else on account of the pleasure to be extracted from them, as we find in Epicureanism of all ages, must be unconditionally rejected as a form of idolatry unworthy of man. But it is quite impossible to find any convincing argument for repudiating all human happiness. Of course, the struggle for joy or happiness, arising out of the plain reality of life itself, cannot be regarded as a duty in its own right; but even if it is not a moral duty it does not (within the obvious limits) contradict moral duty, but rather makes plain the natural and lawful rights of all living things. So in these terms, hedonism may be a legitimate stimulus for economic development, for the expansion of national wealth, comfort, and aesthetic needs and even the 'art industry' so dear to the heart of Sombart (who is here garbling Ruskin's ideas).

But if hedonism of a positive kind appears no more than tolerable from a moral point of view, negative or altruistic hedonism constitutes the prime and most sacred duty of our age. What I am thinking of is the struggle against national poverty, helplessness and destitution. To undertake a dispassionate study of the ascetic ideal of salvation and the seductive teaching of hedonism while the peasantry remains hungry and cold, while mothers of children are worked to death in our factories, while millions of people lead the lives of beasts of burden, with no joy, no light breaking in, would be criminal, savage and hypocritical. To understand the level at which the mass of our people currently live, to build into that life the tastes and demands of civilised existence, and in that sense to win the masses to hedonism is the most solemn and sacred of contemporary duties. Of course, asceticism, the renunciation of pleasure, only has value when it is a free decision; and that freedom presupposes the prior possession of the world's goods. The Buddha was a king's son before becoming an ascetic; Francis of Assisi was the son of a wealthy merchant. But what can be said of those who fast, those who are vegetarians, through no choice of their own, who only see meat on the table two or three times a year, those ascetics who do not wash because they have no soap, who walk barefoot along the railway lines because they cannot afford a ticket? One could go on with such a catalogue. There is one thing only that should be said about such people: it is our obligation to help them free themselves from this involuntary asceticism, to give them what we have determined to be the fundamental condition for the moral life, the condition that is gradually realising itself in history – freedom from poverty. This is the necessary condition (even if it is only a negative one) for the freedom of moral self-determination. These are our obligations in respect of our country and its poor; and the commandments of 'negative hedonism' remain a matter of pressing urgency in the consciousness of modern Russia. Perhaps it is too easy, in consequence of this, to give way to the temptation of seeing in hedonism a general moral principle of a higher order, a positive ethical axiom. But we have already seen what consistent hedonism leads to.

Although it follows that asceticism as a philosophical worldview is to be rejected, there can be no dispute about the significance of the ascetical *principle* in morality. If the meaning of life is not a matter of pleasure but of the goods of the spirit, the inner life of man and of human society represents the spirit's unceasing struggle with sensuality for dominion in man's soul. Economic progress reduces man's dependence on nature understood as an external limit, but does not liberate him from internal dependence on his own body. Thus wealth becomes a spiritual force, influencing the human spirit from within; it changes from a source of limitation to a source of temptation. 'You cannot serve God and mammon' – this saying retains permanent significance. Whichever principle prevails in man, the ideal or the lower and carnal motivation, the latter must always come under the control of the spirit. The proper and legitimate relationship between the diverse needs of spirit and flesh is given by following the path of spiritual combat which the Greek word *askesis*, 'asceticism', denotes – a word which really means an exercise in training for battle. Of course, the forms and stages of asceticism in history vary a good deal. The period in which the spiritual principle of life was being preached among the savage barbarian tribes required heroes of physical asceticism quite unimaginable in our day, when the level of physical requirements and social development is so different. But our age too knows ascetics whose life is a ceaseless process of spiritual attainment [*podvig*], a ceaseless process of sacrifice and self-renunciation, although in these days such ascetics are more often to be met in secular life than in the monastery or the hermitage. The beauty of ascetical or moral achievement remains just as accessible for our own age as it was for the age of monastic ascesis. Is it not still possible in our day for the healthy moral sensibility to be captivated by the image of Francis of Assisi, the apostle of voluntary poverty? Will it really prefer the depraved Cleopatra or the Sun King, in whom some perverse tastes find a kind of aesthetic appeal? The control of sensuality by the spirit, of mammon by God, is, of course, an interior moral act, not necessarily bound to one and the same exterior expression. The latter will be defined by the spirit of the age as much as by the character of the individual. Thus the ascetical principle in morality is not of itself in contradiction to the basic economic law of maximising need and demand, in so far as this latter keeps in sight the task of liberating historical humanity from the hegemony of nature, with a view to the creation of a broader foundation for spiritual culture.

An asceticism that summoned us to renounce the triumphs of civilisation – the railway, the post, the printing press, science and literature – would be reactionary obscurantism, fighting in the cause not of the liberation but of the enslavement of the spirit. And conversely, the increasing sense of human value and the spiritual expansion of personality inevitably expresses itself in the expansion of material demand: we have a good example of this in the whole contemporary movement towards democracy.

Here then, as everywhere in the sphere of moral life, the spiritual side of human nature, the direction of the human will, has definitive significance. Needs and demands can be multiplied so long as this is required by the life of the spirit and by human dignity, but they must equally be curtailed when the life of the spirit requires it. This is a formula free from the excesses both of hedonism and of asceticism. From this point of view we can offer a definition of 'luxury' such as Sombart refuses to give – rightly pointing out that there are no external distinguishing marks for luxury as an empirical phenomenon, and that the conception of it is relative and liable to change. There are indeed no external marks of luxury, as such distinguishing marks can only be internal – though for any particular age it is not difficult to point out its external manifestations as well.

Luxury is the triumph of sensuality over spirit, of mammon over God, whether in the individual soul, or in the whole of a society. Once the cult of gratification, aesthetic or non-aesthetic, has become a guiding principle, we have luxury. Luxury is the reverse side and the constant peril of wealth. Just as in a state of poverty the spirit's liberty is negated by external limitations, so in wealth it falls victim to internal temptation. Luxury and poverty are equally the enemies of culture: there may be as much spiritual poverty in the nobleman's palace as in the pauper's hovel. The spiritual decline that accompanies luxury sooner or later leads to economic decline as well, so that luxury is self-condemned even from an economic point of view. The spiritual state of a nation is very far from being a matter of indifference for its economic life. Nobody would claim that intemperance was preferable to temperance or that moderation in one's requirements was not preferable to extravagance; nevertheless, in our sketches for the future, the dimension of internal struggle between God and mammon is completely ignored. The modern mind, with its excessive mechanisation of life, is particularly given to designing ideal social systems in which people will be virtuous automatically, as it were, without any kind of struggle with themselves. No: virtue is always bestowed and created only by moral conflict; and if our destiny is above all to struggle against poverty and all kinds of tyranny, the destiny of humanity in the future will be, along with other kinds of battle, the struggle against wealth and luxury. Wealth does no more than build the walls of civilisation; within those walls it is equally possible to construct a radiant temple for the spirit and to open a brothel.

It seems to me that this is the attitude to wealth which the gospel enjoins. It does not abolish human happiness or condemn all pleasures of the senses; but it does warn us against the spirit's enslavement to anxiety about riches and the cares of the morrow; it condemns those who 'put their trust in their riches' and commands us to make a decisive choice between the service of God and the service of mammon, claiming that the one is not compatible with the other. The gospel proclaims life 'in spirit and in truth', and addresses itself to the spiritual man; and so it avoids equally the abstraction of asceticism and, still more, the sensuality of hedonism. But it does not pass sentence on culture as such and the economic progress it requires. Mankind should not bury its talent in the ground, as asceticism teaches; it must increase that talent in its history.

Thus the antithesis of hedonism and asceticism, moral dualism of the familiar variety, which presupposes a continuous internal conflict, cannot be resolved by human consciousness or human history. The control of hedonism by the ascetical principle, the discovery of a proper relation between the two, is the task continually set afresh before us, continually finding some sort of resolution, both in the individual life and in the history of the race. The establishment of an authentic civilisation depends on the adequacy and correctness of such a resolution; for true civilisation is undermined equally by one-sided asceticism, which annihilates its problems without solving them (Tolstoy's teachings give us a good example of this), and by one-sided hedonism, which leads to moral degeneration, to the bourgeois mentality. Luxury, spiritual *embourgeoisement*, was one of the strongest poisons corroding the civilisation of antiquity. The barbarians, wholly devoid of culture, were their heirs, people whose only superiority lay in their freedom from the spirit of bourgeois mercantilism, and whose hearts were open to both good and evil. Throughout the whole of the medieval period, the moral ideal or norm was asceticism rather than hedonism. In contrast, contemporary Western culture developed out of the Renaissance and has remained up to now under the sign of that epoch; this is what has shaped its one-sidedly hedonistic character, its self-definition in opposition to the asceticism of the Middle Ages. It may seem overbold to assert that authentic – that is, spiritual – civilisation, which would be equally free from the abstract spiritualism of asceticism and from bourgeois hedonism, has yet to be realised and is still, as hitherto, the desired goal of the world-historical process – although particular historical periods have approximated to the ideal in greater or lesser measure. In any event, it is impossible to say that this situation has arrived in the current state of Western civilisation, which, with its increasing trend towards the hedonistic side of the equation, is rapidly moving further from ideal harmony rather than approximating to it. The human spirit is, so to speak, stupefied by the wealth produced for it; and this state of stupefaction and a sort of spiritual bondage, clearly audible in Sombart's remarks, is not yet a condition in which wealth is fully and freely appropriated for what it is. What Sombart conceives as the ideal is only the first stage in the process of spiritual evolution, which history may yet remedy. But perhaps it is only at one particular moment or in one particular epoch that it is given to a nation to lay bare its true spiritual essence in its entirety, as is typically the case with human individuals. Perhaps, at the end of the day, it is here that we find the real division of labour in human history; diverse nations in distinct historical epochs are given the task of expressing with greater sharpness and definition some specific aspect or condition of historical evolution as a whole. If so, the last word of history has yet to be spoken, and 'normative' or 'ideal' civilisation, the synthesis of medieval and Renaissance culture, the rights of spirit and the rights of flesh, still lies in the future. Which of the nations of history has the destiny of bringing this synthesis to fulfilment?

You must understand that we are here entering an area in which there are no firm proofs, the area where desire and trust begin. But one's gaze rests, willy-nilly, on the destiny of our own people, whose historical future is already clearly before us, who have yet to speak their own distinctive word and fulfil their historic fate. Of course, to think of this national task as a right or privilege, as did the Slavophils in former years, would be to lay quite the wrong foundations and to be guilty of the sin of self-conceit. But indeed, a lofty, even an exaggerated, sense of one's task is bound to accompany the corresponding sense of its solemn obligation upon us. Only in this sense is it possible to speak of 'historic tasks' at all.

We must not ignore or conceal the vision of all the many scars and blemishes disfiguring our life as a nation. Khomyakov, the father of Slavophilism, wrote of these, in the full blaze of his own patriotism: 'When we look at modern Russia, it gives us cause both for joy and for oppression of spirit; we may speak proudly about it to strangers, but are driven to speak quite otherwise among ourselves'. But with all these disfigurements, poverty, ignorance and injustice, there is one sickness that has not yet found a place on the soil of Russia – the bourgeois spirit, the kind of hedonism about which you have heard Sombart speaking today (that was how it seemed to me, at least). Our intelligentsia, which has come to maturity on the anvil of history, under a hammer that shatters glass but tempers steel, considers hedonism or 'bourgeois contentment' to be a type of moral decline, and gives all its sympathy and loyalty to ethical asceticism, to the ideal of self-denial (in its contemporary forms, of course). In this sense it stands closer to the Middle Ages than to the Renaissance. I shall not try to confirm this with evidence and examples from the contemporary context: it is sufficiently well known to my audience without this. But I would turn to the principal object of our nation's pride, the whole of our literary heritage, which as early as Pushkin had already perceived and celebrated the spiritual image of Russian womanhood, and which in its best spokesmen forms an unbroken tradition of protest against bourgeois values: it is the apotheosis of spirituality and of moral asceticism. I think of our great Herzen, who took up the struggle against bourgeois values as if it were the one special focus for his literary activity; I recall the great names of Vladimir Soloviev, Dostoevsky and Tolstoy, who appear and confront the moral life of our society in the last quarter of the nineteenth century, the very age when the voice of Epicurean aestheticism was more and more shrilly heard in the West. There are hardly any great writers on the opposite side among us (not counting the youthful fervour of Pisarev, who was by a narrow margin the contemporary of the ascetic Dobrolyubov). I know of no more instructive a case in this context than Chernyshevsky, in his novel *What is to be Done?*, where alongside the systematic propaganda for utilitarianism and eudaemonism (in terms of which his hero justifies his altruistic feelings and diligently tries to purge them of egotistical motives), we find his principal hero, Nikita Silin, showing himself to be not an aesthetic eudaemonist in the style of Sombart after all, but an ascetic! Just so did Balaam, called upon to curse Israel, pronounce a blessing upon them against his will.

Such is our literature and our intelligentsia. Our bourgeoisie is still too weak to exert a decisive influence on the spiritual life of the people; but bureaucracy, of its very essence, is without spiritual power and can paralyse national development only in externals, and only for a short time. What affects the people at large is the reality of the historical life that lies ahead for them;

and in their present position they are deprived of the principal conditions (though these are only *negative* conditions) for their moral self-definition, their historical existence. Compulsory 'asceticism' and humility, poverty and lack of human rights, still stand in the way of their development. Their liberation, the constructing of the conditions for a life that is human, not merely zoological, is an immediate historical necessity. Our epoch of history stands under the sign of the rights of scientific enquiry and of national economics. The radiant kingdom of the spirit, authentic civilisation, can be built only upon a solid and *material* foundation. But in laying this foundation we are already erecting the building. That is why, once hedonism has been rejected as a moral philosophy, we must, in the realm of actual social relationships, deal above all with the legitimate imperatives of hedonism; we must not in the least contradict them. The understanding of personality, its rights and also its needs in terms of material welfare and property, must be the slogan of our *Russian* renaissance; this will be the watchword of our times, this will be our historical task, our civic duty.

2

'Heroism and the Spiritual Struggle' (1909)

INTRODUCTION

Bulgakov's intellectual development after 1903 took him more and more swiftly in the direction of Orthodoxy, though the final reconciliation did not take place until 1908, on a visit to a remote monastery (movingly described in his *Autobiographical Fragments*[1]). But this period was eventful in all kinds of ways: it saw his most intense involvement in practical politics; his move to Moscow, where he occupied the chair of Political Economy at the Institute of Commerce in Moscow University from 1906 until 1911, when he resigned in protest against Government interference in the university's affairs; and his emergence as a figure of some national importance, not least because of his tireless journalistic activities, reflected in his 1911 collection of essays, *Dva grada*.[2] He had begun to read extensively in Church history and theology: a long essay on Feuerbach, first published in 1905,[3] shows keen appreciation of the developments of German religious thinking in the nineteenth century, and the essays of the following years make increasing reference to writers like Harnack and Troeltsch. He was also reading Carlyle and Ruskin with enthusiasm, and picked up something of the development of Christian socialism in Britain.[4] His

---

[1] *Avtobiograficheskiya zametki* (*Autobiographical Fragments*), posthumously edited and published by Lev Zander (Paris, 1946), pp. 64–6.
[2] *Dva grada* (*Two Cities*), 2 vols. (Moscow, 1911).
[3] *Dva grada*, vol. 1, pp. 1–68.
[4] See the essay on 'social moralism', dealing chiefly with Carlyle, ibid. pp. 106–49. There are references on pp. 108–9 to Kingsley, Maurice, Ludlow and Ruskin, and he had written more extensively on Ruskin in an essay of 1909. The interest in British thought is not too surprising, given his Marxist background: the work of

lengthy studies of 'Primitive Christianity'[5] and 'Apocalyptic and Socialism'[6] are enormously erudite, fully conversant with the most recent Western European scholarship in Church history and the emerging disciplines of social history and the study of ideology.

One of the first activities in which he engaged on his appointment to Moscow was the establishment of a religio-philosophical discussion group, along the lines of the famous Petersburg circle that had met between 1901 and 1903.[7] This group, the 'Vladimir Soloviev Philosophical–Religious Society of Moscow', was, however, more explicitly political in its concerns, and between 1906 and 1908 served as a sounding board for some quite dangerously radical political ideas. The society was dominated by Bulgakov and Evgenii Trubetskoi, but it also included V. Ern and V. Sventitskii, founders of an illegal movement for the reform of Church and state, the 'Christian Brotherhood of Struggle' (*Khristianskoe bratstvo bor'by*).[8] This group, established in 1905, had close links with many members of the Soloviev Society; Bulgakov was an open and vocal supporter, as was another prominent figure in the Society who was to have a decisive influence on Bulgakov, the brilliant polymath Pavel Florensky.[9] Initially the Brotherhood seems to have concentrated on proposals for the disestablishment and democratisation of the Church – a political issue of some urgency and immediacy in 1905, when a number of debates were prompted in the press by a decree from the tsar

---

Engels would have familiarised him with social conditions in England, and he had already discussed the problem of Ireland in his work on capitalism and agriculture (cf. *Dva grada* vol. 1, p. 146).

[5] *Dva grada*, vol. 2, pp. 1–50.

[6] Ibid., pp. 51–127.

[7] Jutta Scherrer's magisterial study, *Die Petersbürger Religiös-Philosophischen Vereinigungen* (Berlin, 1973), remains the best study; see also her article, 'Les "Sociétés philosophiques-religieuses" et la quête idéologique de l'intelligentsia russe avant 1917', CMRS, 15 (1976), pp. 297–314, esp. pp. 310ff., on the Moscow circle.

[8] Jutta Scherrer, 'Intelligentsia, réligion, révolution: premières manifestations d'un socialisme chrétien en Russie, 1905–7', pt. 1, CMRS, 17 (1976), pp. 427–66, esp. pp. 432–45 for details of the development and vision of this group.

[9] The only full-length study in English is Robert Slesinski, *Pavel Florensky: A Metaphysics of Love* (New York, 1984), though this has almost nothing to say about Florensky's political and social ideas (for a brief mention of these, see p. 25, esp. n. 12). His influence was widespread in intellectual circles in Moscow, and he

'HEROISM AND THE SPIRITUAL STRUGGLE' (1909)

apparently blocking the possibility of Church reform by withdrawing it from the agenda of the Council of Ministers.[10] But increasingly the Brotherhood put forward suggestions for wider social reform, supporting a sweeping programme for common ownership of industrial enterprises and public services, and arguing against the legitimacy of unearned income.[11]

If this was to be anything other than an academic exercise, political leverage had to be gained. In the late summer of 1905, the tsar at last gave his approval to a scheme for a national legislative assembly, and political party groupings began to take shape. Bulgakov pressed for a coalition of liberal or leftist Christian candidates for the assembly, and published in the autumn of 1905 a sketch of what their programme might look like.[12] It involved a commitment to redistributive taxation and land reform (i.e. a transfer of land to peasant proprietors), though Bulgakov's consistent and strong advocacy of the individual rights of the citizen prevented this from being simply a collectivist and centralising proposal.[13] At this time, he (and others in the Brotherhood circle) still regarded the state as no more than an instrument for the advancement of the historic movement of the people, not an end or entity in itself.[14] It is noteworthy too that he

is a significant figure in the background of various developments in Russian aesthetics at this time. There is some account of his social thought in Katerina Clark and Michael Holquist, *Mikhail Bakhtin* (Cambridge, Mass., 1984), pp. 135–8. See also Anthony Ugolnik, *The Illuminating Icon* (Grand Rapids, Mich., 1989), pp. 209–15.

[10] See James W. Cunningham, *A Vanquished Hope: The Movement for Church Renewal in Russia, 1905–1906* (Crestwood NY, 1981), pp. 94–105 for some of the background. The referral of proposals for church reform to the Holy Synod rather than the Council of Ministers meant that the existing administration of the Synod – then in the hands of the arch-conservative Konstantin Pobedonostsev – could stifle discussion and veto any recommendations to the tsar.

[11] See Scherrer, 'Intelligentsia, réligion, révolution', pt. 1, pp. 432ff., 445, which makes very clear the anti-capitalist commitments of this group.

[12] 'Neotlozhnaya zadacha: O soyuze khristianskoi politiki' ('An Urgent Task: On the Union for Christian Politics'), *Voprosy zhizni* (*Questions of Life*, the major organ of the Brotherhood and its associates), Sept. 1905, pp. 332–60.

[13] On Bulgakov's concern with civic rights, see, in addition to Scherrer's 'Les "Sociétés philosophiques-réligieuses"' and 'Intelligentsia, réligion, révolution', Pierre Pascal, 'Les grands courants de la pensée russe contemporaine', CMRS, 3 (1962), pp. 5–89, pp. 15–16 on Bulgakov.

[14] Scherrer, 'Intelligentsia, réligion, révolution', pt. 1, pp. 438ff., and *Die Petersbürger Religiös-Philosophischen Vereinigungen*, p. 153. The importance of land reform as an issue at this time is noted by Bastiaan Wielenga, *Lenins Weg zur*

57

assumes that the new social order will be essentially agrarian; but it is hard to say how far this represents a withdrawal from his earlier enthusiasm for industrialisation and how far it is simply a recognition of the inevitability of a basically agrarian society for the foreseeable future. The mixture of peasant proprietorship, wariness of state centralisation and redistributive taxation sounds rather like the 'distributism' or 'guild socialism' of sections of the British left at the same period; and I think Bulgakov would have been happy to be associated with William Morris – or even G. K. Chesterton – on this matter.

At first, the project for a 'Union for Christian Politics' (*Soyuz khristianskoi politiki*) seems to have been open to co-operation with other liberal/leftist groups; but the aggressive secularism of these other embryonic parties rapidly alienated Bulgakov and his associates.[15] The first representative assembly (Duma) met in 1906, and dissolved in chaos: reformist groups were unable to construct coherent and viable policies, and the regime itself showed no signs of willingness to undertake reforms in any case. Some on the extreme left deliberately pushed the situation nearer to the brink, so as to encourage further revolutionary activities (the so-called revolution of December 1905 had been little more than a package of hasty concessions in response to civil disorder), but even the Constitutional Democratic Party (the 'Kadets') had failed to define any very realistic aims, and some reformist moderates broke away from it and attempted to secure a 'centrist' alignment more capable of doing business with an intransigent administration.[16] Prominent in this group was Prince Evgenii Trubetskoi,[17] who was, as we have noted,

Revolution. Eine Konfrontation mit Sergej Bulgakov und Petr Struve im Interesse einer theologischen Besinnung, Munich 1971, pp. 166–170, where Lenin's concern with this question is discussed. Scherrer in a more recent essay draws attention to the role of agricultural issues in hastening Bulgakov's disillusion with the scientific claims of Marxism ('Du marxisme à l'idéalisme: une nouvelle lecture de Bulgakov', CMRS 29 (1988), 481–6, p. 486, n. 16).

[15] Scherrer, 'Intelligentsia, réligion, révolution', pt. 2, CMRS, 18 (1977).
[16] See M. Bohachevsky-Chomiak, *S. N. Trubetskoi: An Intellectual among the Intelligentsia in Prerevolutionary Russia* (Belmont, Mass., 1976), pp. 186–8 and notes on pp. 270–1.
[17] Brother of Sergei Trubetskoi (see Bohachevsky-Chomiak, *S. N. Trubetskoi*), and a substantial philosophical intellect in his own right, author of *Smysl zhizni* (*The Meaning of Life*, Moscow, 1918), and a work on aesthetics recently translated as *Icons: Theology in Colour* (New York, 1973).

closely associated with Bulgakov in the Soloviev Society in Moscow. In 1906, he established a weekly journal, the *Moskovskii ezhedel'nik*, which was designed to be an organ of the reformist centre; Bulgakov published several of his most substantial studies in its pages, including his celebrated essay on Marx. But Bulgakov's increasing reluctance to co-operate with liberals whom he saw as aiming at the destruction of Russia's Christian identity left him isolated even within Trubetskoi's circle.

In 1907, Bulgakov stood for election to the Second Duma as an independent Christian socialist, and served as a representative for the Orel district during the brief life of this body (February to June 1907).[18] His autobiographical notes record something of the depth of his disillusion with what the Duma represented: the sectarianism and extremism of the left guaranteed the practical impotence of the assembly, and the possibility of an effective Christian presence in this kind of democratic politics now appeared more and more remote. He looked back on his aspirations during this period as wholly illusory, and wrote that the main impulse for most of his fellow politicians was the longing to *appear* to be doing something.[19] For the proceedings of the Duma, he had nothing but contempt, and the pages in his autobiographical notes where he recalls the experience of sitting as a deputy are full of despairing anger about the self-indulgence and fractiousness of the assembly.[20] 'In one word', he wrote, 'the Second Duma was for me such a clear revelation of the falsity of the revolutionary idea that I was cured of it as a political goal'.[21]

He never had any desire to return to active politics (though approaches were made to him in 1917).[22] He describes in his autobiographical notes how, in the wake of the traumatic experience of the Duma, he abandoned his former republicanism and developed an intense devotion to the ideal of monarchy

---

[18] See *Avtobiograficheskiya zametki*, pp. 80–1; on the general development of Bulgakov's political activity after 1905, see Wielenga *Lenins Weg zur Revolution*, pp. 254–65.
[19] *Avtobiograficheskiya zametki*, p. 80.
[20] 'Nowhere in the world have I known a place with a more unhealthy atmosphere than the hall and the corridors of the Second Duma' (ibid., p. 80).
[21] Ibid., p. 81.
[22] Ibid., p. 79.

– indeed, to the person of the tsar. He was, he says, fully aware of the corruption of the tsarist system and of the personal weakness and suicidal incompetence of Nicholas II; but he was at the same time struck by a sense of the tsar as carrying the cross for his people, of the tsar not as the presiding authority in a police state but as the symbolic focus of Russia in all its pain and confusion. To be a 'tsarist' in this context was, he says, to accept a share in some of that pain and confusion, and to refuse to put all the personal blame on the tsar as an individual.[23] But this, as Bulgakov realised, had little to do with practical politics: its effect was only to deepen his personal agony over Russia's disintegration and reversion, after 1907, to deeper and deeper stagnation and repression. It is not wholly fair to Bulgakov to say as one commentator has done, that he surrendered to 'the mystique of absolute monarchy';[24] he never became a supporter of absolutism of any kind. The royal authority he was interested in was something more like a sacramental presence, legitimating the political life of the nation and carrying its burdens before God – a powerful and ancient Russian myth. But it is true that after his time as a deputy in the Duma he showed no enthusiasm at all for the discussion of proposals for structural democratic reform; and, as he admits in the autobiography, the tsarist ideal for a time wholly overshadowed any commitment to democracy as a self-evident good: without the sacramental anchorage of political power in the Christian monarch, democracy was simply the perpetuation of the competing self-interests that had paralysed the Duma.

Bulgakov remarks that he has no wish to 'theologise' about monarchical authority; but he clearly believes it is important to underline the sense he had of royal authority as, so to speak, cruciform.[25] And this indicates a link to the more systematic and sustained reflections he was to pursue on the nature of divine

---

[23] Ibid., pp. 81–2.
[24] Christopher Read, *Religion, Revolution and the Russian Intelligentsia, 1900–1912* (London, 1979), pp. 59–60. This is a useful summary of some of Bulgakov's ideas during the period of his political involvement, but suffers from a rather oversimplified political typology and a selective use of Bulgakov's (admittedly copious) writings from these years.
[25] He describes his sense, on seeing the tsar for the first time in Yalta in 1909, of the monarch 'bearing his authority like the cross of Christ' (*Avtobiograficheskiya zametki*, p. 82). Bulgakov goes on to explain that he saw the chaotic degeneration

'Heroism and the Spiritual Struggle' (1909)

power and its expression in *kenosis*, self-emptying. The point is not developed in this context; but it is a significant indication of how one of Bulgakov's major theological motifs was already affecting his thinking in the first decade of the century. It also casts a sidelong light upon the text that follows: what Bulgakov finds morally and spiritually compelling in the image of royal authority (and the reality of the monarchy in the Russia of 1907 and the years following) could almost be characterised as its anti-heroic quality: Nicholas II is not the doer of great deeds, the self-conscious saviour of the nation, but someone bearing what is laid on him, like the monk bearing the duty or the penance imposed by a superior. This essay is more aggressively insistent (paradoxically) on the evils of self-assertion than practically anything else in Bulgakov's work: the longing for the heroic role typical of the Russian intelligentsia is, in Bulgakov's imagination, set against the dogged endurance and constant failure of Russia's absolute monarch.

Read without some of this background in Bulgakov's experience of Russian politics during the first decade of the century, the following essay can sound petulant and negative. Along with the rest of the essays in the volume in which it first appeared, it aroused widespread and vocal criticism from the secular left, and particularly vitriolic abuse from some Marxists (not least from Lenin). *Vekhi: Sbornik statei o russkoi intelligentsii* (*Landmarks: A Collection of Essays on the Russian Intelligentsia*) was published in 1909:[26] it drew together a quite diverse group of contributors, most of whom had been Marxists of one sort or another and all of whom considered that the unadmitted problem of Russia's political culture was the refusal by the Russian intelligentsia to take seriously the spiritual and metaphysical questions necessarily underlying issues about political reconstruction. All would have described themselves as committed to some kind of religious perspective, though by no

of the royal power in the years that followed as a sort of diabolical parody of the high ideals of the Russian tradition. Rasputin could only have happened in Russia, where the ideal of 'the saintly elder directing the monarch' was a powerful folkloric theme (ibid., p. 85).

[26] In Moscow; there is an English translation by Marshall S. Shatz and Judith E. Zimmermann, under the title of *Signposts: A Collection of Articles on the Russian Intelligentsia* (Irvine, Calif., 1986). The word *vekha* can mean any point of orientation – a sign, a beacon or a buoy at sea.

means all were Orthodox Christians.[27] Their diversity lay more in their past and current attitudes to practical political questions: Piotr Struve[28] had been far more sympathetic than Bulgakov ever was to the Kadet party in its early days, and had criticised Bulgakov for his intransigence towards unbelievers; Nikolai Berdyaev[29] was even more sceptical than Bulgakov about the possibilities of strictly political reconstruction, and saw the central theme of a Christian critique of contemporary political options as the affirmation of the radical liberty of the individual and the need for 'inner revolution'. For Berdyaev, the social realm was the sphere of unfreedom, of slavery and 'objectification', instrumental reason. What was needed was the reconstruction of human personality as an anarchic and creative force. Echoes of Nietzsche can be clearly heard in much of Berdyaev's work, and his relation to historical and institutional Christianity was (and was to remain) far from straightforward. In sharp contrast to Bulgakov, he was very critical of the

[27] Of the seven authors, three were Jewish by background, though one of these (S. L. Frank) later joined the Orthodox Church and became a religious philosopher of distinction; see the excellent recent study by Philip Boobbyer, *S. L. Frank: The Life and Work of a Russian Philosopher, 1877–1950* (Athens, Ohio, 1995). The essays and essayists are discussed in Read, *Religion, Revolution and the Russian Intelligentsia*, and there is a good introductory survey in Nicolas Zernov, *The Russian Religious Renaissance of the Twentieth Century* (London, 1963), ch. 5. At the time of *Vekhi*'s publication, Bulgakov was probably nearer the heartlands of Orthodox Christianity than any of the other contributors.

[28] A major figure in liberal politics in the first decade of the century, he had been a prominent 'Legal Marxist', i.e. a member of the group that emerged at the end of the nineteenth century in Russia, moving further and further from socialist activism and supporting policies that would bring Russia more into line with Western developments, especially industrialisation, that in practice required a capitalist economy *before* any progress towards socialism could occur. Scherrer (*Die Petersbürger Religiös-Philosophischen Vereinigungen*, pp. 82–6) has some useful reflections on the factors that distanced this group from the main body of radical intellectuals. Their theoretical commitment to the eventual emergence of socialism freed them from the guilt and dramatic sense of urgency common among Russian radicals, but also opened them up to a more long-term ethical perspective; revolution alone could not act as an ethical touchstone, and they became increasingly interested in neo-Kantianism and other movements in moral philosophy that grounded an ethical idealism for the individual in the present. On Struve and the conflicts between the Legal Marxists and other socialists, see also Wielenga *Lenins Weg zur Revolution* (pp. 93–5 on Struve's evolution in the period just before and after the 1905 revolution).

[29] Probably best introduced through his own reflective autobiography, *Dream and Reality* (London, 1950).

'Heroism and the Spiritual Struggle' (1909)

ascetical and monastic tradition of Orthodox Christianity, despite his enthusiasm for Dostoevsky.[30]

Bulgakov's essay was one of the most substantial and provocative contributions to *Vekhi*, particularly provocative in its demythologising of the self-image of the radical Russian intellectual – the kind of person likely to be involved in the Kadet party as well as in the more overtly revolutionary activities of the Marxist left. Their radicalism is (paradoxically) a function of their rootlessness: Russian cultural history had produced an educated class gravely alienated from all the most serious and creative forces in indigenous Russian culture, not least the Russian religious tradition. Yet the intelligentsia, in spite of itself, has taken on the form of an ersatz religious movement: Bulgakov notes acidly the 'religious' tone of the rhetoric of the Russian left in the debates in the Duma, and (more sympathetically) the genuinely sacrificial and generous impulses of the radicals. But all this is bound up with a fanatical and dogmatic atheism, seen as a necessary aspect of the general assumption of properly 'European' values – a curious development, says Bulgakov, given the religious roots of Western European culture itself. Very interesting here is Bulgakov's strongly worded praise for what we now call the 'Protestant ethic', especially in its English forms. Protestantism is seen as the ground of the development of civic responsibility and political liberties, as well as economic advance; Bulgakov has read his Weber conscientiously. The Enlightenment, in contrast, represents a more apolitical kind of libertarianism, concerned less with civic goods than with a fundamentally pagan individualism and a set of assumptions about human perfectibility that suggest an intrinsic opposition between Christianity and what might generally be called modernity.

Part of the interest of this essay is Bulgakov's attempt to drive a wedge between *political* modernity – that is, the acknowledgement of human rights and the critique of autocracy – and the full-blown ideology of Enlightenment, with its hostility to

---

[30] Ibid., pp. 188–90. Chs. 7 and 9 *passim* demonstrate his unease with the institutional Church and the idea of definitive revelation. See also his *Slavery and Freedom* (London, 1943) on the whole idea of the social realm as the world of alienation. Read, *Religion, Revolution and the Russian Intelligentsia*, pp. 65–77, has a good survey of Berdyaev's contribution to *Vekhi*.

revealed religion and its implicit historical determinism. In insisting upon the religious, indeed, dogmatic, roots of liberal politics, he anticipates some more recent Western debates. But there is more to his critique than this. The greater part of the essay is devoted to outlining the heroic self-image of the revolutionary intellectual; and the thrust of the argument seems to be that this heroic obsession has more to do with 'Enlightenment' than with real political modernity. The struggle for civic responsibility and public justice belongs with the sober discourse of Protestant anthropology; the language of revolution belongs with the substitute theology of Enlightenment individualism, with its steady slippage towards romanticism. It is this pseudo-theology that generates the distinctive pathos of the revolutionary hero, whose cause is legitimated by appeal to suffering and persecution, and promoted in terms of maximal and urgent demands: the whole revolutionary style is alien to labour and negotiation, and so is also inherently aristocratic or elitist. It is impossible, at the end of the day, to derive a genuinely *social* philosophy from the cult of radical heroism.[31]

One of the things that Bulgakov most severely condemns in this analysis is the confusion in revolutionary rhetoric about means and ends. 'Maximalism' about goals seems so often to entail maximalism about methods – which produces, in effect, a sort of moral nihilism, a reduction of moral intervention to the assertion of the individual will. At no point may I be seen to be frustrated; at every point, I must be seen to be making a decisive difference. Hence, as Bulgakov points out, again with some asperity, in a culture obsessed with heroism there are fewer people to do the necessary social maintenance, to secure stability and the prosaic servicing of the kind of order that in fact is able to serve the needs of a populace at large. What are the connections between – as Bulgakov puts it – 'the revolutionary festival' and 'the common daily round', between the carnival of revolution and the construction of a new order? Bulgakov's

---

[31] Compare the discussion in Alasdair Macintyre, *Against the Self-images of the Age: Essays on Ideology and Philosophy* (London, 1971), of a more contemporary style of revolutionary maximalism, the cult of the heroic associated with figures like Che Guevara. In a brief piece on 'Marxism of the Will' (pp. 70–5), Macintyre notes the Kantian intensity and individualism of this ethos, which he christens 'Leninist voluntarism'.

fiercest critic, Lenin, had something not wholly different to say in his assault on the 'infantile disorder' of the extreme revolutionary left.[32]

Paradoxically, the revolutionary intelligentsia still elevates the 'social' as a category above the 'personal'; there is a fascination with the idea of social conditioning and determination at the same time as this obsession with heroism as the triumph of the will. The missing category is one that will allow for the deliberate *education* of the will, and this is a large part of what Bulgakov here understands by the 'personal'. Revolutionary rhetoric has no means of discussing what *virtue* is (to paraphrase Bulgakov in terms that belong more to the debates of the last decade or so); hence the appeal to the idea of *podvizhnichestvo*, the spiritual struggle. The *podvig* in Russian tradition is the 'exploit' that characterises both the hero of folklore and the saintly ascetic, and is here used with reference primarily to the latter.[33] The saint is engaged in the cultivation of a style of personal existence within the limits of the created order, a constantly developing and maturing responsiveness to God amidst the constraints of material life. It thus entails *humility* – not self-abasement, but the willingness to learn, connected with the recognition that the world's ills have roots in each individual self, with its passions and tumults. The effort to improve the external environment is always liable to be seduced by 'heroic maximalism' if it is not accompanied by the cultivation of personal self-criticism, self-discipline and openness to be moulded and corrected by God, the environment itself, history – in fact, all those realities that secretly shape our supposedly individual identities. For Bulgakov this is anything but a passive or world-renouncing ascesis; ideally it should produce a culture of sober and conscientious activism, in which all agents examine their actions and responsibilities in the light of the ideal of *obedience* to God, transferring to 'secular' life the

[32] See Lenin's famous pamphlet on 'Left-wing Communism: An Infantile Disorder', (ET, Beijing, 1965).
[33] The terminology crops up in later works of Bulgakov; ironically, the centrality of the *podvig* is also fundamental in the theology of Bulgakov's rival and critic, Georges Florovsky; see, for example, the latter's classic essay on 'The Predicament of the Christian Historian', in W. Leibrecht (ed.), *Religion and Culture: Essays in Honour of Paul Tillich* (New York, 1959), pp. 140–66 (notes pp. 359–62), a statement of Florovsky's argument for radical indeterminism in human activity.

attitude of the monk to the duties of the monastic life, in which all daily duties are sanctified and unified as examples of obedience.

Bulgakov's essay, therefore, unites certain themes from classical Eastern Christian spirituality with something of the bourgeois Protestant ethic; and, despite his enthusiastic appreciation for Dostoevsky, he is here putting down some markers of caution alongside the nineteenth-century Russian interest in moral extremism. Unlike Berdyaev, he is deeply suspicious of appeals to the anarchic undertow of human personality and the formless creativity of the self. His political and religious concerns alike lead him to stress the need for the disciplined and undramatic virtues of the *citizen*, virtues that were undeniably rare in the Russia of the first decade of this century. In one sense, he is arguing for a good *secular* ethic – that is, an ethic that does not surround the task of creating and maintaining a just society with a pseudo-religious glamour. Of course the radical intelligentsia has suffered, and the state that has inflicted that suffering is an unjust one; but the mystique of revolutionary martyrdom is something for which Bulgakov's distaste is manifest. As he notes, it was one thing to feel sympathy for the persecuted radical before 1905; but such sympathy cannot survive the carrying-over of the dramatic postures of the saintly victim into the business of practical democratic politics. We are reminded sharply of Bulgakov's angry disillusion with the Second Duma, and his abiding conviction that this democratic experiment had been ruined by the irresponsibility of the left.

The essay concludes with a poignant appeal for a Russian renaissance that will not involve further ruptures in an already traumatised national history. Russia has not learned yet to take cognisance of its own history in a constructive way, and the temptation to apocalyptic radicalism is thus all the stronger: We do not know how to think about our past; let us then destroy it, since it is manifestly a past of terror and injustice. In the face of this temptation, the Christian intellectual in Russia has a clear responsibility: to acknowledge the desperate need for political change and social justice, and yet to think through what this might mean for a culture and a population quite different from the already more or less democratised peoples of the West. And if the Russian intelligentsia is capable of returning to religious faith, it will be able to resolve its deepest tensions and release its potential for real social transformation.

As we have seen, Bulgakov, by the time *Vekhi* was published, had practically lost faith in the possibilities of democratic politics in Russia; the appeal at the end of his essay can hardly be read as a hopeful one. *Vekhi* as a whole was taken by the intelligentsia as a counsel of despair, and Lenin's polemic against it argued that it displayed the bankruptcy of the entire non-Marxist left in Russia and the impossibility of 'bourgeois democracy': both the Kadet party and its 'vekhist' critics were ultimately viciously individualistic (and, as Christopher Read has documented,[34] this Leninist analysis flourished in Soviet polemic as late as the 1970s, when various kinds of Western radicalism, from the Frankfurt School to the student risings, were associated with the perspectives of *Vekhi* – in a way that would have surprised its authors considerably). In a sense, Lenin and the outraged intelligentsia democrats were right; what is difficult to discern, though, is precisely what realistic options there were for political action between 1907 and 1917, given the repeated failures of democratic experiments and the increasing reassertion of absolutism, even before the disasters of the war years. Bulgakov can be read as proposing something like Theodor Adorno's 'strategy of hibernation'[35] – the preservation, in so far as it is possible, of social and political vision by small-scale activity and personal fidelity, until such time as political change again becomes possible. Bulgakov's insistence on the need for a kind of personal conversion among the intelligentsia, a rediscovery of the disciplines of personal growth and maturation through a deepened moral and spiritual self-awareness, may sound quietist, or it may speak of the necessary conditions for any serious and reflective public engagement. For the reader, as for him, much depends on where and when you are thinking about all this.

The *Vekhi* essay shows some development from the earlier piece on economics. The most obvious shift, of course, is in the full and explicit use of Christian resources, especially the

---

[34] Read, *Religion, Revolution and the Russian Intelligentsia*, pp. 172–3.
[35] The phrase actually derives from Jürgen Habermas's essay on 'consciousness-raising or Rescuing Critique', *Philosophical–Political Profiles* (London, 1983), pp. 99–110.

vocabulary of monasticism. Perhaps related to this is the more nuanced valuation of humility and asceticism; the essay on economics understandably sets out to distance itself from negative and passive elements in the spiritual tradition, while the *Vekhi* piece has a harder and more sceptical reaction to human aspirations untutored by grace. The earlier work heralds Bulgakov's most active period as a practical politician, and the later reflects his bitterness at the failures of contemporary Russian politics. And, no doubt in reaction to what he saw as the self-indulgent dramatisations of the radical intelligentsia, the Bulgakov of *Vekhi* is far more positive about what are essentially bourgeois ideals than either the earlier or the later Bulgakov, even though the underlying spiritual motivation invoked is far from bourgeois. It is as if Bulgakov is suggesting that the sober virtues of citizenship will always depend upon a kind of secret discipline of humility and self-abnegation as demanding as the obedience of the monk: the apparently dull surface of the good citizen or the good administrator conceals a *spiritual* drama no less intense than that of the radical hero, but one that is more authentic, since it is not performed for an audience and is directed not to self-fulfilment but to the inseparable goals of holiness and the social good. The 'hero' of Bulgakov's critique of heroism is a figure intriguingly close to the Lutheran paradoxes of Kierkegaard or even Bonhoeffer on the hiddenness and anonymity of holiness in the modern context; and his implicit separation between political modernity and the culture of Enlightenment still suggests a complex agenda for future discussion.

Heroism and the Spiritual Struggle

I

Russia has experienced a revolution; but this revolution has not achieved what people expected from it. In many people's minds, and, to a lesser extent, in our age as a whole, the entire legacy still remaining of the positive gains of this movement for liberation has a problematic character. Russian society, exhausted by these earlier exertions and failures, is now in a kind of torpor, a state of apathy, spiritual fragmentation, depression. The Russian state so far shows no sign of that renewal of vigour which it so much needs; as if in a land of dreams, everything is once again frozen into immobility, bound in invincible slumber. Russian society, under the cloud of such a high number of death sentences, an unusually high crime rate, and a general coarsening of manners, has positively regressed. Russian literature is awash with the turbulence of unrestrained pornography and works of sensationalism. Hence the spread of depression and the fact that people have fallen into a state of profound misgiving as to the future of Russia in the longer term. And in any case, as a result of this experience, the rose-tinted utopia of the old-fashioned Westernisers is now already just as much of an impossibility as the naive, rather precious spirituality and faith of the Slavophils. The revolution has brought into question the very capacity for life of Russian society and the Russian state: if we do not reckon with this historical experience, the historical lessons of the revolution, it will be impossible for us to make any kind of affirmation about Russia, impossible simply to repeat what has been said in the past, whether by Slavophils or by Westernisers.

In the wake of the political crisis, a spiritual crisis has also arisen which demands deep and concentrated reflection, *approfondissement*, self-examination and self-criticism. If Russian society is in fact still alive, still capable of living, if it contains hidden in itself the seeds of a future, then this capacity for life must be revealed above and before all else in a willingness and an ability to learn from history. For history is not only chronology, the recording of a succession of bare facts; it is a living experience of good and evil, constituting the condition for spiritual growth. Nothing is so perilous as the deadly immobility of mind and heart in an obstinate conservatism for which it suffices to repeat the past, or simply to keep at bay the lessons of life by means of the mysterious hope for a new 'advance of consciousness', elemental, fortuitous, unplanned.

Reflecting on our experience in the past few years, it is in fact impossible to see in all this a pattern only of historical contingency or a mere play of elemental forces. What has happened here is a pronouncing of historical judgement, a weighing in the balance of the various participants in the historical drama, an auditing of the account of an entire historical epoch. The 'liberation movement' did not lead to the results it should have, and, it seems, *could* have, led to; it brought neither reconciliation nor regeneration, nor did it lead to a strengthening of the Russian political system (although it did leave behind it one seed for the future in the form of the State Assembly, the Duma) or an improvement in the national economy. This was not only because it proved to be too weak for the struggle with the darker forces of history; it was also, to a still greater degree, unable to succeed because it proved itself inadequate to the scope of its task in virtue of the weakness produced by *internal* contradictions. The Russian revolution developed an immense destructive energy, like a huge earthquake, but its constructive powers turned out to be far weaker than the destructive. This bitter knowledge is stored away in the spirits of many, a shared sum of experience. But does it follow that this disillusion is never to find words, never to be plainly expressed, that the question can be posed of how all this comes to be so?

I have already observed that the revolution was an affair of the intelligentsia. Its spiritual direction was in the hands of our intelligentsia with their particular world-view, their conventions and tastes, their social mores. Members of the intelligentsia themselves, of course, do not admit this (this is what being a member of the intelligentsia means), and they will, each according to his own catechism, cast this or that social class in the character of sole motivator of the revolution. We do not deny that without the whole ensemble of historical factors (of which the most important was, of course, a disastrous war), and without the presence of the very serious and vital interests of different social classes and groups, these groups would not have been able to stir from their places and involve themselves in one general ferment; but all the same, we want to insist that the whole baggage of ideas, the whole spiritual arsenal, so to speak, along with the leading fighters and marksmen, agitators and propagandists, were provided for the revolution by the intelligentsia. Spiritually speaking, it was they who gave shape to the instinctive aspirations of the masses, kindled their enthusiasm and, in a word, became the nerves and the brain in the gigantic body of the revolution. In this sense, the revolution is the spiritual child of the intelligentsia; but if so, it follows that its history is the verdict of history upon the intelligentsia.

The spirit of the intelligentsia, this creation of Peter the Great, is at the same time also a key to the future destiny of Russian society and the Russian state. For good or ill, the destiny of Petrine Russia is still in the hands of the intelligentsia, no matter how they have been attacked and persecuted, no matter how weak, even powerless, they have proved to be at this particular historical moment. They represent Peter the Great's 'window thrown open on to Europe', the window through which the atmosphere of the West reached us, an atmosphere both vivifying and poisonous. This handful of people have enjoyed a near-monopoly of European culture and enlightenment in Russia; it is the prime means by which this movement is advanced among Russia's hundred million people; and if Russia is not able to survive the threat of political and national death without such enlightenment, which is so eminently and manifestly the historical vocation of the intelligentsia, how terrifyingly weighty is its responsibility for our country's future, its immediate as much as its remoter future! That is why, for the patriot, who loves his people and is deeply affected by the needs of the Russian state, there is at present no more pressing issue for reflection than the nature of the Russian intelligentsia, and, at the same time, no more oppressive and disquieting anxiety than whether it can rise to the height of its task: whether Russia will receive what the Russian spirit so urgently needs from its cultivated class – enlightened reason and firmness of purpose – or whether, on the contrary, the intelligentsia will join forces with the legacy of the Tatar period, already so prevalent in our state and society, to destroy Russia. Many in Russia after the revolution; and, as a result of their experience of it, went through sharp disillusion with the intelligentsia and became sceptical about its fitness for its historical role; in the specific failures of the revolution they discerned the bankruptcy of the intelligentsia itself. The revolution uncovered, underlined and reinforced those aspects of its spiritual physiognomy that had earlier been foreseen in their full and true significance only by a few people (Dostoevsky above all); it proved to be a kind of spiritual mirror for the whole of Russia, and for the intelligentsia in particular. To be silent about these features now would be not only impermissible but positively criminal. All our hope must now rest upon this – that these years of social decline may also prove to be years of saving penitence, in which spiritual energies can be resurrected and a new people formed and educated, new toilers in the fields and pastures of Russia. Russia is not capable of regeneration so long as its intelligentsia (along with many others) has not been regenerated. The duty of conviction and patriotism is to speak loud and clear on this matter.

The character of the Russian intelligentsia overall is built up under the influence of two basic factors, internal and external. The first was the unbroken and relentless weight of police pressure, capable of flattening out and annihilating a more weak-spirited group; that the intelligentsia preserved its life and energy under such pressure witnesses at all events to the quite exceptional character of its courage and vitality. The isolation from life at large, to which the atmosphere of the *ancien régime* condemned the intelligentsia, reinforced the elements of an 'underground' psychology which already characterised their spiritual profile. It also froze the inner life of the intelligentsia into immobility, sustaining and to a certain extent legitimising its political obsessiveness (a Hannibal-like sworn dedication to the struggle against autocracy), as well as blocking off the possibility of a normal spiritual development. A more favourable external environment for such a development has only now come to exist; it is impossible not to see some spiritual gain resulting from the liberation movement in this respect at least. The second, internal factor determining the character of our intelligentsia is its distinctive world-view and – connected with this – its essential spiritual 'style'. I cannot but see the most fundamental mark of the intelligentsia in its relation to religion. It is not possible to understand the basic character of the revolution without keeping this question of the intelligentsia's relation to religion at the centre of our attention. But Russia's historical future too is bound up with the resolution of the question of how the intelligentsia is to define its stance in respect of religion: whether it remains content with its former deadness in this respect or whether a transformation in this area already awaits us, an authentic revolution in minds and hearts.

II

It has often been remarked (following Dostoevsky) that the 'spiritual profile' of the Russian intelligentsia has some characteristics of a religious nature, occasionally even approximating to Christian qualities. These features developed primarily as a result of its external historical fate: on the one hand, government persecution, creating a self-perception in terms of martyrdom and confession; on the other, a forcible separation from life at large, developing a dreamy and visionary tendency, sometimes a kind of refined preciousness or utopianism, a generally deficient sense of reality. Connected with this is another feature of the intelligentsia: its alienation from the petty bourgeois organisation of life in Western Europe – the values of its daily existence, its labour-intensive economy, and also its pedestrian and constrained character – though this alienation may not last for ever. In the works of Herzen we have a classic expression of the conflict between the Russian intelligentsia and the European bourgeoisie; but the innate tendencies of this mentality have more than once been expressed in more recent Russian literature. The closed and fixed nature of the bourgeois mind is sickening and cloying to the intelligentsia, though we are all aware how much we have to learn, and how urgently, from Western man about the technical side of life and labour.

But the Western bourgeoisie in its turn finds the footloose corps of Russian émigrés repugnant and incomprehensible – nourished as they are by memories of Stenka Razin and Emilian Pugachev, although these are reconceived in terms of contemporary revolutionary jargon; and in recent years this antagonism of spirit seems to have reached an unprecedented pitch. If we try to analyse this anti-bourgeois spirit in the Russian intelligentsia, it appears to be a *mixtum compositum*, made up of very diverse elements. There is a trace here of the inherited aristocratic consciousness – generations of freedom from anxiety about one's daily bread, freedom from the general workaday 'bourgeois' level of existence. There is a significant element of plain 'unformedness', lack of experience of sustained and disciplined labour and of planning the organisation of one's life. But there is also, undoubtedly, a perhaps less marked element of unconsciously religious aversion to the bourgeois soul, 'the kingdom of this world' and its placid self-sufficiency.

A certain unworldliness, the eschatological vision of the City of God, the coming kingdom of righteousness (under a variety of socialist pseudonyms), and so too a burning ardour for the salvation of humanity (from suffering, at least, if not from sin) – these make up the familiar, invariable and distinctive characteristics of the Russian intelligentsia. Pain in the face of the disharmony of life and the yearning for this pain to be overcome are especially characteristic of the major writers among the intelligentsia (Gleb Uspensky, V. Garshin). In this yearning for the City that is to come, in comparison with which earthly reality grows pale, the intelligentsia perhaps preserves, in very recognisable form, the features of the ecclesial life it has lost. How often in the Second Duma have I heard in the passionate speeches of the atheistic left – strange to say! – resonances of Orthodox psychology, suddenly revealing the influence of its spiritual formation and implantation.

In general these conventions of the spirit, nurtured by the Church, explain more than one of the best traits of the Russian intelligentsia, traits that are lost in proportion to its distance and defection from the Church – a certain puritanism, an ethical rigorism, a peculiar sort of asceticism, a general severity or sobriety in personal life. Such leaders of the intelligentsia as, for example, Dobrolyubov and Chernyshevsky (both of them ex-seminarians, both brought up in families of a devout religious character) preserve almost intact their earlier moral character – which, however, is gradually lost by their historical progeny. These Christian features, assimilated piecemeal, unwittingly and involuntarily, through the medium of the general environment, family, nurses, a whole spiritual atmosphere nourished by the Church, shine through in the 'spiritual physiognomy' of the best and greatest among those who were active in the revolution. However, in view of the idea that all real contrasts and opposition in spiritual ethos between Christianity and the intelligentsia can just be blotted out thanks to all this, it is important to establish that these Christian features have only a residual, borrowed, and in a certain sense autistic character, and tend to disappear in the degree to which former Christian *practice* is attenuated as the typical character of the intelligentsia evolves and reveals itself more fully, manifesting itself most powerfully at the time of the revolution, when it casts off the last vestiges of Christianity.

The Russian intelligentsia, especially in earlier generations, also possessed a native sense of guilt in respect of the common people – though this 'social repentance' was, of its nature, directed not towards God but towards 'the people' or 'the proletariat'. Although these feelings in the 'penitent aristocrat' or the '*déclassé* intellectual' have, in their historical origins, a certain flavour of the aristocratic milieu, they do carry the imprint of a particular kind of depth and pathos in the character of the intelligentsia. And to this we must also add its capacity for sacrifice, the consistent readiness for sacrifice among its highest representatives – even a positive quest for the sacrificial. Whatever may be the psychology of this, it certainly reinforces the unworldly cast of mind in the intelligentsia, which makes its ethos so alien to the bourgeois mind and gives it still more the character of a particular sort of religious sensibility.

Nonetheless, despite all this, it is well-known that no body of intellectuals is as consistently atheistic as the Russian. Atheism is the common creed into which those who are received into the bosom of the church of the humanist intelligentsia have to be baptised – not only those who have come from the cultivated classes, but those too who come from the populace at large. The pattern is already fixed from the beginning in the life of

Belinsky, the spiritual father of the Russian intelligentsia. And so, just as every social milieu develops its own mores, its particular beliefs, so the traditional atheism of our intelligentsia becomes itself a comprehensive and distinctive 'style', something not even talked about, as if this silence were a mark of good taste. In the eyes of our intelligentsia, guaranteed enlightenment and culture is synonymous with religious indifferentism and apostasy. There is no debate about this among the differing factions and parties or 'tendencies'; on this point they are at one. It is the pervasive diet of all the debased and impoverished culture found among the intelligentsia, in its papers and journals, its projects and programmes and mores and prejudices – like the blood, oxygenised by breathing, and diffusing itself through the whole organisation. There is no more significant fact than this in the history of the Russian Enlightenment. And on top of this we should recognise that Russian atheism is by no means a form of conscious apostasy, the fruit of complex, painful and protracted labour of mind, heart and will, weighing heavily on the whole life of the personality. On the contrary, it is most frequently sustained by an act of faith and preserves all the marks of a naive religious commitment – though they are all turned upside down. This is unaffected by the fact that it also takes on polemical, dogmatic and would-be scientific forms: such faith preserves at its base an uncritical and unexamined foundational axiom – that science is competent to provide a final solution to the questions of religion, and moreover can solve them only in a negative way. This goes along with a suspicious and uneasy relationship to philosophy – metaphysics in particular, which is rejected and condemned in advance.

This creed is shared equally among the instructed and the uninstructed, the old and the young. It is a philosophy absorbed in adolescence – whose onset is, of course, earlier for some and later for others; and in this phase the rejection of religion is something that is usually taken on lightly and almost naturally, with belief in science and in progress replacing it instantly. Our intelligentsia, once rooted in the soil, remain under the sway of this belief their whole life long, in the majority of cases, continuing to see these questions as adequately resolved and finally decided, hypnotised by the generally prevailing unanimity of opinion about this. Boys grow into mature men; and some of them acquire serious scientific knowledge and become noted specialists. In such a case, they will cast into the scales their authority as 'men of science' in favour of the atheism they learned to profess as adolescents, the atheism that was dogmatically taken for granted in the schoolroom – although in fact, where these issues are concerned, they have no more authority than any reflective and sensitive person. This is how the spiritual atmosphere of our high schools is built up; this is where the embryo intelligentsia is formed. And it is startling how little impression is made upon our intelligentsia by men of profound cultivation, intellect and genius, when such people summon them to an *approfondissement* of their religious sense, to an awakening from their dogmatic slumbers; how little notice was taken of the religious thinkers and writers of the Slavophil movement, of Vladimir Soloviev, Bukharev, Sergei Trubetskoi and others; how deaf our intelligentsia has been to the religious message of Dostoevsky – or even Tolstoy, despite the show of devotion to his name.

It is the dogmatic character of Russian atheism that is its most striking feature, the religious superficiality and frivolity, so to speak, with which it is accepted. But until recently, the problems of religious belief, in all their immense and exceptional seriousness and burning intensity, were not at all noticed or understood by 'cultivated' society in Russia; religion has only been of interest to the extent that it has been tied up with politics, or in relation to the propagation of atheism. There is an astonishing philistinism about religious matters among our intelligentsia. I do not say this simply to accuse, since there are, perhaps, particular historical reasons for this state of affairs, but by way of diagnosing a condition of the spirit. As far as religion is concerned, our intelligentsia has still not advanced beyond the adolescent stage; it is still incapable of thinking seriously about religion and has not allowed itself any conscious religious self-definition. It has never lived through the experience of religious thought and so remains, strictly speaking, not 'above' religion, as it likes to think of itself, but simply outside of it. The best evidence for all this is provided by the historical development of Russian atheism. It was taken over by us from the West (not for nothing was it the first article in the creed of the Russian 'Westerniser'). We accept it as the last word of

Western civilisation, at first in the shape of the Voltairean and materialist philosophy of the French encyclopedists, then in the form of atheist versions of socialism (Belinsky), later still as the kind of materialism popular in the sixties, positivism and Feuerbachian humanism; then, in more modern times, economic materialism and, in recent years, critical philosophy. In the dense foliage of the tree of Western civilisation, with its roots going deep into a history of its own, our attention has been caught by one branch only. We have not known and not wanted to know all the rest, in full confidence that we are grafting ourselves on to the authentic stock of European civilisation. But this civilisation not only has a variety of fruits and a multiplicity of branches, it also has roots nourishing the tree, and to a certain extent countering the effects of a good many poisonous fruits with their healthy sap. So, even negative doctrines have at their origins, among the other powerful and antithetical spiritual currents in their milieu, a psychological and historical significance very different from that which they acquire when they appear in a cultural vacuum and claim to provide a structure for the essential basis of an enlightened and civilised life in Russia. *Si duo idem dicunt, non est idem.* No culture was ever yet built on such a foundation.

It is often forgotten these days that Western European culture has religious roots to a very high degree; a good half of it is constructed on a religious basis with its foundations deep in the Middle Ages and the Reformation. Whatever may have been our attitude in the past to Reformation dogmatics and Protestantism in general, there is no denying that the Reformation provoked an immense spiritual advance in the whole of the Western world, including even those parts that remained faithful to Catholicism but were compelled to find renewal through controversy with their foes. The new personality of European humanity was, in this sense, born in the Reformation era, and this origin has left its mark: political freedom, liberty of conscience, human and civic rights were all proclaimed by the Reformation (at least in England). The significance of Protestantism, especially the Reformed tradition, Calvinism and Puritanism, for economic development has become clear in recent studies; the outworking of individualism in this tradition offered a welcome and apt structure of thought for those taking a leading role in the growth of national economies. Also in connection with Protestantism, very importantly, there occurred the development of modern science and, more particularly, modern philosophy. And the whole of this development advanced in precise and steady historical succession and order, without great gulfs and avalanches. The cultural history of the Western European world presents itself as a single connected whole, in which both the medieval and the Reformation epochs live on and still have their indispensable place alongside the tendencies and movements of more recent times.

Already in the Reformation era, the spiritual channel which was to be decisive for the Russian intelligentsia had been marked out. Alongside the Reformation, there was a revival of some of the features of paganism in the humanist Renaissance, the resurrection of classical antiquity. In parallel with the religious individualism of the Reformation, a neo-pagan kind of individualism was also gaining strength, exalting natural and unregenerate humanity. In this perspective, humanity was good and beautiful in virtue of its own nature, which was only disfigured by external conditions; all that was needed was to restore the natural condition of humanity, and all would be accomplished. Here is the root of all sorts of different theories about the law of nature, as also of modern doctrines about progress and the unlimited power of reforms in the external life of humanity to resolve the human tragedy – the root, therefore, of the whole of modern humanism and socialism. The apparent closeness in external form of religious individualism and pagan individualism does not cancel out their profound internal difference; so it is that we see in recent history not only a parallel development but also a conflict between these two currents of thought. In the history of ideas, the motifs of humanistic individualism are signally reinforced in the epoch of the so-called *Aufklärung,* in the seventeenth, eighteenth and part of the nineteenth centuries. It is the Enlightenment that draws the most radical negative conclusions from the original premises of humanism: in the religious sphere it moves, by way of both rationalism and empiricism, towards positivism and materialism; in ethics, by way of 'natural morality', to utilitarianism and hedonism. Materialistic brands of socialism can also be considered as a late-autumnal fruit of the Enlightenment.

This general tendency of thought, which is in part a result of the fragmentation of the Reformation heritage, and is itself one of the factors promoting fragmentation in the spiritual life of the West, has been especially influential in recent history. It is the inspiration of the great French revolution and of most of the revolutions of the nineteenth century; and, at another level, it has also provided a spiritual foundation for the European mercantile bourgeois mentality, whose dominance superseded the 'heroic age' of the Enlightenment. However, it is important not to forget that, although the face of the earth in Europe is so largely disfigured by the wide diffusion of Enlightenment philosophy among the mass of the population and is still under the ice-cap of bourgeois culture, the Enlightenment never played and does not now play a wholly exclusive or even a dominant role in the history of culture. The tree of European culture is still nourished, even if imperceptibly, by the spiritual sap of its ancient religious roots coursing through its pores. These roots, this healthy historical conservatism, are what guarantees the durability of the tree itself; although, to the extent that the Enlightenment permeates the root and bole, it sets in motion the process of wasting and decline. It is impossible, therefore, to conceive of Western European civilisation as irreligious in its historical foundations, despite the fact that it has increasingly become so in recent generations. Our own intelligentsia in their enthusiasm for all things Western have not got beyond a merely external appropriation of the modern political and social ideas of the West, by taking them on board in association with the most extreme and strident forms of Enlightenment philosophy. But in the Russian intelligentsia's option for the West, there is no essential accord with Western civilisation in its organic entirety. For the Russian intellectual, the role of the 'dark age' of the medieval period, the entire Reformation epoch with its immense spiritual advances, the whole development of scientific and philosophical thought apart from its extreme Enlightenment forms, all these pale into insignificance in historical perspective. First came barbarism, then civilisation shone forth – i.e. the Enlightenment, materialism, atheism, socialism: there you have the beautifully simple philosophy of history characteristic of the average Russian intellectual. And so, in the present conflicts over the formation of Russian culture, it is necessary to contend – among other things – for a far deeper and more historically aware 'pro-Western' stance.

Why has it turned out that our intelligentsia has been so ready to adopt these particular dogmas of the Enlightenment? Many historical reasons might be adduced for this, but it is a familiar enough truth that this choice is also a *free act* on the part of the intelligentsia themselves, for which they are accordingly to be held accountable before nation and history.

In any event, it is especially thanks to this option on their part that the interconnections in Russia's cultural and educational life have been shattered; and this rupture is the cause of the spiritual sickness afflicting our nation.

III

Having rejected Christianity and its established forms of life, our intelligentsia takes for granted, along with atheism – or more precisely, *instead* of atheism – the dogmas of a religion of the human-as-divine, in one or other of its variants, as elaborated by the Western Enlightenment. What seems to be the basic dogma characteristic of all its different forms is the belief in the natural perfection of the human and the illimitable nature of the progress achieved by human powers – but human powers that are, at the same time, conceived in mechanistic terms. Just as all evil is to be explained by disorders external to human social life, so there can be no personal guilt or responsibility; the entire task of social construction consists in the conquest of these external disorders by – naturally enough – external reforms. Once providence and any sort of primordial plan realising itself in history have been denied, humanity puts itself in the place of providence and sees itself as its own saviour. This self-evaluation does not seem to interfere with the manifestly contradictory belief in a mechanistic account of the human, sometimes in terms of a crudely materialistic understanding of historical process, which explains it in terms of the activity of elemental forces (as with economic materialism); yet the human person remains, for all this, the sole reasonable and conscious agent, his or her own providence. Such was the typical frame of mind in the West, where it appeared in an age of cultural flowering, profoundly aware of human possibilities, and given added psychological colouring by the sense of cultural self-satisfaction characteristic of the expansion of bourgeois prosperity. From the point of view of any religious evaluation, this self-deifying of the European mercantile bourgeoisie – common to socialism and individualism alike – looks like a repellent case of self-satisfaction and spiritual larceny, a temporary deadening of religious consciousness; but in fact in the West this 'humanity-as-divine', once having been through its *Sturm und Drang*, has long since become, though no-one can say for how long, tame and placid – as has European socialism. In any case, it has so far proved powerless to destroy the laboriously constructed vault of European culture (although this is what it would in fact involve if it persisted long enough) and the spiritual health of the European people. Age-long tradition and the historical disciplines of labour have already practically triumphed over the influence of self-deification. But it is otherwise in Russia, in the face of the ruptures that have happened here, breaking the connections between the periods of our history. The religion of the human-as-divine, and its essential core, the idea of self-deification, have been accepted in Russia not only with the ordinary fervour of youth but also with the adolescent's ignorance of life and of his own capacity, and so have assumed almost feverish forms. Thus inspired, our intelligentsia has developed the sense of a vocation to play the role of providence for the nation at large. It recognised itself as the solitary bearer of illumination and of European culture in this country, where – as it seemed to them – everything hitherto had been steeped in impenetrable darkness, everything was barbarous and foreign. The intelligentsia acknowledged its spiritual guardianship over Russia, and set out to determine its salvation, as understood and conceived by itself.

The intelligentsia thus came to stand in relation to Russian history and contemporary society in the position of an *heroic* challenging force engaged in *heroic* conflict, a position resting on the intelligentsia's own self-valuation. *Heroism* is, I believe, the word that reveals the fundamental nature of the intelligentsia world-view and ideal; more particularly, a heroism of self-apotheosis. The entire 'economy' of its spiritual power is based on this self-perception.

The isolated position of the intellectual in this country, his uprootedness from the native soil, his harsh and difficult historical milieu, his lack of serious knowledge and historical experience – all this has stimulated the psychology of such 'heroism'. The intellectual, especially at certain particular times, has fallen into a state of heroic ecstasy which has a manifestly hysterical colouring. Russia must be saved, and the intelligentsia can and must be shown to be its saviour, in general and even in specific, named and particular, instances; and without it there is no saviour and no salvation. Nothing so firmly reinforces the psychology of heroism than external persecution, oppression, conflict with its environment, danger and even destruction. And, as we know, Russian history is not lacking in this respect; the Russian intelligentsia has evolved and matured in an atmosphere of uninterrupted martyrdom. It is impossible not to bow down in reverence before their consecrated suffering. But such a genuflection before these sufferings in their immense past and heavy present scale, before this involuntary 'crucifixion', does not oblige us to keep silence about what still remains true, what we cannot pass over in silence, even in the name of piety towards the intelligentsia's martyrology.

So it is suffering and oppression above all that secure the canonisation of the hero, both in his own eyes and in those of the people around him. And just as, in consequence of the most deplorable features of Russian life, such a fate so often overtakes the intellectual at a young age, so this self-perception develops very early on; and the rest of his life then simply exhibits a consistent movement in a direction already established. Anyone can, without any trouble, find plenty of examples in literature, and from their own observation of life, of how, on the one side, you have the crippling effects of a police state, depriving people of the possibility of useful work, and how, on the other, this very fact aids in the elaboration of a certain 'aristocratic' quality of spiritual life, and – so to speak – the sense of a 'patented' and authorised heroic style in its sacrificial activity. It is a matter for bitter reflection how much the psychology of Russian intelligentsia 'heroism' owes to the pressure of resisting the influence of the police state, and how great this influence was, not only for people's external fate but upon their spirits and their world-view as well. In any event, the influences stemming from Western 'Enlightenment', the religion of the human-as-divine and self-apotheosis, found an unexpected but powerful ally in the prevailing conditions of life in Russia. If the youthful intellectual, a male or female student, say, has any remaining doubt as to whether he or she is ripe for an historical mission to save their native land, the fact that the Department of Internal Affairs takes this ripeness for granted removes all remaining traces of uncertainty. The transformation of Russian youth or of yesterday's average citizen into the heroic mould, with the interior labour demanded for such a transformation, in fact requires an uncomplicated and usually brief process of appropriating certain dogmas of the religion of the human-as-divine and the quasi-scientific 'programme' of some party or other that corresponds to the change in personal self-perception; after which the stage trappings of heroism grow up of their own accord. In the furthest future, refinements of suffering, bitterness at the harshness of authority and at the burdensome loss and sacrifice required, simply bring to perfection the building-up of this type of personality. Whatever may then befall them, they will certainly no longer doubt their mission.

The heroic intellectual is thus not content with the role of a humble worker (even if he is in fact obliged to confine himself to this); his vision is of being the saviour of humanity or, at least, of the Russian people. What is necessary for him (in his dreams, of course) is the heroic maximum, not a half-baked minimum. Maximalism is an inalienable part of that intelligentsia heroism which revealed itself with such astonishing clarity at the time of the revolution. This was not a feature of one party only; this maximalist impulse is the very soul of heroism, since the hero cannot be reconciled to small things. Even if he sees no present or even future possibility of realising this maximum, it is this alone which occupies his thoughts. He makes a leap of historical imagination, and, with little interest in the path he has leapt over, directs his gaze solely on the luminous point that marks the very limit of the historical horizon. Such maximalism shows clear signs of sickness, self-hypnosis, at the level of ideas; it paralyses thought and furthers fanaticism, it is deaf to the voice of life. This offers some sort of answer to the historical question of why, during the revolution, it was the most extreme tendencies that prevailed, tendencies which meant that the immediate tasks of the moment were all defined in a more and more 'maximalist' way (to the point of seeking the establishment of a republican or anarchist society). In this way, these more extreme and clearly senseless tendencies became more powerful and influential, and, given the general leftward drift of our pusillanimous and passive society, which so easily submits to *force majeure*, they squeezed out all the more moderate trends (suffice it to recall the hatred expressed by the 'left bloc' for the 'Kadet' party).

Every hero has his own mode of saving the human race and must work this out for his social programme. Usually this means taking on the programme of one of the existing political parties or sects, which, indistinguishable in their totality (being mostly based on materialist socialism or even, more recently, anarchism), go their different ways in terms of methods. It would be wrong to think that these party political programmes have any psychological correspondence with what they mostly pretend to be – parliamentary parties as found in Western Europe; this is something far greater. It is a religious *creed*, a self-authenticating method of saving humanity, an ideological monolith which can only be accepted or rejected. In the name of belief in whatever the programme is that presents itself, the best element in the intelligentsia subjects itself to the sacrifice of life and welfare, freedom and happiness. Although these programmes are usually presented as 'scientific', which increases their attractiveness, it is better to say nothing about the degree of their actual 'scientific' status; indeed, the most fervent of their adherents, considering the degree of their maturity and education, may in any case turn out to be the worst possible judges in this matter.

All feel themselves to be heroes, equally elected to be saviours and agents of providence – but all are not equally at one as to the ways and means of achieving this salvation. And since in fact the same central chords of the soul are touched by all the discordant variety of programmes, partisan dissensions become entirely non-negotiable. The intelligentsia, smitten with 'Jacobinism', struggling towards a 'seizure of power', a 'dictatorship' in the name of the people's salvation, inevitably breaks up and dissolves into mutually hostile factions; and this is more sharply felt the more the 'heroic' temperature rises. Impatience and mutual controversy are such familiar characteristics of our partisan intelligentsia that we need only mention them in passing. Something like self-poisoning is going on in the life and activity of the intelligentsia. It is of the very essence of heroism that it presupposes a passive object to be worked on – the 'people' or the 'humanity' being saved – amongst whom the hero, individual or collective, is invariably and exclusively conceived as a solitary figure. Once there is more than one hero or heroic project on the scene, rivalry and division are inevitable, since it is impossible to establish more than one 'dictatorship' at the same time. Heroism as a global attitude to the world is a principle making for separation, not unification; it produces rivals, not fellow-workers.

Our intelligentsia, almost uniformly involved in struggling for collectivism, for the possibility of conciliarity [*sobornost'*] in the life of human beings, appeared in its general ethos as anticonciliar, anticollective, since it carries in itself the principle of 'heroic' self-assertion. The hero is, in a certain degree, a superman, standing to his neighbours in the arrogant and hectoring posture of a saviour. For all its struggles for democracy, the intelligentsia is only a particular manifestation of class pride, 'aristocratism', setting itself disdainfully over against the life of the 'natives' or 'locals'. Anyone who has lived in intelligentsia circles will be perfectly familiar with this disdain and self-conceit, this consciousness of one's own infallibility and contempt for all who think otherwise, this abstract dogmatism in which all teaching is cast in such circles.

As a result of its maximalism, the intelligentsia remains remote from arguments alike of historical realism and of scientific knowledge. Socialism itself is for them not a cumulative concept meaning progressive socio-economic transformation and consisting in a sequence of specific and entirely concrete reforms; not an 'historical movement', but a transhistorical 'ultimate goal' (in the terminology of the well-known Bernstein controversy), for which a great historical leap forward must be accomplished by an act of heroism on the part of the intelligentsia. Hence the lack of any sense of historical actuality and the absolute geometrical straight lines in which opinion and judgement operate – the famous 'principled' character of the intelligentsia. It seems that there is no word so often on their lips as this; everything is judged on 'principle', i.e. in fact *abstractly*, with no acquaintance with the complexity of an actual situation, frequently shaking off the constraints and difficulties of undertaking the proper analysis of circumstances that is required. Anyone who has had dealings with the intelligentsia at work will be familiar with the cost of their 'principled' unpracticality, which leads often enough to 'straining at gnats and swallowing camels'.

This maximalism constitutes the greatest obstacle to raising the level of general culture, especially in those matters which it considers to be its speciality, questions of a social and political nature. Once it has inspired itself with the idea that the end and the means of the movement are already fixed, and fixed, moreover, 'scientifically', then of course it loses interest in studying the mediating connections that bring the goal nearer. Whether consciously or not, the intelligentsia lives in an atmosphere of expectation, the expectation of a social miracle, a global cataclysm; it lives in a 'chiliastic' frame of mind.

Heroism struggles for the salvation of humankind by its *own* powers and, moreover, by *external* means; hence the exceptional value ascribed to the heroic deed, the maximal incarnation of the programme of maximalism. It is necessary to move something, to achieve something beyond ordinary power, yielding up in this cause whatever is most costly and precious, even life itself: such is the basic imperative of heroism. Becoming a hero, becoming a saviour of humanity is possible through heroic deeds, ultimately beyond the bounds of mundane daily duty. This dream that lives in the soul of the intelligentsia, though realised only in some individuals, grows to universal proportions as a criterion of judgement and discernment in life. The achieving of such an heroic deed is both extraordinarily burdensome, since it requires a struggle against the extremely powerful instincts of fear and attachment to life, and extraordinarily simple, since it demands an effort of will that lasts only for a relatively short period of time, though the results conceived and expected from it are so highly esteemed.

Sometimes the enthusiasm for leaving life behind that results from an inability to come to terms with it, the inability to bear the burden of living, merges indistinguishably into heroic self-abnegation, so that the question must, reluctantly, be allowed to arise: is this heroism or suicide? Indeed, the intelligentsia's calendar can commemorate many such heroes, who have performed prodigious feats in terms of suffering and protracted efforts of will, yet, in spite of the differences arising from the capacities of different individuals, still have the same tone or ethos in this respect.

Obviously, this attitude to the world is far better suited to the stormier moments of history than to its more serene periods, which are so oppressively tedious for heroes. The greatest opportunity for heroic action is when irrational 'heightening of awareness', exaltation, intoxicated lust for combat create an atmosphere of heroic daring and adventurousness; all these things are the active element of heroism. Hence the enormous power of revolutionary romanticism among our intelligentsia, their celebrated 'revolutionary spirit'. We must not overlook the fact that revolution is understood in a *negative* way; it has no independent content but is characterised purely and simply as the denial of what it destroys. Thus the 'pathos', the emotional tone, of revolution is hatred and destructiveness. But one of the major figures of the intelligentsia, Bakunin, had already formulated the notion that the spin of destruction was simultaneously the spirit of creation; and this belief is a central nerve in the psychology of heroism. It simplifies the job of historical construction; on such an understanding, what this requires above all is strength of muscle and nerve, temperament and mettle. And, looking at the record of the Russian revolution, more than one case of such simplified understanding comes to mind . . . . .

The psychology of intelligentsia heroism is shaped above all by the social groups and external conditions amongst which its character is most clearly revealed in the full consistency of undeviating maximalism. In our society, it is the young student world that presents just this happy combination of circumstances. Thanks to its physiological and psychological immaturity, its lack of life experience and scientific knowledge, and its compensating fervour and self-confidence, thanks to its privileged social position – but a position not yet as isolated as the world of the Western bourgeois student – our educated youth has become the most finished paradigm of heroic maximalism. And if the essential embodiment of spiritual experience in

Christianity is *starchestvo* [the nurturing work of an 'elder', a spiritual father], then for our intelligentsia this role naturally comes to be played by student youth. *Spiritual 'paedocracy'*, the government of children, is the greatest evil of our society, and at the same time a symptomatic manifestation of the heroic ideals of the intelligentsia, its fundamental trait set out in accentuated or exaggerated form. This abnormal relationship, in which the judgements and opinions of the student generation turn out to be normative guiding influences for their elders, turns the natural order of things upside down, and is equally destructive for both parties. Historically speaking, this spiritual hegemony is connected with the leading role actually played by students in their irruptions into Russian history; psychologically, it is to be explained by spiritual fashions among the intelligentsia which remain throughout life – in its most lively and vigorous representatives – identical with those of student youth as far as world-views are concerned. Hence the profoundly bad and widespread indifference and, much worse, the covert or even open approval with which some among us view the way in which our young people, devoid of knowledge and experience, are fired by the heroic ideals of the intelligentsia to involve themselves in social experiments that are serious and dangerous in their consequences, and which, of course, in their actual execution only strengthen the arm of reaction. There has been hardly any adequately self-critical reflection on, or any appraisal of, the fact that we have groups whose membership is extremely youthful and immature committed to the most 'maximalist' actions and programmes. Worse still, many take this to be entirely natural. In the days of the revolution, 'student' became the name by which members of the intelligentsia were popularly known.

Every stage of life has its advantages, and youth, with its still latent capacities, usually has a good many of them. Anyone concerned for the future will be concerned about the younger generation. But to be spiritually dependent on them, to seek their favour and approbation, to wait on their opinions and take them as a standard of judgement, this is evidence of the spiritual weakness of a society. In any case, it is a distinctive sign of the whole age we live in and of the essential structure of intelligentsia heroism that the ideal of the Christian saint, the *podvizhnik* involved in the spiritual struggle, should have been ousted by the image of the revolutionary student.

IV

As recent years, alas, have shown, maximalist means are linked with maximalist goals. In this lack of fastidiousness about means, the heroic attitude of 'everything is permitted' (which Dostoevsky had prophetically depicted in *Crime and Punishment* and *The Devils*), the nature of intelligentsia heroism in its commitment to the human-as-divine finds its supreme articulation. In this context we can clearly see the process of self-deification at work, the putting of oneself in the place of God or of providence – and that not only in terms of goals and plans but in the ways and means of realising them as well. I set out to realise my own idea, and for the sake of it I free myself from all ordinary morality; I give myself rights not only over the property but over the life and death of others, if this is what is needed for realising my idea. Within every maximalist is a little Napoleon of socialism or anarchism. Amoralism or (to use an older term) nihilism is the necessary consequence of self-deification, and it is here that the danger of self-deification lies hidden, the danger of internal disintegration, the inevitable fall that lies ahead. And the bitter disillusion that so many experienced in the revolution, the indelible remembered images of rampant self-will, acquisitiveness, mass terror, all this was manifestly more than a contingent effect of revolutionary action; it was the outworking of those spiritual potentialities that are necessarily bound up in the psychology of self-deification.

In fact, the path of heroism is open only for a few chosen souls and, what is more, only in exceptional moments of history: in the intervals between these moments, life is just the ordinary daily round. Now the intelligentsia is not made up entirely of heroic characters. Without the actual reality of heroic living, or at least the possibility of its appearance, 'heroism' becomes mere pretence, a seductive pose; a peculiar spirit of heroic bigotry develops, a permanent 'principled' opposition, an exaggerated sense of being in the right and a weakened consciousness of obligation and personal responsibility overall. The ordinary citizen, in some respects above and in some respects below the level of the milieu in which he lives, begins to speak of himself with arrogance as soon as he has donned the uniform of the intelligentsia. This evil is particularly noticeable in provincial life in our country. Self-deification in one's own estimation is well fitted for producing a certain inflated pretentiousness. A man deprived of absolute norms and firm principles for personal and social behaviour will replenish his store from the resources of self-will and self-definition. This is why nihilism is such an appalling scourge, a dreadful spiritual cancer eating away at our society. The heroic 'everything is permitted' is imperceptibly replaced by a plain lack of principle in all things, as far as personal life and conduct are concerned, the issues that fill up the span of ordinary mundane existence. This is one of the main reasons for the fact that in our society, with such an abundance of heroes, there is such a dearth of conscientious and disciplined people equipped for serious work, and the same younger generation so committed to heroism, the generation to whom their elders look for their own self-definition, so easily and imperceptibly changes into 'superfluous' people or Chekhovian and Gogolesque characters, ending up in wine and gambling, if not worse. The clear-eyed genius of Pushkin lifts the veil on a possible future for Lensky, who dies with such tragic untimeliness, and sees in it only an unrelievedly prosaic landscape. Make the mental experiment of doing the same thing in relation to some other young man, one who is now surrounded by the aureole of heroism, seeing him in later years simply in the role of an ordinary worker, when the affectation of heroism has disappeared, leaving in his soul only the vacuity of nihilism. Not for nothing did Nekrasov, the poetic voice of the intelligentsia, author of 'A Knight for an Hour', sense that an early death is the ultimate apotheosis of intelligentsia heroism.

> Do not grieve so foolishly for him:
> It is good to die young!
> Relentless mediocrity had no chance
> To cast its shadow upon him.

This affectation of heroism, with all its superficiality and transitoriness, explains the extraordinarily irresolute character of the taste and style of the intelligentsia, their beliefs and attitudes, changing according to the whims of fashion. Many are astounded at the radical changes of mind which have occurred over the last four years – the transition from the heroic revolutionary mindset to the nihilistic and pornographic – and also at the present epidemic of suicide, which they mistakenly explain with reference only to political reaction and the heavy pressures of Russian life.

But both this course of events and its attendant hysteria appear natural to the intelligentsia; it prompts no alteration in their essential nature, which only shows itself more fully as the revolutionary festival gives place to the common daily round. False heroism does not go unpunished. The spiritual condition of the intelligentsia cannot but give cause for serious alarm. Far greater unrest is provoked by the spiritual attrition of the younger generation, and especially the fate of the children of the intelligentsia. Inconstant, cut off from the organic structures of life, devoid of any abiding support, the intelligentsia, with its atheism, its blinkered rationalism and general lack of fixed direction and firm principle in daily life, hand on all these characteristics to their children as well, the only difference being that these latter are deprived even in their infancy of the healthy nourishment that their parents received from the folk environment.

In the milieu of intelligentsia life, the ideas of *personal* morality, *personal* self-development, the attainment of *personality* itself are extremely unpopular (and conversely, the word 'social' has a peculiar, sacramental character). Although the intelligentsia's attitude to the world presents itself as the ultimate self-affirmation of personality, the self-deification of personality, the intelligentsia mercilessly castigates this same ideal of personality in its theoretical pronouncements, almost always reducing it without remainder to the sum of environmental influences and the elemental forces of history (in conformity with the general doctrine of the Enlightenment). The intelligentsia does not want to allow that there is any living and creative energy bound up in personality, and remains deaf to everything that touches closely on this problem; deaf not only to Christian doctrine, but even to the teachings of Tolstoy (in which there can certainly be found a healthy element witnessing to the ideal of a personal process of deeper penetration into the life of the self), and to all philosophical doctrines that compel attention to this question.

Meanwhile, it is precisely this lack of an adequate doctrine of personality that constitutes the intelligentsia's chief weakness. The distortion of personality, the falsity of the ideal held up for its development, is the root cause from which the weaknesses and defects of our intelligentsia arise, its historical bankruptcy. The intelligentsia must be set on the right path from within, not from without – a task it can only perform for itself, through free, spiritual growth and achievement [*podvig*], invisible but entirely real.

V

The peculiar nature of intelligentsia heroism becomes clearer to us if we compare it with its polar opposite in the spiritual realm – Christian heroism or, more precisely, the Christian spiritual struggle [*podvizhnichestvo*]; for, in Christian terms, the hero is the 'spiritual athlete' [*podvizhnik*]. The fundamental difference here is not so much external as internal and religious. The hero, casting himself in the role of providence, arrogates to himself, in virtue of this usurpation, not only a greater responsibility than can be borne, but also a greater task than a human being can compass. The Christian *podvizhnik* trusts in a divine providence, without whose will not a hair falls from the head. In his eyes, both history and the unique life of a human individual are realisations of this divine purpose, although in particular details the divine economy of things is beyond his grasp; here he must humble himself in the *podvig* of faith. Thanks to this, he is liberated from heroic posturing and pretension. His attention is concentrated on his immediate task, his concrete obligations and the fulfilling of them with strict fidelity and without delay. Naturally, both the determining and the fulfilling of these obligations sometimes requires no less wide a horizon, no less breadth of awareness, than the heroism the intelligentsia lays claim to. Here, however, the concentration is on a consciousness of personal duty and its fulfilment, on self-control; and this shifting of the centre of attention onto the self and its obligations, this liberation from a false image of oneself as the (uninvited) saviour of the world and the arrogance that invariably goes with it, restores health to the soul, filling it with the sense of a wholesome Christian humility. Dostoevsky, in his Pushkin lecture, called the Russian intelligentsia to this spiritual self-renunciation, this sacrifice of the arrogant ego of the intelligentsia in the name of a greater holiness: 'Humble yourself, proud man, and, above all else, break down your pride ... Conquer yourself, quiet yourself – and you will begin a great work, you will make others free, you will see good days, for your life is fulfilled'.

In the milieu of the intelligentsia, no word is so unpopular as *humility*; there are few notions so prone to incomprehension and distortion, few notions on which it is so easy for intelligentsia demagogy to sharpen its teeth; and this, you could say, is the best evidence of all as to the spiritual nature of the intelligentsia. It lays bare its arrogance, the arrogance that rests upon the self-apotheosis of heroism. At the same time, humility, according to the unanimous witness of the Church, is the primary and fundamental virtue; but even outside the Christian sphere it is a quality that has its own full integrity, testifying, wherever it is seen, to a high level of spiritual development. It should be easy even for a member of the intelligentsia to understand that for our scholars and savants, for example, the deeper and wider their knowledge, the greater their sense of being merely at the brink of the abyss of their ignorance; that success in knowledge is, for such people, accompanied by a growing understanding of their ignorance, an increase of intellectual humility. This is confirmed by the biographies of the greatest scholars. Conversely, confident self-sufficiency, the expectation of reaching a fully satisfactory level of knowledge by one's own unaided powers, is a sure and certain symptom of scientific immaturity, or simply youthfulness.

The same sense of a profound dissatisfaction with one's own achievements and their failure to produce something conformable to one's ideal of beauty – which is the task of art – is no less characteristic of our artists, for whom their work inevitably becomes a torment, even though it is only in this work that they discover their true life. You will find no true artist who is without this sense of abiding dissatisfaction with his creation – which could be called a kind of humility before beauty. And the same sensation of the limited character of individual powers and resources in the face of ever-expanding tasks holds of the philosophical thinker, the civic activist, the planner of social policy, and many more.

But if the natural and necessary character of humility can be relatively easily understood in these specific areas of human activity, why does it appear so difficult where the central sphere of spiritual life, moral and religious self-awareness and self-examination, is concerned? This is where the decisive significance of one or another higher-level criterion or ideal of personal life becomes plain: will this criterion of self-examination be the image of perfect divine personality, incarnate in Christ, or the self-deifying human agent in one or another of its limited earthly shapes (humanity, the people, the proletariat, the superman) – i.e., in the long run, the self-sufficient ego, which sets before itself only itself in an heroic posture? The *podvizhnik* looks at the limited and distorted world of human sin and suffering, especially as it exists in his own self, with the purified eyes of the spirit, and in so doing brings to light new imperfections; the sense of distance from the ideal is intensified. In other words, the ethical development of personality is accompanied by an increasing awareness of one's imperfection, or (which comes to the same thing) is expressed in humility before God and 'walking in the sight of God' (as this is expounded in the consistent testimony of ecclesial and patristic literature). And this distinction between heroic and Christian self-valuation penetrates the furthest corners of the soul, its whole sense of itself.

As a result of the absence of an ideal of personality (or, more precisely, the *distortion* of this ideal), all that relates to the religious 'culture' of personality, its development and discipline, inevitably continues to be completely neglected among the intelligentsia. There is a lack of any of the absolute norms and values which are necessary for such cultivation, and which religion alone can provide. Above all, there is no understanding or awareness of sin – so much so that the very word has almost as barbarous and alien a sound in the ears of the intelligentsia as 'humility'. All the power of sin, its tormenting weight, the ubiquity and profundity of its influence on the whole of human life, in a word, the entire tragedy of the human condition, from which, in God's eternal plan, only Golgotha can provide deliverance, all this remains wholly outside the consciousness of the intelligentsia, who are still, as it were, in religious infancy – not *above* sin, but *below* the level at which they might be aware of it. Along with Rousseau and the Enlightenment, they have put their trust in the essential goodness of the natural man, believing that the doctrine of original sin and the radical corruption of human nature is a superstitious myth that has no correspondence with moral experience. Thus there is overall no particular concern about the cultivation of personality (the much-despised business of 'self-improvement'), nor any sense that there should be; all one's energies should be entirely expended on the struggle to improve the environment. While they declare personality to be the product of the environment, they offer this very same thing, personality, as the agent for improving the environment, like Baron Munchausen pulling himself out of the quagmire by his own hair.

Many features in the structure of the intelligentsia's life and soul and, alas, many of the sadder aspects and events of our revolution can be explained by this repudiation of the sense of sin, and a certain nervousness, to say the least, in mentioning it – features also of the spiritual decay that followed in the wake of the revolution. The intelligentsia has been feeding itself with many piquant dishes from the table of Western civilisation, finally surfeiting and disordering a stomach that was damaged to start with; is it not time to recall the plain and coarse but entirely healthy and nutritious diet of the old Mosaic decalogue, or to move on from there to the New Testament?....

Heroic maximalism is wholly projected outwards, wholly directed towards the attainment of external goals; as regards personal life, over and above the heroic act and all that goes with it, this maximalism turns out to be minimalism – i.e. it simply leaves the personal dimension out of its purview. Hence too its incompetence in forming and perfecting a stable, disciplined personality, capable of real work, standing on its own feet, not on the crest of a wave of public hysteria which will in due course sink down again. Every representative of the intelligentsia is defined by this combination of maximalism and minimalism, in which maximal claims can be advanced with the most minimal foundation in personality. This is equally true in the sphere of scientific knowledge as in experience of life and self-discipline; and this is thrown into high relief in the unnatural hegemony enjoyed by student youth, in our 'spiritual paedocracy'.

The world is understood very differently in the Christian spiritual struggle. In complete contrast to the arrogance of intelligentsia heroism, this struggle is above all a matter of maximalism in personal relations, in the demands made on oneself; and conversely, the harshness of external maximalism is here significantly softened. The Christian 'hero', the *podvizhnik* (in our admittedly rather provisional terminology), does not set himself to do the job of providence, and so does not link the destiny of history or humanity to his or anyone else's individual efforts). In his activity, he looks above all to the fulfilment of his duty before God, to the keeping of God's commandments; he is constantly turned Godward. He is obliged to fulfil this duty before God with the greatest possible completeness, and equally obliged to show both the greatest possible energy and the greatest degree of selflessness in discerning what constitutes this duty and its active performance. In a certain sense he too is bound to maximalism in action, but it is a wholly different sense. One of the most common misunderstandings where humility is concerned (one, moreover, that is not always *bona fide*) is that Christian humility, the interior and visible conflict with self, self-will, self-deification, is always to be interpreted in terms of passivity at the exterior level, as a reconciliation with evil, as inertia and even servility, or at least inactivity in the external sense; and in all this, the Christian spiritual struggle is confused with what is only one of its many forms (though a highly important one) – monasticism. But the struggle, understood as the internal establishing of personal reality, is compatible with all kinds of external activity, in so far as they do not contradict its basic principle.

Christian humility is particularly ardent in its opposition to the 'revolutionary' frame of mind. Without going into this question in detail, I want only to point out that revolution – i.e. revolution as a particular programme of political action – is not able of itself to settle the question of the spirit and ideals that should inspire it. When Dmitri Donskoi set out with the blessing of St Sergius to fight the Tatars, this was a revolutionary action in the political sense, a revolt against legally constituted authority; but at the same time it was, I believe, an act of Christian spiritual achievement in the souls of those involved, inseparably united to the active virtue of humility. And, conversely, the recent revolution, in so far as it was based on atheism, was remote in spirit not only from Christian humility but from Christianity in general. In the same way, there is an enormous spiritual difference between the Puritan revolution in England and the atheist revolution in France, as there is between Cromwell and Marat or Robespierre, between Ryleev or, more generally, the Christians among the Decembrists and more recent revolutionary activists.

In fact, of course, there may, in appropriate historical circumstances, be particular actions that can be called heroic, yet are wholly compatible with the psychology of Christian spiritual struggle; they are done not in the agent's own name, but in God's, not in an heroic spirit but in the spirit of interior labour and struggle, so that although they are 'heroic' in outward form their religious psychology is wholly distanced from what that word suggests. 'The Kingdom of Heaven suffers violence, and men of violence enter it by force' (Mt 11.2): 'violence' is required from all, the maximal effort of our energy is called out for the actualising of the good. But such violent exertion does not give us the right to the pretensions of the heroic self-image, the right of spiritual arrogance, since it is no more than the fulfilling of a duty: 'When you have done all that is commanded you, say, We are unprofitable servants; we have done no more than our duty' (Lk 17.10).

The Christian struggle is a matter of unremitting self-control, war with the lower and sinful levels of one's ego, ascesis of spirit. If heroism is characterised by the brief flare of intensity and the aspiration to do great deeds, here, in contrast, the norm that appears is far more of an even flow, 'moderation', a sustained habit of life, unwavering self-discipline, endurance and perseverance – precisely the qualities lacking in the intelligentsia. Faithful performance of one's duty, bearing of one's own cross, repudiation of self (not only in external things, but even more in the interior sense) and leaving the rest to providence – these are the marks of authentic spiritual labour. In monastic practice, there is a very fine expression for this religious and practical idea – 'obedience' [*poslushanie*]. This is the term applied to any and every particular job assigned to a monk, applied equally to all tasks, whether study or heavy physical labour, so long as they are done as a matter of religious duty. This notion can be extended beyond the boundaries of the monastic life and applied to all work of whatever kind it may be. The physician and the engineer, the professor and the political activist, the manufacturer and his workers can all of them in the fulfilling of their duties find themselves guided not by their own personal interest, spiritual or material, but by conscience and the imperative of duty in carrying out their 'obediences'. This discipline of obedience, this 'secular' asceticism (*innerweltliche Askese*, as the Germans say), has had immense influence over the development of personality in diverse sorts of work in Western Europe – a development still perceptible in our own day.

The reverse side of the maximalism of the intelligentsia appears in their historical restlessness, their lack of historical patience or temperance, the striving to bring about a social miracle – the practical negation of their theoretical commitment to evolutionism. In contrast, the discipline of 'obedience' should assist the development of patience in the face of history, self-mastery, stability of life; it teaches us how to endure the burdens of history, the yoke of obedience in history; it creates a certain 'earthiness', a sense of connectedness with the past and grateful indebtedness to it – something which is now so easily forgotten for the sake of the future. It restores the moral bond between children and parents.

Pure humanistic progress, in contrast, means contempt for one's forebears, a turning away from one's past and a wholesale condemnation of it, an ingratitude that is both historical and frequently, simply personal, a legal act of spiritual separation between fathers and children. The hero creates history according to his plan, he – so to speak – initiates history out of the resources of his own selfhood, and considers the realities of the world as raw material, passive objects for his influence to work on. The rupture of historical continuity in sensibility and will makes this inevitable.

The foregoing parallel allows us to draw a general conclusion about the relation between intelligentsia heroism and the Christian spiritual struggle. Beneath a certain external similarity there is no inner relationship at all between them, not even an underlying contingent one. The task of heroism is the external salvation of humankind (or more exactly, the future members of humankind) by its own powers and planning, 'in its own name'; the hero is the person who, in the highest degree, brings his idea to realisation, even if he loses his life for its sake. He is a 'man-God'. The task of the Christian struggle is to transform one's own life by the imperceptible process of self-renunciation, obedience; to perform one's work with whole-hearted endeavour, self-discipline, self-mastery, but also to see both it and oneself as an instrument of providence. The Christian saint is the person who, in the highest degree, reorders his personal will and the whole of his empirical personality as far as possible, through an uninterrupted and unremitting ascetic effort [*podvig*], so as to let it be wholly permeated by the will of God. The image of this total 'permeation' is the figure of the 'God-man', the one who comes 'not to do his own will, but the will of his Father', 'he who comes in the name of the Lord'.

The distinction between Christian heroism (at least in theory) and intelligentsia heroism, which, historically speaking, has borrowed certain of its basic dogmas from Christianity (especially the ideas of the identical status of all people, the absolute worth of human personality, equality and fraternity) is liable to be generally minimised these days rather than exaggerated. This tendency is assisted above all by the intelligentsia's incomprehension of how great a gulf actually lies between atheism and Christianity, an incomprehension that has more than once led to the image of Christ being 'improved', with typical self-assurance, set free from its 'ecclesiastical distortion' so as to bring into clearer outline its social democratic or revolutionary socialist character. We already have an instance of this in Belinsky, the father of the Russian intelligentsia. This has happened more than once – a process that is not only in poor taste but intolerable for religious sensibilities. But in other respects the intelligentsia has taken no interest in this rapprochement as such, resorting to it primarily in relation to political goals for the sake of facilitating 'agitation'.

Heroism and the Spiritual Struggle

There is another far more subtle and seductive, though no less blasphemous, falsehood, that has come to be repeated in various forms particularly often in recent years: this is the assertion that the maximalism of the intelligentsia and its revolutionary spirit – shown, in my view, to be spiritually grounded upon atheism – is distinguished in essence from Christianity only by its lack of explicit religious confession. Substitute the name of Marx or of Mikhailovsky for that of Christ, *Capital* for the Gospel or, better, the Apocalypse (for ease of citation), or, indeed, change nothing at all, and it remains only to reinforce the revolutionary spirit of the intelligentsia, to carry forward the revolutionary action of the intelligentsia, for a 'new religious consciousness' to come to birth out of all this (as if there were not already a sufficient example of what this carrying through of an intelligentsia revolution involves, as an example that brings to light all its spiritual potential, in the shape of the great French Revolution). If in the days before the revolution it was relatively easy to confuse the suffering and persecuted member of the intelligentsia, bearing on his shoulders the burden of the heroic battle against bureaucratic absolutism, with the Christian martyr, this has become far more problematic in the wake of the spiritual self-disclosure of the intelligentsia during the actual period of the revolution.

At the present time it is also possible to observe a distortion of Christianity perpetrated by the intelligentsia that is particularly characteristic of our own epoch – the appropriation of Christian vocabulary and ideas for the maintenance of the whole spiritual physiognomy of intelligentsia heroism. All of us who are Christians from an intelligentsia background will find this combination of ideas deeply rooted in ourselves. It is very easy for intelligentsia heroism, wrapping itself in Christian garments and sincerely understanding its intelligentsia-based experiences and conventions of heroic pathos in terms of the righteous indignation of the Christian believer, to present itself as a Christian, ecclesial revolutionary programme, setting its new form of sanctity, its new religious consciousness, against the deceits of the 'historic' Church. The same 'Christianising' representative of the intelligentsia, frequently unable these days to meet the ordinary requirements laid upon a member of the 'historic Church', very readily feels he is a Martin Luther, or, still more, the prophetic bearer of the 'new religious consciousness', called not only to renew the life of the Church but to create new forms for it, if not practically a new religion. Equally in the sphere of secular politics, the customary maximalism of the intelligentsia which sustains the revolutionary programme is simply 'seasoned' with Christian terminology or Christian texts and presented in the guise of genuine Christianity at work in politics. This intelligentsia brand of Christianity leaves untouched all that is supremely anti-religious in the context of intelligentsia heroism, especially its inner animating structure; it is a compromise between contradictory and conflicting principles, which has only a temporary and transient significance and is without any independent vitality. It is superfluous for contemporary intelligentsia heroism and impossible for Christianity. Like every other religion, Christianity is jealous; it is powerful in human beings only when it takes hold of their whole identity, soul, heart and will. There is no way in which this contrast can be obscured or softened.

Just as there is no kind of interior identity in substance between the martyrs of early Christianity and those of the revolution, despite all the external similarities in their struggles, so too there is no identity between intelligentsia heroism and Christian ascetic achievement, again despite all similarities in external manifestation (which may otherwise be granted, though only practically and provisionally). There is still a great gulf fixed, and it is impossible to be simultaneously on both sides. One must die for the other to be born, and, to the degree that one dies, the other grows and consolidates itself. There is the true correlation between the two world-views. It is necessary to 'repent', i.e. to see everything afresh, to change one's mind, to pass judgement on one's former interior life in all its depths, its twists and turns, so as to be born into a new life. That is why the first word in the proclamation of the gospel is a summons to repentance, founded upon self-knowledge and self-assessment. 'Repent (*metanoeite*), for the Kingdom of Heaven is at hand' (Mt 3.1–2, 4.17; Mk 1.14–15). The new soul must come to birth, the new 'inner man', which will be born and will develop and strengthen itself in the living-out of spiritual struggle. We are not talking about a political change or a party programme (the intelligentsia is normally incapable of conceiving regeneration in any other terms) or indeed *any* kind of programme, but about something far greater – human personhood itself; not the action but the agent. This regeneration is accomplished invisibly in the soul of man; but if invisible agencies can be seen to be effective even in the physical world, so in the moral realm their power cannot be gainsaid simply on the grounds that they cannot be sketched out in the itemised paragraphs of a manifesto.

A long and hard road lies ahead for the Russian intelligentsia, the road of personal re-education, on which there are no great leaps forward, no cataclysms, and victory comes only through stubborn self-discipline. Russia needs new labourers in all spheres of her life: in the state, for the realisation of political reform; in economics, for the improvement of the nation's economic life; in culture, for work that will carry forward the enlightenment of Russia; in the Church, to raise its educational level, among clergy and hierarchs. Such new people, if Russia can wait for them, will surely want to seek new practical paths for service as well as the concrete programmes already existing, and these will, I believe, emerge through their self-denying efforts.

VI

In relation to the Russian people, whose service is a fundamental principle for them, the intelligentsia oscillates continually and unavoidably between two extremes, uncritical worship of the people and spiritual aristocratism. The need to show this uncritical reverence in one form or another (in the form of old-fashioned populism, originating with Herzen and based on a belief in the essentially socialist character of the Russian people, or in the more recent Marxist form, in which only one section of the people, the proletariat, rather than the nation as a whole, is reckoned as having this character) arises from the very foundations of the intelligentsia's creed. But a contrary principle also arises necessarily from these same foundations – an attitude of arrogance towards the people as the object upon which salvific influence is to be exerted, as children who need a nanny to educate them in 'awareness', who are unenlightened in the intelligentsia's sense of the word.

Our literature is full of indications of the spiritual divorce between the intelligentsia and the people. Dostoevsky thought that this had been prophetically foreshadowed in Pushkin's work, first in the figure of the eternal vagabond Aleko, later in Eugène Onegin, opening the way to a whole succession of portraits of 'superfluous people'. And in fact the sense of rootedness, authentic historical blood-ties, shared interest, love for one's history and aesthetic appreciation of it, all these are strikingly rare among the intelligentsia; they have only two predominating colours on their palette, black for the past and rose-coloured for the future (and, in contrast, how much more clearly the spiritual greatness and acuity of perception of our major writers appears! They put down their roots deep in the history of Russia and bring out from these depths works like *Boris Godunov*, *The Song of the Merchant Kalashnikov*, or *War and Peace*). Generally, history provides only the raw material on which a theoretical schema must be imposed, whatever schema prevails in men's minds at a given moment (e.g. the theory of class war), or else raw material to serve the aims of propagandists and agitators.

The cosmopolitan nature of the Russian intelligentsia is well known. Educated in the abstract schemata of the Enlightenment, the member of the intelligentsia most naturally takes on the pose of a Marquis de Posa, feels himself to be a 'citizen of the world'; and this cosmopolitanism of the void, this lack of healthy rational sentiment which so stands in the way of a maturing of national self-awareness, is closely linked with the fact that the intelligentsia remain outsiders in relation to the life of the people.

The intelligentsia has yet to think through those national problems that have thus far occupied the attention only of the Slavophils; they have been content with 'natural' explanations for the origins of folk identity – a trend originating with Chernyshevsky, who laboured assiduously to destroy any awareness of the self-evident importance of the national problem, and persisting to our own time in the work of the Marxists who resolve it without remainder into the terms of class war.

The idea of a nation rests not only upon ethnographic and

historical foundations but, above all, on a religio-cultural base. It is founded upon a religio-cultural 'messianism', the mould in which the whole conscious sensibility of a people is necessarily cast. So it was in the case of the greatest bearer of the religious and messianic ideal – ancient Israel; so it is with every great nation in history. The struggle for national autonomy, for the preservation of national identity and its defence, is only a negative expression of this ideal, which has value only in connection with its positive and intelligent maintenance. This, indeed, was how the national ideal was understood by those who have given strongest expression to our folk consciousness – Dostoevsky, the Slavophils, Vladimir Soloviev – who linked this self-awareness with the idea of a universal mission for the Russian Church or Russian culture. Such an understanding of the national ideal in no way leads to nationalistic exclusivity; on the contrary, it alone can provide a positive image on which to ground the idea of a brotherhood of nations, rather than a non-national, atomistic ideal of world citizenship or the 'proletariat of all nations', cutting loose from their roots. The idea of nationhood, understood in this way, is a necessary positive condition for the progress of civilisation. The cosmopolitanism of our intelligentsia creates a great deal of difficulty for it, difficulties that are bound to arise in the attempt at the practical resolution of national problems; but it also involves paying a high price, the death of a whole dimension of the soul, that dimension, moreover, which is most directly orientated towards the life of the people. This is why – among other things – such cosmopolitanism is so easily exploited by the representatives of militant, chauvinistic nationalism, who, thanks to this, appear to have a monopoly of patriotism.

But the deepest gulf between intelligentsia and people is not caused simply by this, which is really only a derivative and second-order schism. The fundamental division is still to do with attitudes to religion. The world-view of the people and their spiritual outlook are determined by Christian belief. However great the distance between ideal and reality in this matter, however ignorant or unenlightened our people, their ideal is still Christ and his teaching and their norm of behaviour is the Christian spiritual struggle. What else has constituted the whole history of our people but this struggle, in the first days of our nation's oppression at the hands of the Tatars, then later at the hands of the Muscovite and Petrine state? Through the centuries-long history of affliction, we have stayed at our post, guarding Western civilisation from the barbaric peoples and the desert sands of Asia, in this harsh climate of ours with its perpetual famines and cold and hardships. If our people have been able to bear all this and still preserve its strength of soul, to come out alive, however much maimed by it all, it is solely because it has had a wellspring of spiritual power in its creed and in the ideals of Christian struggle and discipline, providing a firm foundation for its national health and vitality.

So too the light that burned in the monastic houses, where the *people* have flocked across the ages, seeking moral nurture and instruction, has illuminated Russia with these ideals, with the light of Christ. To the extent that they have actually received this light, the common people of Russia, for all their illiteracy, are – let me say it bluntly – spiritually more enlightened than her intelligentsia. But it is precisely in this central respect above all, in what touches the belief of the common people, that the intelligentsia's relation to them has been and still is characterised by incomprehension and even contempt.

So what contact there is between the intelligentsia and the people is primarily a collision between two systems of belief, two religions; and the intelligentsia's influence is seen above all in the way in which, having demolished the practice of popular religion, it proceeds to lay waste the soul of the people, removing the age-old foundations of its life, foundations that have hitherto remained unshakeable. But what has it to put in their place? How does it understand the task of educating the people? In a way dictated by the Enlightenment – that is to say, as the development of the intellect and the augmentation of knowledge. What is more, because of the lack of time and of capability, and, more seriously, the deficiencies in the actual formation of our would-be enlighteners themselves, the performance of this task is replaced by dogmatic exposition of whatever doctrine prevails at any given time in a given party (all this, of course, under the rubric of strict scientific method), or else by the mere transmission of fragments of knowledge from various spheres. This brings into very sharp focus both our general lack of culture, the inadequacy of our schools and their textbooks, and also, above all, the absence of plain literacy. For the members of the intelligentsia, these educational tasks are inseparably bound up with political and partisan projects, for which the outer forms of education are no more than a necessary means.

We have seen already how the soul of the people trembles after being injected with a significant dose of 'education' in the sense defined, how tragic is its reaction to this spiritual devastation. This reaction has appeared in the form of extremes of lawlessness, at first under the pretext of ideals, then without even any pretence of justification. The intelligentsia nursed the mistaken idea that Russian education and Russian culture could be erected on an atheistic foundation, in total disregard for the religious cultivation of personality, substituting for this a simple transmission of knowledge. Human personhood is not only intellect; it is, above all, will, character; and the neglect of this brings a cruel nemesis. To destroy the age-long foundations of life of the people in religious and ethical principles is to set free its darker elements, so much in evidence in Russian history, deeply infected by the evils of Tatar rule and the instincts of these nomadic conquerors. In the history of the Russian soul there is a constant struggle between the legacies of St Sergius's monastic community on the one hand and that of the Zaporozhian Cossacks and the hordes that made up the regiments of the usurpers Razin and Pugachev on the other. These terrifying, unrestrained, elemental forces, with their destructive nihilism, have only an apparent proximity to the revolutionary intelligentsia, though the latter take them to be partners in the same 'revolutionist' spirit; but, in fact, they have a very ancient ancestry, significantly older than that of the intelligentsia. The Russian state has, with great labour, triumphed over these forces, harnessing them, setting limits to them, but it has never wholly mastered them. One aspect of the influence of intelligentsia 'enlightenment' has been to awaken these sleeping instincts and to turn Russia back to a condition of chaos in which all that has been achieved in Russia's history by such labour and sacrifice is weakened. Such are the lessons of these recent years, such is the morality of popular revolution.

Thus there are clear and fundamental reasons for the deep spiritual conflict that has been tearing Russia apart in our times, the division of Russia into two separate halves, left-wing and right-wing blocs, 'Black Hundreds' and 'Red Hundreds'. Party division, based on differences in political ideas, social position or property interests, is a common and widespread phenomenon in countries that have a national representative system, and, in one sense, this is a necessary evil. But this division is nowhere so profound as in Russia; nowhere else has it so gravely fragmented the spiritual and cultural unity of the nation. Even the socialist parties of Western Europe that most sharply stand apart from the structures of 'bourgeois' society are still in fact organic parts of that society; they do not seek to dismantle its whole cultural framework. Our separation between right and left is distinguished in having for its object not only a differentiation in political ideals, but also, overwhelmingly, a differentiation of world-views or creeds. If you want a more accurate analogy in Western European history, a far closer one is furnished by the division between Catholics and Protestants in the successive religious wars of the Reformation era than by contemporary political parties. An analysis of these 'left' and 'right' blocs into their basic spiritual elements is enough to make this clear. Russian enlightenment, to whose service the Russian intelligentsia is called, has had to contend with the long-lasting heritage of the Tatar period, which has eaten deeply into all sorts of areas in our national life, with the arbitrariness of bureaucratic absolutism and the way it has rendered the state itself impotent. It had to contend in earlier days with a right wing committed to the maintenance of serfdom and corporal punishment, and, in our own time, with the institution of capital punishment, with the general worsening of morals – contending with all these for the sake of a better standard of life. It is this aim that the ideals of the so-called 'liberation movement' amount to – the movement whose heavy burden the intelligentsia has taken upon its shoulders; and in this struggle it has also acquired many martyr's crowns. But, unfortunately for the life of the Russian people, the intelligentsia also bound up this struggle inextricably with its own negative world-view. Thus, for those to whom the faith of the people was a precious treasure and who felt themselves called to defend it – above all, for members of the Church – it became necessary to fight against the influence of the intelligentsia among the people so as to defend the people's faith. The religious element was mingled with the conflict of political and cultural ideas; but despite all the seriousness of the religious struggle, and all its menacing significance for the future of Russia, the intelligentsia is still unable to understand what is at stake. The almost universal exodus of the intelligentsia from the Church, and the cultural isolation in which the Church found itself as a result, constituted an ultimate stage in the steady worsening of the historical situation. It is obvious that, for anyone who has faith in the mystical life of the Church, no definitive significance can attach to whatever particular outer form may clothe it at any given moment in history; whatever it may be, it cannot and must not be allowed to breed any doubt about the Church's ultimate triumph, when its clear illumination will shine upon all. However, considering the Church at the empirical level and in the Russian context, as a factor in the historical process, we cannot reckon it insignificant that the educated classes in Russia have almost universally decided for atheism. This spiritual bloodletting is bound to be reflected finally in the whole cultural and intellectual milieu of those who remained in the Church. Among the intelligentsia there is a general smug satisfaction at the many blemishes in the Church's life, which we do not in any way want to minimise or deny (bearing in mind too, though, that all the positive aspects of Church life are neither understood nor even known among the intelligentsia). But does our intelligentsia have the right so to criticise the life of the Church so long as it remains bound to its former indifferentism towards or programmatic rejection of religion, so long as it sees in religion no more than darkness and folly?

An 'ecclesial' intelligentsia, uniting an authentic Christianity with a *genuinely* enlightened and clear grasp of the cultural and historical task before us (a grasp so often lacking in the representatives of the contemporary Church), if it could be brought to birth, would answer to the needs of our history and our people. Even if such a group in its turn were condemned to persecution and oppression, which the intelligentsia has so long endured for the sake of its atheistic ideals, it would still have an enormous historical and religio-ethical significance, and its image and reputation in the national soul would be something quite distinctive.

But so long as the intelligentsia devotes the whole of its

cultural energy to the destruction of popular faith, the defence of this faith more and more takes on, with a tragic inevitability, the character of a struggle not only against the intelligentsia but also against enlightenment itself, given that this has in fact been diffused solely through the intelligentsia; obscurantism becomes the means of defending religion. This is an unnatural situation for both sides of the debate and it has become more acute in recent years; it is this that has made our present situation so particularly painful. And to all this must also be added the fact that this struggle to defend popular faith against the intelligentsia is exploited as an excuse by the self-interested forces of reaction – by spectators and fishers in troubled waters: the struggle for faith comes to be interwoven with these interests in a single historical and psychological complex making for habits of thought that are taken for granted, historical associations of ideas, which both supporters and opponents begin to think of as self-evident and indissoluble. The two poles carry opposite electrical charges. The present appalling prevalence of a narrow group mentality turns these parties into defensive *laagers*; the same psychological milieu, conservative and authoritarian, is created in both. The nation splits in two, and its best energies are dissipated in sterile conflict.

Such a situation is the product of the whole of our spiritual past; our present task is to overcome this schism, to rise above it, understanding that its roots do not lie in some ideal internal necessity but simply in the power of historical facts. It is time to set about unravelling the Gordian knot of our history.

VII

The soul of the Russian intelligentsia is a tissue of contradictions, like the whole life of our country, and it generates contradictory sentiments. It is impossible not to love it, impossible not to be repelled by it. Alongside all the negative features, presenting the symptoms of philistinism and historical immaturity, all the features that must be conquered, there are also traits of spiritual beauty that shine through in the marks of suffering on their faces and make them seem like some quite distinctive, rare and delicate flower adorning the harsh landscape of our

Heroism and the Spiritual Struggle

history; as if the intelligentsia were itself that 'flower', soaked in tears and blood, which appears in the vision of one of its noblest representatives, in the great and generous heart of Garshin.

Alongside the 'antichrist' principle in the intelligentsia, an elevated religious potential can also be sensed, a new historical embodiment waiting for spirit and life to be breathed into it. This eager quest for the City of God, the struggle for the fulfilment of God's will on earth as in heaven, is something profoundly different from the impulse towards secure worldly well-being in bourgeois culture. The horrors of the intelligentsia's maximalism, with all its practical uselessness, are the result of a distorted religious sensibility; but this can be overcome by religious renewal.

The Russian intelligentsia is naturally religious. In *The Devils*, Dostoyevsky compared Russia, and above all its intelligentsia, with the Gadarene demoniac in the gospel, whom Christ alone could heal, and who found health and restoration only at the feet of the Saviour. This comparison has lost none of its force today. A legion of evil spirits has entered the massive frame of Russia, shaking it with convulsions, torturing and maiming it. Only by spiritual struggle, invisible but of great proportions, is it possible for it to be healed and set free from this legion. The intelligentsia has rejected Christ and turned away from his face; it has cast out his image from its heart and deprived itself of the interior light of life. And, along with the whole of its native land, it is now paying the price for this betrayal, this religious suicide. Yet, strangely, it is not within its power to forget this wound to its heart, to restore equilibrium in its soul, to calm itself after the devastation it has inflicted on itself. Having denied Christ, it still bears his imprint upon its heart; it tosses and turns in unconscious pining for him, not knowing where to look for the slaking of its spiritual thirst. And this agitating restlessness, this transcendent vision of a transcendent righteousness, leaves its distinctive mark; it gives the intelligentsia a strange ecstatic, unbalanced character, as if it were indeed 'possessed'. Like the beautiful Shulamite when she has lost her bridegroom: on her bed by night, in the streets and squares, she seeks him whom her soul loves. She asks the watchmen in the city if they have seen her beloved; but the watchmen that go about the city give her no answer, but instead beat her and wound her (Song of Songs 3.1–3, 4.1). Yet all the time the beloved, the one whom her soul longs for, is so close at hand. He stands at the door and knocks – at the door of the heart of the intelligentsia, that proud and disobedient heart. Will his knocking ever be heard?

3

The Unfading Light (1917)

INTRODUCTION

The image of 'Sophia', the divine wisdom personified, had already played a significant role in Russian religious thought before Bulgakov. Its origins have been much debated: the iconography of late medieval Russia had on occasion depicted a winged and enthroned female figure identified as divine Wisdom; but commentators have tended to interpret this as representing Christ in his character as God's wisdom (see, for example, I Cor. 1.24, and the consistent patristic tradition identifying Old Testament references to wisdom as designations of Christ).[1] No theological reflection on this theme seems to be traceable before the late nineteenth century, and the more immediate influences in the speculation of this period are German hermeticism and Jewish Kabbalah. The 'eternal feminine' of Goethe and the German Romantics, the notion found in German mystics like Jakob Böhme of a kind of eternal potentiality over against the actuality of divine life, and the originally Gnostic mythology, taken up by Jewish mystical speculation, of a feminine world-soul embodying the divine life in a

---

[1] The history of Russian iconography related to this subject is treated at length in Pavel Florensky, *Stolp i utverzhdenie istiny* (*The Pillar and Ground of Truth*, Moscow, 1914), discussed later in this introduction. The Christological interpretation of this tradition in Byzantium and Russia is authoritatively advanced by Georges Florovsky in 'Christ, the Wisdom of God, in Byzantine Theology', (résumé), *Résumés des rapports et communications, 6ème Congrès International d'Etudes Byzantines, Alger, 2–7 octobre 1939, Supplément* (Paris, 1940), pp. 255–260; reprinted (under the title 'The Hagia Sophia Churches') in *Aspects of Church History – The Collected Works of Georges Florovsky* vol. 4, Gen. Ed. Richard S. Haugh (Belmont, Mass., 1975), pp. 131–5. A complete version of this paper does not seem to have survived; since the planned Byzantine Congress did not take place, there may never have been a full text, though there *is* a slightly longer study of the subject in a Russian essay of Florovsky's published in 1932, to which I have not had access.

self-alienated or even 'fallen' form – all this combines to create a powerful and evocative, if not always clear or coherent, cluster of ideas that connects cosmology, Trinitarian theology, the doctrine of the incarnation and the doctrine of the Church. The rather clumsy name of 'sophiology' has been commonly given to speculative essays in this vein.

Vladimir Soloviev (1853–1900) was the first Russian writer to elaborate a system along these lines.[2] He is, by any account, a wholly remarkable figure, poet and publicist, social theorist and speculative philosopher, author of a brief and brilliantly poignant piece of apocalyptic fiction in his last years, advocate of reunion between Eastern and Western Churches. His own vision of Sophia is coloured, on his own eloquent admission, by three experiences in which he believed he 'saw' the form of Wisdom in a beautiful female figure.[3] For him, Sophia is primarily a kind of ideal form of humanity – but humanity conceived as the crown of the cosmic order, containing within itself the whole of creation. However, this is not a static ideal in the mind of God: it is in some (rather elusive) sense an active 'other' to God, a striving towards full realisation within the cosmos of the freedom and love of the divine life. It is a 'concrete universal', the comprehensive unity (*vseedinstvo*) in which all particular and exclusive perspectives are overcome;[4] as the ground of cosmic harmony, it is also the basis upon which knowledge is possible, since true knowledge is always participation in the reality of what is known. To know is to share in the hidden harmonies of things, to transcend the atomistic perspective that is reinforced for us by the impenetrability of (fallen) material bodies.[5]

[2] On Soloviev, see particularly the admirable survey by Jonathan Sutton, *The Religious Philosophy of Vladimir Soloviev* (London, 1988).
[3] Recorded in his poem 'Three Encounters: Moscow, London and Egypt'. Hans Urs von Balthasar, in a penetrating chapter on Soloviev (*The Glory of the Lord: A Theological Aesthetics. Vol. III: Studies in Theological Style: Lay Styles*, trans. Andrew Louth *et al.* (Edinburgh, 1986), pp. 279–352, suggests that these should be interpreted as visions of Our Lady (p. 292).
[4] Soloviev's *Lectures on Godmanhood*, trans. P. Zouboff (Poughkeepsie, NY, 1944) remain the best source for this vision.
[5] See, for example, *Lectures III* on this theme; further elaboration in *Kritika otvlechennykh nachal* (*A Critique of Abstract Principles*, Moscow, 1877–80), ch. 33, and a good summary in N. O. Lossky, *History of Russian Philosophy* (London, 1952), pp. 99–100.

All this is, in Soloviev's earlier work, set out fundamentally as a general cosmological theory; but as his thought develops and extends, it takes on a more clearly theological character. The ground and rationale of Sophia as cosmic harmony is the second person of the Trinity, the Logos, active divine reason. The fallenness of the world results from the freely chosen alienation of Sophia from the Logos (the Gnostic background of Soloviev's thought is very much in evidence here); and it is Christ incarnate who restores the lost unity between Logos and Sophia. Christ wholly and perfectly renounces the self-assertion which alienated Sophia from her divine home, and so initiates a universal reconciliation through the Church, which is an 'organism' activated by the Holy Spirit in which all that belongs to the limited ego is gradually eroded.[6] There is more than a hint of the notion that the multiplicity of human selves is a consequence of the Fall – a notion somewhat in tension with the strongly underlined conviction that created persons are indefinable and irreducible.[7] This latter owes something to the assumption that the trinitarian life is the 'realised ideal' of the harmony of perfect love, the renunciation of self-defence and self-assertion.[8] If there is any resolution of this tension, it is to be found partly in the shifts between the earlier and the later works of Soloviev, partly in the fact that what seems most to worry Soloviev is *physical* plurality, which involves the mutual impenetrability already mentioned.

The status of Sophia for Soloviev is thus significantly fluid. She is what the world is meant to be, a reconciled whole centred upon humanity restored to mutual communion and communion with God. As such, she is what we might call a primordial expression of the divine self-communication in the Logos. She is also in some important respect distinct from the Logos, endowed with the freedom to turn away from God; hence the present state of creation, divided and unfree. Yet, as reconciled

---

[6] See especially *God, Man and the Church*, trans. D. Attwater (London, 1938), e.g. pp. 138–9.
[7] *Lectures VIII* has a robust doctrine of the substantial and indeed supra-temporal human self (see, for example, p. 126); but a late work like *Opravdanie dobra* (*The Justification of the Good*, Moscow, 1897 and 1899) is more ambivalent about multiplicity.
[8] See especially *Lectures VII*.

by and with the Logos, she is the principle leading the world towards its final goal. Critics have, from the earliest to the most recent days, expressed their puzzlement over how exactly all this hangs together in Soloviev's thought;[9] I suspect that some of the trouble derives from trying to read Soloviev's language as attempting a chronological 'story' of the spiritual universe. His vision is perhaps more kaleidoscopic: Sophia is primarily the world's ideal form and *therefore* a principle working towards the reconciled future through the unclarities of the present; she is set free so to work in virtue of Christ's self-identification with her in the incarnation; outside that, or 'prior' to that, she is not free to move towards reconciliation, and her natural indeterminacy – freedom, if you like – is vulnerable to fragmentation or atomisation. Of course, this leaves plenty of problems still unresolved. What sort of agency or indeed personality is being ascribed to Sophia (in anything other than a mythical sense)? Is the reconciliation of the cosmos now assured because of the incarnation (Soloviev's last writings suggest that the possibility of tragic catastrophe is still very much alive[10])? And how does the agency and freedom of Sophia relate to the agency of particular created subjects? But Soloviev's own preferred idiom of exposition is not well suited to giving crisp and unambiguous answers to such queries.

If it is true that later Russian metaphysics is largely a series of footnotes to Soloviev, this should not be understood as

[9] Lossky, *History of Russian Philosophy*, pp. 127–31; more briefly, F. C. Copleston, *Russian Religious Philosophy: Selected Aspects* (Tunbridge Wells and Notre Dame, 1988), pp. 86–7.

[10] The famous 'Tale of Antichrist', which forms the climax of *Tri razgovora* (*Three Conversations*, Moscow, 1899), is the *locus classicus* for this theme (there is an English translation in *A Solovyov Anthology*, ed. S. L. Frank (London, 1950), pp. 229–48). A recent essay on this text, however, (Judith Deutsch Kornblatt, 'Soloviev on Salvation: The Story of the "Short Story on the Antichrist"' in *Russian Religious Thought*, eds. Judith Deutsch Kornblatt and Richard F. Gustafson (Madison, Wisc., 1996), pp. 68–87) argues that the story is a lot more complex and ironic than commentators have allowed, and that its real point is the need for the presence and intervention of the one agent who is both divine and human, Christ, at the point where human response to evil fails; but also that this presence and intervention is still through human response of a certain kind – specifically and surprisingly, in the 'oral' continuation of the 'Tale', by the resistance of the Jewish people to the Antichrist, which opens the way for the Second Coming. It is a persuasive reading.

implying an uncritical reception. Later writers[11] return obsessively to the theme of Sophia, but hardly any of them fail to correct, amplify and gloss Soloviev's insights, often quite radically. Among these, however, one in particular was to influence Bulgakov's appropriation of the 'sophiological' tradition. Pavel Florensky has already been mentioned as a figure in the circles Bulgakov moved in during his experiments in Christian socialism; but it was not as a political or social thinker that Florensky made his greatest impact on Bulgakov. In the first decade of the century, Florensky was engaged in a vastly ambitious intellectual project, whose final form was not to appear until 1914, a project which represents his response to various aspects of the Russian cultural milieu of the 'Silver Age'. The characteristic interests of the Russian Symbolists in the mystical depths of language, even in the occult, are already in evidence in Florensky's essays during these years. From 1908 to 1914, various lengthy articles, most of them in the *Bogoslovskii vestnik* (*Theological Messenger*) of Moscow, elaborated a metaphysical scheme of some complexity, expressed in an elevated (not to say overheated) style and supported by an extraordinary amount of recondite learning.[12] The general tenor of these essays had to do with the theme of knowledge as participation and the consequent inadequacy of bare logical formulation for a truthful doctrine of knowledge. Logic depends upon the principle of identity: that is, for logical purposes, each subject or substance is what it is and is not what is other. But a world of mutually impenetrable entities cannot be the world that is known to art and to faith – or even to contemporary science (Florensky was aware of some of the epistemological shocks that physics was beginning to unleash upon the intellectual world[13]). An

---

[11] Particularly the brothers Evgenii and Sergei Trubetskoi, in addition to Florensky and Bulgakov. Among younger writers, N. O. Lossky, L. P. Karsavin and S. L. Frank develop a very similar metaphysic, though with reservations about the personalised metaphor of Sophia; V. V. Zenkovsky uses the language of Sophia more readily and stands close to Bulgakov, though without Bulgakov's range and detail (and socio-cultural interests).

[12] Robert Slesinski, *Pavel Florensky: A Metaphysics of Love* (Crestwood, NY, 1984), traces his literary production in these years (pp. 40–3).

[13] On Florensky's acquaintance with mathematics and science, see Leonid Sabaneeff, 'Pavel Florensky: Priest, Scientist, and Mystic', *Russian Review*, 20 (1961), pp. 312–25. His initial training was in mathematics and physics.

adequate metaphysic – which must be a religious metaphysic – has to deal with the fundamental *antinomies* of knowing,[14] and must provide an account of a world in which identity and otherness are always in tension, no identity being conceivable without its other, and therefore being strictly unreal, untrue, when considered as a subject posited in itself. What makes this more than a rather overexcited Hegelianism is Florensky's interest in a kind of cosmic vitalism, at once more materialistic than Hegel and more consciously mythological and personal. The cosmos has an 'ideal personality' at its heart, a 'fourth hypostasis' standing not exactly alongside the three subsistent subjects of the divine Trinity, but in some sense in apposition to them.[15]

This is Florensky's Sophia. The vision is developed with far more explicit reference to the liturgical and iconographic tradition of the Eastern Church than was the case with Soloviev, though its roots are no less eclectic.[16] But it is true, as Bulgakov was later to remark, that Florensky's sophiological speculation grows a bit more directly from manifestly ecclesial and theological arguments than might at first appear.[17] In the final drawing-together of his essays in the monumental *Stolp i utverzhdenie istiny* (*The Pillar and Ground of Truth*) of 1914,[18] the discussion of Sophia follows several chapters about the work of the Spirit and the triumph of divine grace over sinful egotism, culminating in a strong and original account of the significance of the body in the processes of salvation or reconciliation. Grace becomes literally visible in the transfigured saint, because the body is never simply a material object; it is the total 'Gestalt' of the human person and so reflects the relations in which the person stands, to others and to the creator. Life in the Church, when it is what it should be (i.e. in the mature saint), reveals a creaturely nature not imprisoned by the violence of *mere*

---

[14] Florensky, *Stolp*, pp. 146ff., 485–9.
[15] *Stolp*, pp. 323–4, 349ff.
[16] *Stolp*, Excursus XXIV on iconography, and pp. 358–82; pp. 388ff. on the liturgy. For a summary, see Slesinski, *Pavel Florensky*, pp. 185–91.
[17] Bulgakov, *The Wisdom of God: A Brief Summary of Sophiology* (London, 1937), now reprinted as *Sophia, the Wisdom of God* (Hudson, NY, 1993), p. 10.
[18] As Slesinski remarks (*Pavel Florensky*, p. 43), a critical edition of this text is highly desirable, since the stages of its composition are complicated.

THE UNFADING LIGHT (1917)

materiality, the impenetrable and would-be neutral surfaces of the fallen bodies we are familiar with.[19] And to speak of Sophia is to speak of what makes this ecclesial radiance or beauty possible.

Sophia is the concrete presence of the ideal world – primarily in the mind or purpose of God, derivatively therefore in the created order itself. Sophia is the outgoing, self-abandoning divine love, shaping what is other, creating a harmonious but distinct image of itself.[20] As such, it has a share in the divine life, though not as a divine subject.[21] Since the Logos, the second person of the Trinity, is the ground of the created order *as* order, Sophia is in a very particular sense the counterpart – the 'bride' – of the Logos, existing in and for the Logos.[22] And, as the Bride of Christ, Sophia is thus obviously 'the Church in its heavenly aspect'.[23] From this in turn we may deduce that the true vocation of the Church is precisely the revelation of the world as grounded in divine love; and it fulfils this task by realising love in its own life, by showing what 'consubstantiality' means, the loving interpenetration and co-presence of all apparently distinct subjects through their universal participation in the primordial outgoing of the trinitarian love as Sophia.[24] In this movement into creation, the consubstantial love of the Trinity actively and continuously transforms creation, realising its 'ideal personality'.

This is a sketchy and unsatisfactory summary of a very complex picture, but it will at least indicate some of the ways in which Florensky echoes but also corrects or supplements Soloviev. In both, Sophia is the ideal world – not simply as a primordial 'world of ideas' in the mind of God, but an active principle, an eschatological presence. Florensky, however has more to say about *interpersonal* relation as the locus of Sophia in creation,[25] and thus appears to be more positive about the

---

[19] E.g. *Stolp*, pp. 264–6, 292–3.
[20] E.g. *Stolp*, pp. 212–14, 325–9.
[21] *Stolp*, pp. 212, 349.
[22] *Stolp*, p. 329.
[23] *Stolp*, p. 350.
[24] E.g. *Stolp*, pp. 346, 349.
[25] Sophia is experienced not so much (as we might perhaps expect) in ecclesial relations but in 'friendship' (*Stolp*, pp. 393–464, *passim*); this was one feature of *Stolp* that attracted fierce criticism from more conservative Orthodox.

status of contingent difference or otherness within the world; and he also criticises Soloviev for blurring the distinction between the divine and the created *nature* by suggesting that Sophia is identical with the essence of the divine Person.[26] In fact, this latter is not wholly fair to Soloviev, and it cannot be said that Florensky fully succeeds in clarifying the question. On balance, though, it is true that Florensky's Sophia is more generally envisaged as the *effect* of the divine love and the divine action – hence the curious 'fourth hypostasis' language. Florensky's extensive and fascinating interpretations of the icons of Sophia in medieval and post-medieval Russian tradition goes well beyond anything in Soloviev, and brings together themes in Christology, Mariology and ecclesiology in a heady mixture.[27] This aspect of Florensky's work has clear influences on what Bulgakov was later to produce.

But in fact Florensky's *magnum opus* appeared two years *after* Bulgakov's first and least-known essay in sophiology, the *Philosophy of Economic Activity*, which constituted his doctoral thesis at Moscow and was published – to some critical bewilderment – in 1912.[28] No-one could deny that the influence of Florensky in Bulgakov's general thinking was enormous in the years leading up to the publication of this work, the years which had seen Bulgakov's formal return to Orthodox sacramental practice in 1908.[29] But there is little trace before 1912 of the Sophia theme, even in Bulgakov's essays on Soloviev. An excellent recent study of Bulgakov's early doctrine of Sophia concludes that only in or around 1910 does Bulgakov begin to look hard at the *metaphysical* issues raised by Soloviev, as opposed to general questions about the relation between Christianity and the material world in relation to political, social and artistic practice.[30] It is, of course, unimaginable that Bulgakov did not read the articles Florensky was publishing – including

---

[26] *Stolp*, p. 775, n. 701.
[27] Slesinski, *Pavel Florensky*, pp. 182–5.
[28] I have not had access to the full text of the Russian original, and refer to the French translation by Constantin Andronikof, *Philosophie de l'économie* (Paris, 1987).
[29] See above, pp. 55–6.
[30] Bernice Glatzer Rosenthal, 'The Nature and Function of Sophia in Sergei Bulgakov's Prerevolutionary Thought', Kornblatt and Gustafson (eds.), *Russian Religious Thought*, pp. 154–75, esp. pp. 156–8.

the piece that was to become the chapter on Sophia in *Stolp*, which appeared in 1911.[31] But the reader of the *Philosophy of Economic Activity* will be aware of a very different intellectual climate prevailing. Florensky does not feature in the argument; and while there is allusion to Soloviev, it is Schelling who is more fully discussed as a source for Bulgakov's speculations here.[32] Metaphysical argument is deployed with some sophistication, and the backbone of Bulgakov's exposition is a bold attempt to provide a response to the theories of Kant and Hegel about knowledge that will have at its centre a commitment to transforming action.[33] For all its eccentricity, it reveals how seriously Bulgakov took the task of engaging with the 'mainstream' European intellectual tradition. It is a very impressive – if often infuriating – book.

The central question posed is about the nature of the subject. Bulgakov, true to his earlier Marxist convictions, insists that a subject who is only or even primarily a subject of *knowledge* is an abstraction. The actual subject is an agent involved in *labour*:

> Labour, which is the actuality of human existence, objectivising human being beyond its own limits and making the world 'objective' to us, is a living link between subject and object, the bridge by which the ego may go out into the world of [other] realities and which connects that world indivisibly with itself. Thanks to the fact of labour, there is no such thing as a pure subject, as idealism would hold, nor a pure object, as materialism claims: there is a living unity, at once subject and object. Only by examining it from this or that angle by some kind of methodological abstraction can you divide it. But the polarised, 'doubled' state of [our present] being is only transcended in the Absolute, which is at once both subject and object to itself. And the concept of the Absolute also excludes any *going-out* from subject into object: its character as subject-object is posited by a

---

[31] In *Bogoslovskii vestnik*, 2 (1911), pp. 135–61, 582–613.
[32] See *Philosophie de l'économie*, pp. 50–8 in particular.
[33] In the summary of his doctoral defence, published as 'Filosofiya khozyaistva' in *Russkaya Mysl'*, 5 (1913), pp. 70–9, he memorably describes his aim as interpreting 'Marx in the spirit of Böhme' and 'Kant in the spirit of Marx' (p. 77); cf. *Philosophie de l'économie*, pp. 57–8, 88–92, 210–18.

unique, self-identical and extra-temporal act. This is the mystery of the life of the Holy Trinity in itself.[34]

On this basis, we cannot conceive knowledge as the 'unfolding before us of a kind of theatrical representation'; *knowledge is labour*, willed and active engagement in changing the world.[35] To make sense of the world is not simply to interpret it, but to make new and orderly patterns within it. Knowing is thus an 'economic' activity, it is production and the constituting of value. The very notion of production is, says Bulgakov, problematic unless it is understood within the context of a programme for the 'humanisation' of the world; and it is because of this that we need not only an integral and transformative theory of knowledge as one of the forms of transforming engagement but also an overarching theory of *what* the transformations are that are appropriate to the kind of beings we are and of how transforming activity finds coherence.[36]

Kantian and Neo-Kantian philosophy presupposed a 'transcendental subject' of all human knowledge; that is to say, it grounded all particular acts of cognition in a regulative ideal of universal validity against which these particular acts could be measured.[37] Bulgakov is clear that, unless this ideal has some kind of extra-mental existence, it guarantees nothing.[38] But the salient point is that, on his own account of knowledge, there must equally be a transcendental subject of *labour*, a transformative principle existing outside the ensemble of human effort but grounding the unity and intelligibility of our actions in changing the world; and this is where Sophia enters the picture, as a 'World-soul', the ultimate subject of human productivity.[39] Thus the transcendental subject of production is both a principle in the cosmos at large but also a kind of universal Adam, an ideal human subject (since humanity is the agent of intelligent production in the world we know).[40] And here Bulgakov, like Soloviev and, to a lesser extent, Florensky, alludes to the

[34] *Philosophie de l'économie*, p. 74.
[35] Ibid., p. 75.
[36] Ibid., pp. 77–9.
[37] Ibid., pp. 84–5.
[38] Ibid., p. 86.
[39] Ibid., pp. 87–90.
[40] Ibid., pp. 92–6.

Gnostic and Kabbalistic ideas of the 'heavenly Man', the Adam Kadmon of Jewish mysticism, in whose unfallen creativity God's own labour is worked and fulfilled within creation.[41] The transcendental subject is thus also that which will work against social fragmentation, renewing our sense of the communal character of the human enterprise: 'Social ideals are a formulation within historical reality of what is already existent in metaphysical reality.'[42] In our present condition, all is fractured; 'objective' reality is understood as by definition 'impermeable' to the subject, the spirit; and relations in space and time are seen as external, the collocation of atoms. Materialism rests content with such an account, denying the ways in which all distinctively human activity refuses to accept this. Whatever certain kinds of scientific philosophy claim, a model of the world as essentially conflictual will not do; and this attitude needs purging from economics when it attempts to establish itself as a quasi-mechanical science, deterministic and shaped by 'natural' conflict. The economic subject needs to relearn what his or her relation to their own body already teaches: here I know that my physical actions follow determined causal patterns, and I know just as directly that they communicate meaning, and therefore freedom.[43]

> We might well cite here the famous formulation of the idealists, so ineptly taken up by Marxism: *freedom is necessity brought to consciousness*. Freedom and necessity as polar opposites will not disappear except in the situation where power and will coincide; and that happens only in function of the growth of economic power. But that power and freedom do not depend naturally upon the content of the will. Man can will diverse things, he can situate himself by his will either above or below his true self, he can serve God or Satan, Christ or Antichrist; and this is how his spiritual liberty is manifested. Only, being an incarnate spirit, and thus inseparable from the world and capable of acting within it, he still has need of acquiring economic power; and he has the capacity so to do.[44]

[41] See particularly *Lectures III* for Soloviev's development of the 'Adam Kadmon' image.
[42] *Philosophie de l'économie*, p. 97.
[43] Ibid., p. 166.
[44] Ibid., p. 167.

It is up to the human agent what is communicated by his or her acts, what meanings are constructed by the way in which the transformation of the world is undertaken. Of course I act under constraints, the rule of nature; but my meanings remain to be defined.

Here is indeed what a recent commentator has called the beginning of an Orthodox 'work ethic'.[45] The earlier interest in material economic development as a proper spiritual goal, the conviction that certain kinds of control over the environment are necessary for moral and spiritual flourishing, is here given a formidable philosophical grounding – and, incidentally, related more closely than before to the enterprise of *artistic* production.[46] As has been pointed out by the same commentator, Bulgakov does not offer any real guidance on practical and political issues, 'desired, permissible and prohibited actions'; and there is a definite Promethean streak in the rhetoric.[47] As an *ethical* treatise, it is almost as eccentric as it is if read as a work of ordinary economic theory. A second volume was planned, to deal with ethics more directly and to draw out the eschatological foundations of ethics, but it was never written – perhaps partly because Bulgakov ceased to be a professional university teacher in 1911.[48]

Svet nevechernii (*The Unfading Light*) was published in 1917 though a good deal of the text had already appeared in the form of long articles.[49] Bulgakov certainly regarded it as a

---

[45] Bernice Glatzer Rosenthal, 'The Search for a Russian Orthodox Work Ethic', in *Between Tsar and People: Educated Society and the Quest for Public Identity in Late Imperial Russia*, eds. E. W. Clowes, S. E. Kassow and J. L. West (Princeton, 1991), pp. 57–74, an essay concentrating on Bulgakov's early work and on the *Philosophy of Economic Activity* in particular.

[46] *Philosophie de l'économie*, pp. 99–102, explicitly puts art alongside other forms of creative production and already hints at the delineation of the spheres of economics as *maintenance* of the conditions for distinctively human life and art and religious practice as embodying the eschatological hope that will be developed further in Bulgakov's later work.

[47] Rosenthal, 'The Search for a Russian Orthodox Work Ethic', p. 71.

[48] He resigned his position in protest at state interference in the university.

[49] As with Florensky's *Stolp*, a critical discussion of the evolution of the text would be of great interest. The journal *Voprosy filosofii i psikhologii* (*Questions of Philosophy and Psychology*) published the bulk of the material that would form the introductory chapter of *Svet* in 1914, the discussion of negative theology and some of the material on the created order in 1915, and the section on Sophia in the

THE UNFADING LIGHT (1917)

kind of sequel to the *Philosophy of Economic Activity*, but it is not by any means the second volume he had projected. It is far more explicitly theological than its predecessor, revealing an extraordinarily broad range of reading in the Greek Fathers; long before most Orthodox, let alone Western, scholars discovered the significance of Maximus the Confessor or Gregory Palamas, Bulgakov discusses them with some authority, making connections that later scholars would devote much energy to exploring.[50] In this strand of the Byzantine tradition, he finds not only the foundation of the theology of negation which he develops at length here, but also a vision of the transfiguration of the cosmos by the penetration of divine energy. In Palamas's famous and controversial proposals for distinguishing between the essence, *ousia*, and the action, *energeia*, of God, he sees a foreshadowing of what he wants to say about Sophia. Later Russian theologians who claimed that Palamas had already solved Bulgakov's problems without his compromising and eclectic conceptuality do not seem to have discussed his novel and careful treatment of Palamas in this work.[51]

Florensky's presence is more clearly in evidence than in the earlier work – though even here it should not be overrated. His work is several times referred to for its discussion of the 'antinomic' nature of concrete thinking[52] and for the material on the iconographic and liturgical background to sophiology,[53] but it is

---

created order in 1916. A 'fragment' on 'art and theurgy' appeared in 1916 in *Russkaya mysl'*, 12. I have not found any other published antecedents for material in Part III of *Svet*.

[50] On Maximus as an exponent of apophatic theology, see *Svet*, pp. 121–3; on the overcoming of sexual polarity in the new creation, pp. 291–2; there are several further citations from Maximus. On Palamas, see pp. 124–6 on apophaticism and the distinction between the unknowable essence of God and his self-communication in *energeia*, and pp. 308–9 on the relative superiority of human beings to angels because of the *incarnate* character of the human self.

[51] A fascinating item on this can be found in *Simvol*, 29 (1993), pp. 199–216, which publishes for the first time correspondence from Georges Florovsky to Bulgakov in 1926; Florovsky argues that Sophia can in no sense be called an hypostasis because it is an *energeia* of God, a work or relation of grace. Palamas is referred to (p. 206) as offering a clear resolution of the problem Bulgakov's sophiology tries to address.

[52] *Svet*, pp. 96, 150 (referring to a 1909 essay on Kant), 227.

[53] *Svet*, p. 213, n. 2.

not discussed in detail. However, the fascination with Kabbalism and the interest in aesthetics certainly reflect the impress of Florensky's mind as well as Soloviev's. A further very important presence is Nikolai Fyodorov (1828–1903), a writer who had already made a considerable impression on Bulgakov, and is discussed in several earlier works.[54] Fyodorov, schoolteacher, clerk, librarian, friend of most of the major Russian intellects of the later nineteenth century, is still an enigmatic figure, whose *Philosophy of the Common Task*, posthumously published, is really a vast notebook of speculations and projects, the work of an undisciplined genius, inconsistent and occasionally ludicrous, but replete with insight.[55] Fyodorov certainly foreshadows the way in which Bulgakov unites the question of knowledge with that of action: the 'common task' is the restoration of true kinship between agents, and indeed between the agents of the past and the present. Its ultimate goal is the resurrection of the dead – which Fyodorov seems to have thought, at least sometimes, to be a realisable project for future technology.[56] But more important for Bulgakov is the vision of the world as a *task* for humankind, as an environment to be humanised and revealed as entirely transparent to human and divine meanings as they are defined for us in Christ, the supreme agent of resurrection and image of resurrected life. What exactly Bulgakov made of some of Fyodorov's more uncritically reactionary ideas about Russian politics (he was a staunch defender of monarchical autocracy) is hard to discern. The significant influence is in the area of Bulgakov's sense of the human vocation, the importance he consistently gives to creativity in human action and relation; introducing a substantial section in *Svet* devoted to Fyodorov's philosophy, Bulgakov says that '*Fyodorov transforms economic activity into theurgy*, or, more accurately,

---

[54] Bulgakov devoted an essay to him in 1908, reprinted in *Dva grada* (*Two Cities*), 2 vols. (Moscow, 1911), vol. 2, pp. 260–77, and he is briefly mentioned in *Philosophie de l'économie* (p. 104).
[55] The only English monograph is George M. Young, Jr., *Nikolai Fedorov: An Introduction* (Belmont, Mass., 1979), which has excellent documentation and a fine bibliography. A very attractive brief introduction in English is 'The Supramoralist: Nikolai Fyodorov' by the late Donald Nicholl, published in the posthumous collection of his papers, *Triumphs of the Spirit in Russia* (London, 1997), pp. 67–118.
[56] Young, *Nikolai Fedorov*, pp. 93–113, esp. pp. 110ff.

THE UNFADING LIGHT (1917)

pours them indiscriminately and inseparably into the same mould'.[57] And this prompts Bulgakov to explore the *distinction* between what he calls 'theurgy', human action wholly absorbed into God's action, and a quasi-magical exaltation of human economic–technological achievement. Fyodorov is certainly confused, in Bulgakov's eyes, but it is a confusion that forces his critics to work harder, to extract what is of lasting importance.

Svet begins with a long meditation on the nature of religious consciousness, insisting, as we should expect, on the concreteness, the integral and practical nature, of religious belief, which is a living participation in divine truth; there can be no purely conceptual or abstract philosophical system; like Marx, Bulgakov judges Hegel's system to fall finally on the abstract side, and to reduce to theoretical form realities that can only be apprehended in the openness of historical action.[58] This leads on to a very erudite survey of the tradition of negative theology: God is 'nothing', not a determinate object, and so not amenable to conceptual finality. God's relation to creation is thus a complex matter to think through. God is not a part of creation, nor is he the inner life of creation, yet he is its ground; in him is the potential of creation, however exactly we are to interpret that.[59] The Absolute exists in relation to an Other, exists *relatively*; how are we to conceive this except by thinking through what the ground is *in* God for relation and otherness? Otherwise expressed, this is a question about what it might be to conceive of love as the essence of the divine life; and so we come to the definition of Sophia.

The first extract here from *Svet* elaborates this, in ways which clearly reflect Florensky's ideas quite closely (notice the 'fourth hypostasis' language); what takes it beyond Florensky, however, is the notion that Sophia is, from one point of view, revelatory of what it is to be God; it displays the rationale for the divine life as trinitarian. Or rather, perhaps, Sophia as the eternal object of divine trinitarian love reflects the divine nature, its

---

[57] *Svet*, p. 360; pp. 360–8 is a careful critical discussion of Fyodorov on the resurrection, repudiating it as a possible *literal* expectation but affirming his vision as expressing the confident aspiration for universal reconciliation.
[58] Ibid., pp. 83ff.
[59] We shall return to this problem in the introduction to the next extract; and see *Svet*, pp. 101–2.

eternal ground, so faithfully that we can speak of Sophia *within* God. Hence the difficult idea that Sophia is 'the loving of love', the act of God's love towards a love that is posited beyond itself, a yearning or eros (there is more on this later) towards the divine. As the ground of everything determinate, Sophia is the womb of the world, the Eternal Feminine.

The concept of eros in creation is explored in the second extract. All things await with eager longing the revelation of what they fundamentally are, all things press towards beauty. Dostoevsky's 'Beauty will save the world' is one of Bulgakov's favourite quotations; but he is careful to insist that this is not a religious transposition of aestheticism. The beauty that saves is God's Sophia acting within the created sphere and pushing it to its eschatological goal, not any finite aesthetic achievement.

And so, in the third extract, to the body, the material order, and its destiny. The sophiological perspective dissolves crude oppositions between spirit and body, and allows us to imagine a world that is not only self-aware but *sensually* aware of itself. All earthly realities are grounded in an ideal reality that is also a kind of eternally self-aware *materiality*, since there is no thought without matter and concrete action.[60] The fourth extract reproduced here follows this through with a distinction between matter as contingently experienced and bodiliness, the state of ideal embodiment in universal harmony toward which the world yearns. We have some sense even now of the interconnectedness of the material world, and so can begin to make sense of the sophianic hope for bodily transfiguration.

Bulgakov has so far concentrated on the directly theological and metaphysical; in the third and final section of the book, he turns to the destiny of historical humanity, developing further the ideas sketched in the *Philosophy of Economic Activity* about economics and art, and offering some openings for the elaboration of an ethic. Very significantly, Bulgakov sees the basis of ethics in the call to active co-operation with the sophianic transfiguration of the world; if you separate the idea from bodiliness, you end up with an extrinsic and formal ethic,

---

[60] Bulgakov has a discussion of Plotinus at this point (pp. 245–7) which does more justice than some professional Plotinus scholars to Plotinus's notion of a kind of matter *within* the intellectual world, a passive medium for the activity of intellectual form to transfigure.

THE UNFADING LIGHT (1917)

abstract duty, as in Kant, which bears not at all on a world in which the characteristic *human* business is the transforming of an environment.[61] But this transformation is grounded in and enabled by 'theurgy' – supremely, of course, the sacramental activity of the Church, but also, it seems, the action of the mature saint.[62] The twin human enterprises of art and economics are both to be understood relative to theurgy. If either of them mistakes itself for the other, or if either is simply confused with theurgy, disaster follows. Economic action is necessarily historical, the labour of realising this world as a human world, exercising Adam's sovereignty, poised between freedom and necessity; but it has no eschatology in itself. It is the material basis for there being a history at all.[63] Art is erotic, desiring and anticipating the eschatological transformation of matter; it goes beyond the functional.[64] Both are transformative activities, but are only fully and properly so in relation to each other. Art alone, forgetting its materiality, its share in the common world of bodies and so of ethics, becomes aestheticism. As such, it will be destructive of and parasitic on the body.[65] There is a powerful essay of Bulgakov's, first published in 1915, on an early Picasso exhibition, in which he argues that Picasso shows a fundamental hatred of the body and the feminine, in contrast to artists like Matisse and Cézanne;[66] these pages in *Svet* give the background for such a judgement. But economics alone is equally dangerous, forgetting that it is only one aspect of the human task, fundamental but not determinative; it is disfigured into 'economism' the philosophy of *homo economicus* beloved of both capitalism and Marxism.[67] Here Bulgakov repeats, with far more theoretical elaboration, the themes that had preoccupied him since the early years of the century. It is also possible for art and economics to seek to change places: art tries to be

---

[61] *Svet*, p. 258.
[62] *Svet*, pp. 373–7 in particular.
[63] *Svet*, pp. 368–9.
[64] *Svet*, pp. 356, 370ff.
[65] *Svet*, p. 358.
[66] 'Trup krasota' ('The Corpse of Beauty'), *Russkaya mysl'*, 8 (1915), pp. 10–106; reprinted in Bulgakov's collection *Tikhiya dumy* (*Quiet Thoughts*, Moscow, 1918), pp. 32–52. Part of the text is translated in *A Bulgakov Anthology*, ed. James Pain and Nicolas Zernov (London, 1976), pp. 67–72.
[67] *Svet*, pp. 359ff.

practical and effective, to follow or to set practical social goals, and economics tries to create radically new imaginative and moral possibilities.[68] Only in concert with each other and with the Church's theurgy do they remain aspects of Sophia, bound in to the genuine human vocation of transfiguring the material world under God.

The last three extracts represent parts of this ambitious overview of human destiny. Bulgakov is vigorously engaged in a number of cultural and political debates in this concluding section of the book, and it is in many ways overloaded and repetitive (he was never a terse writer at the best of times). But it is a discussion of quite remarkable prescience as well as originality. The modern reader may well recognise the problems caused by a messianic approach to market economics in the West and a deterministic confidence in the renewal of social morality by economic planning in the old communist East. We might also reflect on Bulgakov's conviction that the secularisation of art means ultimately a contempt for the body: whether manifested in dead sheep in formaldehyde or earrings made from aborted foetuses or simply in the rampant conceptualism of what habitually appears in the major annual submissions for awards, the condition of contemporary visual art needs some moral and theological reflection, and Bulgakov has some suggestive starting points. But the final text of all prompts even deeper reflection. Here Bulgakov takes up again his earlier criticisms of a spiritually moribund conservatism disguising itself as a theocracy, and, once again, shows a striking prescience in his outlining of the tension between loyalty to a minimalist administration safeguarding basic rights and the apocalyptic desire for transfigured relations. It is a tantalising text (the concluding two sections of *The Unfading Light*, not included in this volume, fill it out a bit), but what Bulgakov points towards is a finely balanced model of the relation between Church and civil or legal society. The Church cannot and should not try to impose its own eschatological categories on the management of society; but the management of society needs the passion and maximalism of the Church to remind it of the limits of its own authority. As we shall see, Bulgakov was to remain broadly

---

[68] *Svet*, pp. 358–60.

faithful to this vision throughout his career, steering a difficult path between the traditional Orthodox political ethic of ecclesial detachment or passivity and the transferring to the political realm of the apocalyptic themes and rhetoric appropriate to faith, a confusion which he poignantly identified years before and which had a peculiar pertinence in 1917.[69]

Svet is a difficult book to assess, and there is a distinct shortage of detailed critical discussions of it.[70] Some of the sophiological speculation he would later qualify; the language of Sophia as 'fourth hypostasis' was abandoned in the 1920s,[71] and the complex proposals about the materiality of the divine ideas and the self-sensing of ideal forms are not further explored. But it is a watershed in his work. It represents the fullest statement of his socio-cultural criticism, the culmination of over a decade's intense thinking and writing about the foundations of (in the broadest sense) political activity, and the most mature account of an aesthetic which had been sketched and retouched many times in earlier and more ephemeral works. The major new element was the detailed theological discussion, and it was this that was to dominate his writing increasingly after 1917.

---

[69] It is a theme of several essays in *Dva grada*, particularly the first two, on Feuerbach and Marx, and the immense essay on 'Apocalyptic and Socialism' in the second volume.

[70] Rosenthal, 'The Nature and Function of Sophia in Bulgakov's Prerevolutionary Thought', is a valuable contribution, but only a relatively brief one.

[71] See the introduction to the next extract for an account of his revisions to some of the ideas of *Svet* in a paper of 1925.

The Unfading Light

1. [Sophia: Divine Wisdom and Divine Love]*

God is love: and this love is not a quality or property, not a predicate, but the very essence of Godhead. And in this divine love, each hypostasis, surrendering itself in love, finds itself in the other hypostases and thus actualises the unity of Godhead. In the Trinity, the absolutely personal character of the Godhead, its *hypostatic* nature, is united with the absolutely *transpersonal* character of its threefoldness – 'trinity in unity and unity in trinity'. In the revelation of the three hypostases we see the qualitative distinctions that exist within the trinitarian life. Divine fatherhood, substantiality, outpouring are the properties of the first hypostasis; of the second, distinctness, *logos*, the power to structure and order – and this is the 'heart' of God, the dimension in which the Father loves the Son; the third, the Holy Spirit, is aware both of Father and Son, finds itself in them and rejoices in the divine love. Thus the Trinity is revealed to the world in the threefold unity of Father, Son and Spirit, as an intimate internal relationship, and so as the self-revelatory activity of the divine life. In the Godhead itself it is impossible to allow any kind of 'order of succession' or progressive development, for the Trinity has its transcendent existence from all eternity in one inseparable act of love and identity. The divine life in the Trinity is complete and absolute in itself. It has no need of any external fulfilment or disclosure. It is entire in itself, and if we can speak of such fulness becoming yet more full, this is not from the point of view of the Godhead but in respect of what is not divine: the life of that which is not divine or is external to the divine may be drawn into the fulness of the

---

* pp. 211–14.

divine life. In no sense, however, is there any evolutionary necessity for the Godhead, as if the destiny of creating were laid upon God, a destiny without which his self-manifestation would be imperfect: creation is the gift of a free and generous love – grace, mercy and benevolence. The radiance of love flows out from the divine fulness; the divinity in its superabundance goes forth from itself and illuminates the darkness of the non-divine nothingness, the realm of non-being. The Godhead, which knows nothing of envy or grasping, or any possibility of augmenting its own limitlessness and absoluteness, desires to call even the realm of non-being, the life of what is not divine, into its own love. The Godhead in its divine liberality, in self-renouncing love, longs for what is not itself, not divine, and so goes forth from its selfhood in creating.

But in structuring for itself a world that will be external to itself, the Godhead *ipso facto* establishes between itself and the world a kind of frontier; and this frontier, which by definition stands *between* God and the world, creator and creature, is neither the one nor the other, but something quite distinct, simultaneously itself united with and divided from both God and creation (a kind of *metaxu* in Plato's sense). This angel of creation, the beginning of the ways of God, is 'holy wisdom', Sophia. It is the *loving of love*. The divine triunity, God-as-love, complete in itself, sufficient to itself, the eternal divine actuality, substantive love, posits (in the metaphysical sense) an object for this divine love beyond itself; it loves this object and pours into it the lifegiving power of the trihypostatic love itself. Of course, this object of love is not simply an abstract idea or a lifeless mirror; it can only be a living being, with a personal, hypostatic life. And this love [in the object] is Sophia, the eternal object of the divine love, bliss, joy and gratuitous delight or 'play'. It is impossible to think of Sophia, the divine 'idea', as no more than an ideal representation, devoid of concrete life and the power of being. That which God is, essentially and so from before all ages, beyond all time (we are well aware of the inappropriate-ness of these expressions, but we make use of them in the absence of any more fitting words in human language), this must be conceived in the sense of what is supremely *real*, *ens realissimum*; more particularly, it is the divine 'idea', divine Sophia, that possesses this supremely real reality. Sophia is not only the object of love, but the subject of love directed towards a corresponding love, and in this mutual love it receives all things and *is all things*. As the loving activity of love and as love *for* love, Sophia possesses a personality, a face; it is a subject, a person, or, to use the terminology of theology, a *hypostasis*. It is of course distinct from the hypostases of the Holy Trinity, it is an individual reality of another order, a fourth hypostasis. It does not share in the intra-divine life: it is *not* God, and so does not turn the Trinity into a quaternity of hypostases. However, it is the first principle of the new, *created* plurality of hypostases; this multiplicity of hypostases (human and angelic) is its consequence, a multiplicity existing in sophianic relation to the divine. Yet it is itself not internal to the divine world, it does not enter into the self-enclosed absolute fulness of that realm. However, it is granted access to it by the unutterable condescension of the love of God, and, thanks to this fact, able to reveal the mysteries of the Godhead in its depths, and to rejoice, to 'play' in God's presence. The life of the Trinity is an eternal act of self-giving, the self-emptying of the persons in their divine love. Holy Wisdom also gives itself to the divine love, and receives its gifts in return, the revelation of its mystery. But it gives itself in a different way from the divine persons, who remain unchangeably one consubstantial Godhead, wholly realising themselves in that Godhead and its self-identity. Sophia, on the other hand, *receives*, having nothing to give; it contains only what it has received. By the self-giving of the divine love, it becomes pregnant with the totality of all things. In this sense, we can call it *feminine*, receptive; it is the 'eternal feminine'. At the same time, it is the ideal, intelligible world, the whole, the authentic *hen kai pan*, 'pan-unity'.

The mystery of the world is this 'femininity'. The world in its feminine 'principle' (*archē, bereshith*) is 'begotten' before it is created; and from this divine seed which revelation implants in it, the world is created out of nothing. This begetting, of course, is not distinct *in principle* from that act of begetting by which the Father eternally brings forth the only-begotten and beloved Son from his own bosom, everlastingly, timelessly, sexlessly, and in him and through him begets those divine offspring who are born, not of flesh and blood, but of God. The generation of the world in Wisdom is the act of the whole Trinity in each of its persons, reaching out to realise itself in a receptive reality, the eternal feminine, which thus becomes the principle of a world, *natura naturans*, forming the foundation for *natura naturata*, the created universe.

This 'fourth hypostasis', receiving in itself the revelation of the divine mysteries, mediates *through* itself and *for* itself the differentiation, the order, of the internal sequence of the divine triunity. It takes into itself the single and complete Godhead in its tripersonality, as Father, Son and Spirit. In so far as it receives its substance from the Father it is the creation and the daughter of God. As that which knows and is known by the divine Logos, it is the bride of the Son (as in the Song of Songs), the spouse of the Lamb (as in the New Testament, especially the Apocalypse). As the receiver of the outpouring of the Spirit's gifts, it is the Church, and so too the mother of the Son who was incarnate from the flesh of Mary by the outpouring of the Spirit into her – Mary, the heart of the Church; and as such Sophia is also the ideal soul of creation, Sophia is beauty. All these are interlinked – the daughter and the bride, the spouse and the mother, of the threefold reality which is the Good, the True and the Beautiful, the Trinity itself, within the world: all this is what divine Wisdom is. The second hypostasis, Christ, is pre-eminently the one turned towards Sophia, as he is the light of the world and all things come into being through him (Jn 1); by receiving the light of the Logos, Sophia itself becomes Christ-as-Wisdom, the Logos in the world, and, as such, the object of the Father's love, poured out upon it in the gifts of the Spirit. It is worth noting that Sophia in iconography and liturgy is sometimes identified almost completely with Christ, or at least with his powers and attributes (this is the conception behind Justinian's Church of Hagia Sophia in Constantinople), sometimes with the Mother of God (the celebration of Holy Wisdom is formally associated with that of the Dormition of the Virgin), sometimes with the Church in glory, in heaven and on earth, sometimes with the feminine image of the Bride in the Song of Songs (in certain icons), sometimes even with the cosmos itself.

But what is this 'eternal feminine' in its metaphysical substance? Is it a creature? No, for it was never created. The beginning of creation is nothingness, non-being, the *apeiron*, the void. But in Sophia there is no 'no', only a 'yes' to everything; no non-being, which is a mark of the life of *individual* being, exclusive and self-determining being, breaking up the plenitude of positive and universal unity. Sophia, although it is not the Absolute or God, and does not possess what God possesses, is the direct and absolute *image* of God; it is free from immersion in the nothingness that is native to worldly existence. Thus it is impossible to apply the predicates of *being* to it in the sense in which we apply them to the created world. As such, Wisdom is securely at one in itself; however, apart from its own defined being, it is the indefinable and unfathomable frontier between being or createdness and that which is more than being, the essence of God. It is neither being nor what is more than being; it is one and many, a single *yes* without a *no*, an affirmation without a negation, light without darkness. *It is what being, of itself, does not possess*, i.e., it *is* and it is *not*: immanent in being on the one hand, transcendent to being on the other, free from its grasp. Its place is *between* God and the world, and so it is fixed between being and what transcends being, never becoming either the one or the other, never revealing both at the same time.

2. [The Destiny of Creation]*

Methexis, the participation of matter in ideal form, is also *erōs*, the desire of 'earth' for 'heaven'. The ideal form or entelechy is at once both a datum, the 'root' of being, so to speak, and a project, a reaching forward towards the limits of realisation. It is a painful struggle, the individual thing seeking its own ideal and eternal essence, a self-creation and self-generation. The soul goes in search of itself, like the Shulamite [in the Song of Songs] wandering through the streets of the city in search of her beloved: she asks of all creatures if they have seen him whom her soul loves. She is weakened by her passionate longing for union with him, her longing to transcend herself and 'bear herself anew in beauty'. The whole of nature 'groans and travails' in its 'subjection to futility', its 'bondage to decay', the

---

* pp. 242–4.

bondage to which it is consigned in its materiality, its opacity, the whole of its continuing failure to be what it is. Like plants, all things long for the light, so that they may come to full flower, understand their sophianic being; does not the beauty of flowers in bloom preserve a kind of living symbol of the sophianic content of the natural order? Is not their generative power a self-evident sign of this?

All living things instinctively strive towards grace and beauty, harmony of movement, an inner rhythm in their life. What we call the feral, the 'bestial' in the pejorative sense, is a disease, a deformation of the animal world: to the eye of the artist it is granted to see the more-than-animal, almost human, grief over its own condition in the eyes of a creature. Perhaps the birds of the air speak most plainly of the purity, the 'ideality' of the animal world, the birds which glorify God by their very existence. 'Liberation' from bondage to 'futility', sophianic illumination, transfiguration into beauty, is what every creature thirsts for; but for this very reason the 'speech' of creation is tongue-tied. Only in the human soul, the poor, frightened, weak *psychē*, do we have final, intimate and secure knowledge. But what then could be more plausible than the conclusion that our present ego is *not* the real 'I', since our eternal essence, our divine genius, is something quite other than our empirical personality, our body, character and psychology? *It is impossible to achieve true reconciliation with oneself*; and unreconciledness is perhaps the supreme dignity of man: 'If I must boast, I will boast of the things that show my weakness' (II Cor. 11.30). This sense of unreconciledness can be banished from the heart, suppressed in the soul, only by total spiritual degeneration. Alcibiades utters immortal and inspired words to Socrates, words which must be repeated by every soul confronted face to face by the divine being, confronted by a kind of mirror held up to its own imperfection and disfigurement. In these words, the passion of the entire Platonic scheme finds expression; and in the avowals of Alcibiades–Plato it is the psyche itself that is speaking out of an awareness of the erotic nature of its very being:

> Whenever I listen to him [Socrates], my heart beats faster than if I were in a religious frenzy, and tears run down my face, and I

observe that numbers of other people have the same experience. Nothing of this kind ever used to happen to me when I listened to Pericles and other good speakers; I recognized that they spoke well, but my soul was not thrown into confusion and dismay by the thought that my life was no better than a slave's. That is the condition to which I have often been reduced by our modern Marsyas, with the result that it seems to be impossible to go on living in my present state.
[*Symposium* 215e; trans. W. Hamilton (Harmondsworth, 1951), p. 101]

Is not the awakening of the soul from the deep sleep of non-being or half-being something accomplished in each one of us as we encounter on our path through life a true 'friend', a Socrates of our own, and suddenly see *ourselves* in him or through him, suddenly perceive the 'unfreedom' of our condition? This dividedness in our consciousness, this sense that 'I' am not truly myself, is the real evidence in our interior life of the truth of Platonism, which applies not only to the soul but to the body as well. Somewhere in the depths of the soul, everyone feels themselves to be an 'Endymion' with a light, harmonious and beautiful body of the kind that shines through in Greek sculpture or the plastic fluidity of dance – not a lame 'ugly duckling' with an awkward body alien to any sort of gracefulness. It is impossible to be reconciled with this, for it is impossible to rejoice in ugliness. Every man is aware of a higher self within himself, a kind of 'genius' allotted to each one – for each one has his place in the *pleroma* of total humanity, each corresponds to his own particular ray from the light of Sophia.

But this 'genius' is something he does not know how to uncover in himself; he cannot dig down far enough to unloose the Castalian spring of inspiration, although he may by now be fainting from thirst. All that he does falls short of this, quantitatively and qualitatively; when the soul wants to sing, it comes out with inarticulate and discordant sounds. Only in those geniuses who are the ambassadors, the plenipotentiaries, of the human race does this inner quality of genius show itself outwardly, this hidden but universally shared quality which is our real and substantial participation in Sophia. The mere existence of such figures is disturbing to people in general, like the shriek of a crane from the sky's heights. All long to fly in those blue heights, and feel their lack of wings as an injury, an affront. All are beautiful, endowed with genius, sophianic in the ground of their being, their ideality, their vocation; but alas, they are not so in their concrete existence. And the task of earthly humanity's creative power is, ultimately, to lay bare its true and eternal image, to reveal itself. It is therefore 'erotic' in tone, to the extent that all creativity is a self-constituting, self-creating force. All earthly life is consummated in the discovery of one's own true face. And the 'science of all sciences', the 'spiritual art' of the ascetic, confronts man directly with this vocation to create an 'inner man', to discover his true essence by working on himself – a long and arduous task, the attainment of an 'artistry' of the spiritual life. This path is not only a straight one but is also essentially the one and only path, since all other paths in the creative life lead finally to recognisable goals, only in so far as they coincide with *this* path and share its depth and reality. Art, understood as a 'rebirth in beauty', is a discovery through itself and so also *in* itself of the sophianic character of creation, a breaking through non-being or half-being into substantial reality. However, it is precisely in this breakthrough that a limit is set to man's self-transfiguration, in so far as man remains, so to speak, his own prisoner. And this is how there comes to be that seductive duality in the life of the poet, thanks to which he is simultaneously a messenger from the celestial realms and 'the vilest of earth's offspring' – 'Beauty will save the world': this means that the world will be perceptibly transformed into Sophia – but not by the creative or self-creative action of men. It will be achieved by the creative act of God, bringing to ripeness the 'good fruit' of creation – by the outpouring of the gifts of the Spirit. The unveiling of the world in its true beauty is 'the holy city Jerusalem coming down out of heaven from God, having the glory of God' (Rev. 21.10–11). Beauty, as the unceasing force that strives within every being towards the realisation of its own *logos*, its eternal life, is the inner law of the world, the force that forms the world, the demiurge of the cosmos. It holds the world in being, uniting both its static and its dynamic elements; and in the fulness of time its victory will be accomplished, and it will indeed 'save the world'.

3. [The Meaning of Bodily Existence]*

Christianity accords to the body a positive and absolute significance. The body is not merely a consequence of sin or of a fall from some higher state, a *katabolē*, it is a primordially established reality. The basic Christian dogma of the incarnation – 'the word was made flesh' – along with the Christian devotion to the Mother of God associated with this doctrine, the belief in the fleshly resurrection and ascension of the Son of God and his sitting on the right hand of the Father, all of this is so clearly opposed to any kind of Neoplatonic, Buddhist, spiritualistic or idealistic rejection of the body that it would be superfluous to labour the point. It is particularly noteworthy that Christ is designated 'saviour of the body' in the New Testament (*autos sōtēr tou sōmatos*, Eph. 5.23), and 'the head of the body, the Church' (*kai autos estin hē kephalē tou sōmatos, tēs ekklēsias*, Col. 1.18). The Church is repeatedly called 'the body of Christ'. 'Even so husbands should love their wives as their own bodies. He who loves his wife loves himself. For no man ever hates his own flesh, but nourishes it, as Christ does the Church, because we are members of his body. "For this reason a man shall leave his father and mother and be joined to his wife, and the two shall become one" [Gen. 2.24]. This is a great mystery, and I take it to mean Christ and the Church' (Eph. 5.28–32). The Church is 'his body, the fulness of him who fills all in all' (Eph. 1.23).

Of course, it is possible to resolve all this into allegory and, if one wishes, to 'understand these things spiritually'. However, this would be not only to do exegetical violence to the textual data of the New Testament, but also to fail to reckon with the whole spirit of the Old Testament, with its evident love of the body and affirmation of bodily life. In particular, we should be obliged to treat as uninterrupted allegory the holy eroticism of the Song of Songs, which simply cannot be read either as a purely lyrical or as a purely didactic work, but penetrates to a deeper and more serious level of symbolic realism. It would also be necessary to ignore the Church's teaching on the sacrament of marriage and to exclude on principle what Christianity has

* pp. 248–52.

allowed in fact. It would be to outlaw the whole of the Church's relation to the natural world of material flesh, all that has been expressed in liturgical and sacramental action – not only in the Eucharist but in the practice of blessing water, bread, fruit, flowers, houses, and so on. It would involve us in repudiating the entire tradition of ecclesiastical art – iconography, architecture, music, singing, etc. In a word, it would mean expelling from Christianity everything that idealistic and spiritualistic iconoclasts (in the broadest sense) call religious 'materialism' or simply 'paganism'. But Christianity is not only a religion of salvation for the soul; it is also for the salvation of the spiritualised and glorified body. Alone among the world religions, Christianity does not punish the body but glorifies it, because Christ not only saves the soul from sin, he is also the 'saviour of the body'. Christianity is the apotheosis of the body and holds out a great promise for its redemption.

But what exactly is this 'body' we are speaking of? What is bodiliness? It is often defined in negative terms, as the opposite of 'spirituality', as the 'non-spiritual'. In the first place, such a definition is as unsatisfactory as any other purely negative definition; and in the second place, it is not true, if this negation is understood as total contradiction or exclusion. In its essence, bodiliness is absolutely *not* the opposite of spirit, because there exists a spiritual bodiliness, the 'spiritual body' St Paul speaks of in I Cor. 15.44: 'If there is a physical body there is also a spiritual (*pneumatikon*) body' and indeed this kind of bodiliness contains in itself the ontological norm of bodily life. Bodiliness in the sense of a denial of the spiritual is only one particular *state* the body may be in, and a diseased state at that: it does not belong to its essence. Holy corporeality, the body of the Church, is spiritual and spirit-bearing; thus its essence cannot in any way be defined as *non-spirit*, but must also have some positive definition. This essence must be seen in the life of the *senses* as a specific and distinct element in life, separate from spirit but in no way alien or contradictory to it. The life of the senses is clearly distinguishable both from the substantial volitional core of the personality and from the way in which thought, the rational perception and contemplation of ideal reality, participates in the Logos. But *sense* experience of ideal realities in their embodied form *belongs with* will and thinking.

Moralists and philosophers, ascetics and mystics, have grown used to despising the life of the senses, and the very word 'sensuality' has acquired associations and connotations that cannot easily be forgotten: for some, the life of the senses is the sinful bondage of spirit to flesh, something, at any rate, that needs to be subdued; for others, it is a filthy and degrading, though irremovable, alloy in the life of the spirit, sullying the purity of its transcendental or logical patterns, a necessary 'trampoline' for thought, or an insoluble sediment at the bottom of the gnoseological retort that cannot be evaporated by any quantity of idealist reagents. How much more easily the idealist philosophers would breathe if it were indeed possible to 'think away', to relegate to the status of pure blind sensation (*Empfindung*), all the dead weight of ballast stored in the hold of the *Critique of Pure Reason*! Fichte's cosmogony rounds itself off, so to speak, attaining formal completion by way of the reflection of the 'I' in the mirror of the 'not-I', as if it were possible to get by with logical impulses alone, without any need for the irritant provided by the external goad of the world in all its crudity. With what artistry and solid consistency Hegel's dialectical world is constructed, as if it sufficed to 'deduce' the alienation of spirit in material form – in the face of the facts of concrete experience, where there is no escape from some sort of mysterious commerce between the two realms. Would the triumph of materialism, the dark Ahriman, the realm of Lucifer be possible if matter had not been conceived as a permanent vexation, obstinately refusing to be *completely* enlightened and idealised? Yet Hegel's logical schematisms, for all their splendour, designed as they are to embrace the scale of the whole world, cannot bring a single speck of dust into existence – something real, perceptible to the senses, not just ideal. *Res*, real existence, is to be found in bodiliness, accessibility to the senses; and although idealism does not know what to do with this bodiliness except fastidiously to banish it from its own Kingdom of Light, yet it is the Spirit of Darkness, laughing in triumph, who holds the key to reality, for all his logical crudity. For there is more comfort to be had as the humblest doorkeeper on earth than as a wanderer in the shadowlands of the idealist's Hades, even vested with the highest dignities.

We have already touched on one of the fundamental marks of

bodily existence – accessibility to sense experience. It is in this that the *reality* of the world, the power of existence, consists. It stands at the very frontier of the logical differentiation between light and darkness; it is, so to speak, hidden in the idea, its secret 'supporting' structure. It cannot be expressed in word or thought, and it would be a mistake to try to reason about it: one can only accept it, state its existence. This is why the problem of the existence of an external world is so heavy a cross for idealist philosophy, for this reality is not something established by conceptual means; it is perceptible only to the senses, and in this respect it is what makes logical and alogical principles inseparable – an inseparability characteristic of all actual existence. The ideal and the real are distinguishable only in thought, not in actuality. And if reality consists in accessibility to the senses, in bodiliness, which exists only 'on the outside' of the idea, then pure ideality is pure illusion or abstraction. Following through this train of thought, we come inevitably to the ultimate question of cosmology, the question of the reality of the idea: is it properly conceived as a higher principle of being, postulated by reason, like the Platonic ideas in respect of their separability and organic integrity? Is sensible existence, bodiliness, appropriate to such ideas, a palpable existence that constitutes the basis of their reality, or should we understand them as no more than logical abstractions, as *nomina rerum* once again? Is the ideal basis of existence a matter only of ideal schemata that possess in themselves a poorer, more meagre and one-dimensional existence than they have when 'mixed' with the realities of our world, or should we, on the contrary, ascribe to them a reality *in sensu eminentissimo*, a supremely real reality, *realitas realissima*? In the idealist understanding of Platonism, the Platonic system is stripped of all its vital meaning and assimilated to contemporary idealism of the Husserlian type, an inoffensive but impotent affair of 'intentionality' and 'ideation'.

The idea must rather be understood as what causes the *fulness* of reality – i.e. as a kind of sensible existence, bodiliness. The Platonic idea possesses a bodily form, a kind of refined materiality. And it is impossible to conceive separate ideal forms, devoid of qualities, one-dimensional monads that possess the capacity only for mutual repulsion and thus give rise to a general sense of impermeability in things, and yet are without 'boundaries', so that they have no qualities to *individuate* one over against another. The idea is a body concretely characterised and individuated, in no sense a repetition of any other: each idea is aware *of* itself *in* itself, i.e. it has an individual 'body'. It is a material entelechy.

Thus the idea not only *knows* itself but *senses* itself. This spiritual sensuality, the perceptibility of the idea, is *beauty*. Beauty is as much the absolute foundational principle of the world as is *logos*. It is the revelation of the third divine hypostasis, the Holy Spirit. Beauty, as 'spiritual sensuality', possesses of necessity; some kind of material substrate which is 'surrendered' to the beauty [of form] that will nurture it and bring it to full perfection. In other words, beauty presupposes a *materiality in general* or *reality in general* which, when it is wholly shot through with beauty, can be perceived as the determinate form of the ideal world, its alogical substrate. *Reality in general* is to be recognised in a unique spiritual sensation corresponding to the blind sensation of reality that we have in our physical musculature. For this *general* sensation of reality, over and above particular sensation, indisputably exists and is perceived metalogically; it constitutes an insurmountable – though not a logical – obstacle for idealist metaphysics of the Hegelian variety, which is bound to capitulate, however much this is concealed, before the alogical aspect of the logical process. Without this materiality or reality in the idea, there is no beauty; we could have only a *conception* of beauty. A certain *apeiron* (indeterminacy), hidden in ideal form and thus never revealing its chaotic character, constitutes the secret underlying element in all beauty. Chaos in the world of ideas never shows itself as such, for it is entirely and without remainder dissolved in *cosmos*; but it is still perfectly real. Chaos exists only so that a real cosmos may be possible.

So we arrive at the notion of some sort of *matter as a postulate of reason*, representing the foundation of bodiliness within Sophia itself, so that, in the context of Sophia, this indeterminate element does not appear as a weakness or defect of any kind, but, on the contrary, as powerful and resourceful, as the materiality thanks to which Sophia is the *ens realissimum*, *ontos ōn*, not an idealist phantom. We have an important presentiment of this truth in Plotinus's profound doctrine of *two* kinds of matter – the 'meonic' matter of our world, lying in bondage to evil, and the matter postulated by reason, which is the necessary substrate for *nous*, making it possible for *nous* to reveal its ideal content. *Nous* in Plotinus's sense corresponds exactly (as has already been observed) to the Christian Sophia, in that it unveils to the world the power of the transcendent divinity of the One; however, thanks to his emanationist pantheism, the true hierarchical relation between *hen* and *nous* is obscured, so that the latter comes to occupy a kind of intermediate position between the second hypostasis, the Logos, and Sophia in the proper sense. Plotinus's own real conception of this is different, for he does indeed think of the postulated materiality as belonging to the realm of *nous*, but not to the One, i.e., not to the transcendental Absolute. So too, in Christian belief, the inner trinitarian life of the Godhead, God in himself, belongs in the sphere of absolute and unknowable mystery for all creatures ... But God, revealing himself in Sophia, makes himself known in his tripersonal selfhood as creator – God the Father, the Logos, and the life-giving Spirit; and this giving of life also involves the gift of an awareness [in every subject] of the self coming to full realisation in its ideal form, *perceiving* itself as living, activating the power of the cosmos and triumphing over chaos. The grace of the Holy Spirit brings to light the holiness of sensible existence, creates a holy fleshliness, the 'good harvest' of the earth. Beauty is pre-eminently a revelation of the Holy Spirit.

4. [The Destiny of The Body]*

'There are celestial bodies and there are terrestrial bodies' – *kai sōmata epourania kai sōmata epigeia* (I Cor. 15.40) – says the apostle, referring to the whole range of polarities between holy or spiritual bodiliness and its earthly or fleshly counterpart. In what does the difference consist? It is obviously connected with the characteristics of the 'earth' as the raw material of earthly

---

* pp. 257–9.

physicality. What we mean by the 'earth' is the materiality common to all things, bringing forth from its bosom vegetable and animal matter and, finally, human fleshliness. The earth is materiality in general as it exists in the diverse species of fleshliness of which Paul speaks: 'Not all flesh is alike (*ou pasa sarx hē autē sarx*), but there is one kind for men, another for animals, another for birds and another for fish' (I Cor. 15.39). The 'earth', as a reality set over against 'heaven', is no more than the potentiality for a spiritualised materiality, a blending together of this spiritual potential with nothingness, a kind of primordial 'mixing', as in Plato's *Timaeus*. The meonic basis of materiality remains only potential in the *spiritual* body, as it is there overcome and finally mastered by the idea; but in the 'earthly' body it affirms its own actuality, so that the idea becomes no more than a distant goal to be striven after. This is how process, development, growth arise. The 'earth', in this sense, is spiritual bodiliness *in the process of becoming*, hastening on its way to becoming the 'new earth' that will be manifest at the end of the cosmic process, when the dark and obscure mass of materiality will become 'as it were a sea of glass, like crystal' (Rev. 4.6). Earthly flesh as such is weighed down by matter or 'nothingness', i.e. by inertia, by gravity, by grossness. We can see this mysterious overcoming of matter by the idea in every moment when there emerges 'the countenance of the rose from the dark clods of earth', in the appearing of trees, flowers, grass; earth striving to produce a body for itself, to unveil in itself its own ideal form. This is also what is accomplished in *art*, as it irradiates matter with ideality. Ultimately, man himself can be said to produce himself by the labour of the spirit, constructing a higher ego for himself and in this process transforming his body as well.

Body and matter are by no means identical, in the usual sense of the term; the connection of bodiliness with matter is an enigma, no less mysterious than the connection between soul and body. The notion of an idea existing in a disembodied state is a fiction, an abstraction: *nulla idea sine corpore*. The whole earth is potentially a 'body'; from its original condition as 'without form and void', it proceeds to clothe itself continuously throughout the six days of creation. Everything comes from the earth and returns to the earth. The earth in this sense is

'God's acre', the graveyard that preserves bodies for resurrection: it is of *this* earth that it is said, 'Dust [earth] thou art and unto dust shalt thou return'. Between bodiliness and materiality there is an antagonism which finds religious and practical expression in asceticism; and on the soil of this antagonism there arises a false opposition between spirit and flesh, which is expressed in one-sided spiritualism and one-sided materialism. The earth, as 'flesh', obscures, conceals and resists the idea or entelechy; and this is what produces the sense of fleshliness as the principle of sin and limitation or frustration. Both the sighings of Plato and the lament of the great apostle ('Wretched man that I am! Who will deliver me from this body of death?' [Rom. 7.24]) relate essentially to this body of *flesh*. The same is true of Paul's testimony to the two 'laws' that are present in man, struggling against each other (Rom. 7.23). Here is the ontological core of morality, with its tool of a categorical imperative, ceaselessly convicting us, pronouncing judgement on a human will rendered impotent by the flesh.

The whole world is *one* material reality, *one* body, in which, however, each material entelechy must arrive at a wholly individual perception of itself. Because of our sense of space or extension, our awareness of the connectedness of things is weaker than our awareness of their separateness: thus the impermeability of extended or spatial reality becomes axiomatic for empirical cognition (this throws light on the theological doubts as to how one and the same eucharistic sacrifice can be offered timelessly and simultaneously in many places in such a way that, each time, the Lord unites himself completely with each and every communicant). Nevertheless, the unity of bodily reality cannot be completely fragmented in the world of spatial extension: it is indirectly confirmed by the bodily functions of nutrition and breathing, the exchange of material essence, the general interconnectedness of existence. But the individuality of bodies is not negated by this, despite the fact that attempts to define this individuality in language familiar to us, the language of material corporeality, has led to antinomy and aporia. The universal fact of the permeability of bodies is quite compatible with a notion of *dynamic* individuality, a centre upon which diverse incarnated spiritual realities converge; though this individuality is itself also expressed in the purposive connection of these spiritual realities with determinate bodily units (cells). This understanding of bodily individuality is indissolubly linked to the doctrine of the incarnation. The Lord takes flesh not only in the sense of a generalised participation in [worldly] reality, but in a perfectly concrete sense: he became incarnate in an individual body, lived and suffered in it, and rose from the dead in it, leaving the grave empty – empty in the simple sense of having no material body in it. This is underlined by the account of the grave-clothes and the 'napkin which was about his head' (Jn 20.7) being left behind. In him, indeed, the whole creation is potentially resurrected and will at some time be really resurrected, since it is all in a certain sense Christ's body, having some sort of share in the life of his Church. But although Christ has the whole of fleshly existence as his body, he also possesses a particular body of his own, the body in which he ascended to heaven and 'sitteth on the right hand of the Father'. The proclamation that individual bodies will rise from the dead was what originally constituted the good news of the Christian gospel (we may recall Paul's preaching at the Areopagus in Athens, and the sceptical reaction of the Athenian 'spiritualists' of his day [Acts 17.32]). This question has been considered time and again in Christian literature; and the recognition of [the significance of] the individual body is the basis for the practice of venerating the relics of saints.

5. [Economic Activity and 'Theurgy']*

Economic activity constantly seeks to transcend itself, not only by extending its domain into the artistic realm, but also in exertion within its own proper sphere, in its own inner dynamic. It is striving to become not only *one* sphere of life, but the *only* one, or the ultimately definitive one, recognising no extra-economic or supra-economic court of appeal. The result is *economism* as a fundamental perception of the world, a worldview. Its classic expression is 'economic materialism', a many-faced and many-faceted phenomenon, although it has come to be associated with the name of one of its boldest exponents,

* pp. 358–60, 368–9.

Karl Marx. Man is aware of his being in the world only as an economic subject (economic man, *homo economicus*), for whom economic activity is pure commercialism: economic instinct or egoism is laid down as the foundation of life itself. This egoism is simply the pure manifestation of the universal, metaphysical egoism of creation as a whole. Economic activity founded upon egoism is inevitably afflicted by disharmony and strife, personal and communal ('class war'), and there is no possibility of any ultimate harmonising of this economic egoism which would lead it towards that 'solidarity' of which socialist thinking makes so much. Economic egoism is an elemental force which is in need of regulation, both external and internal (spiritual and ascetical); left to itself, liberated from all restraint, it becomes a destructive power. Where economics is concerned, it is just as wrong to turn away from it in disgust as to be enslaved by its concerns. Economic labour is imposed upon us as a penalty for sin, and we are bound to see it as a duty [*poslushanie*, literally 'obedience'] laid upon all mankind. There is nothing in common between the fastidious aristocratic distaste for economic activity and that freedom from economic concern which the gospel enjoins: this freedom aims not at neglect or contempt but at spiritual mastery.

Economic activity should never be allowed to become autonomous, making itself an end in itself, as economism would like to have it – growth in wealth for the sake of growth in wealth. It must retain its significance as no more than a means for the good life; and this is how the religious ideal of economics appears as its proper measure and criterion. The *spirit* of economic activity is defined by this ideal and the ascetical self-regulation that goes with it. This spirit will not be bound to particular determinate [social] forms, but defines itself from within. The characteristic style of economic activity will correspond to the spiritual style of its epoch; so, for example, there is a clear enough connection between capitalism and modern European humanism.

Two problems can be distinguished in economic activity, leading to a twofold struggle: the struggle against poverty at both the natural and the communal level – i.e. the strictly economic struggle and the social. This battle against poverty (or, in the language of the economist, 'the development of the forces of production') is a universal and laborious task requiring our obedience – the 'curse' upon the earth that is laid upon [fallen] humanity. In the process, a 'social politics' appears, directed at the overcoming or at least the moderating of the consequences of egoism in human relations. Can we ultimately solve both problems? Can we overcome poverty by the 'development of the forces of production' and also solve the social question by practical social reform, as the socialists believe? The second task is obviously subordinate to the first – or, at least, it cannot be dealt with in isolation from the first. But what is the term for this development of productive forces? *Is* there such a term? Does economic activity have not only a history but an eschatology as well? Can it not transcend itself and pass over into the supra-economic sphere, so that the economic age of human history (Marx's *Vorgeschichte*, 'prehistory') is over and done with? Might it be that man, possessed of full economic sustenance in the world, being a 'demiurge' in the world, is called also to become a *cosmourgos*, a restorer of life to the dead, a guardian of the present, a godfather to the future? Might it be that the economic labour of the human microcosm will take away death from the macrocosm of the universe and deliver the earth from its curse? [...]

Economic activity, in so far as it is bound up with the earth's curse, does *not* have an eschatological task transcending the limits of the mortal life of this present age, which alone is its territory. Thus it cannot, within its own proper limits, fulfil or complete itself; like human life overall, it requires interruption for its own fulfilment. This does not mean forgetting that temporal existence has its own depths, depths that also lead to eternity, where time finds its full integration, even though we cannot at present fathom how this might come about. But in temporal perspective, economic activity is a 'malign infinity', knowing no fulfilment. To the extent that history is shaped in and through economic activity (understood in the broadest sense), it is in and through economic activity that the historical *body* of humanity takes shape, the body that must be 'changed' by resurrection, when the entire world will appear as a potential 'body' for humanity. In economic work, man realises this world for himself, constructs his cosmic body and becomes concretely aware of it, realises the authority primordially bestowed on him. Even in his 'housekeeping' role, man retains some reflection of the royal splendour of Adam.

But the consequence of his fall is that he does not so much govern the world as the world governs him, since the covering of material corporeality means that he is overshadowed by the world, and his body is swathed in Adam and Eve's 'garments of skin'. So, in the sphere of economic behaviour, the gospel presents an ideal not of freedom *in* and *through* economic work but of freedom *from* it; it summons us to a belief in miracle that flies in the face of worldly inertia, it exhorts us to be miracle workers, not mechanics, in relation to the world, healers, not physicians. Economic activity is only tolerated by the gospel; it is reconciled with the gospel only in the way any other aspect of the burdensome existence of this present age is reconciled, and no more than that. All the efforts of modern economism are guided by a kind of prophetic energy towards an eternalising of the life of this present age, towards a denial of the limits of life as it is lived in discrete human personalities, or, indeed, in the whole of this contingent world. In diverse forms, this is what scientific economic theory, especially socialist doctrine, speaks of: what they aim at – under the guise of freedom by means of increased 'wealth' – is the consolidation of man's economic *slavery*, promising to realise the contradictory ideal of a freedom both *magical* and economic. This is why, for Christianity, with its qualitatively higher notion of freedom, what is to be celebrated is not power but weakness, not wealth but poverty, not the wisdom of this world with its economic magic, but divine folly [*yurodstvo*].

Economic activity, then, in its own proper sphere of proceeding, has no eschatology; when it tries to go down this path, it falls into pseudo-eschatology, it chases lying and deceitful phantoms. This pseudo-eschatology is rooted in a false estimate of economic activity, in a forgetfulness of its conditional and relative character. Our age is marked not only by a blossoming of economic activity isolated from other considerations but also by an economism disguised as a form of spiritual self-awareness; and it is at the same time characterised by an extension and exaggeration of economic eschatologism. Thus the religious consciousness is obscured not only in individual thinkers, but also in the mass of the people, cut off from mystical relation with the land itself: this can be seen in those socialists who prized so much a frenzied, blind and sacrificial pseudo-eschatology, their raptures recalling in the Christian era the messianic expectations of the Hebrew world. But now, in the middle of a world war, these economistic towers of Babel are crumbling. To anyone with eyes to see, it is becoming clear that the enterprise of building these structures, conceived from that day to this in the same grandiose terms, here faces failure. Yet again, the magical kingdom built from the stuff of this world has not succeeded – and thank God it has not. This same sequence of historical events has compelled people to look longingly for a *different* kingdom, 'not of this world'. The 'new history' [of Marxism and other radical movements] has not succeeded; but this very failure, by deepening the human experience of good and evil, paves the way for the global crisis of history and creation. And the failure of all worldly history is also, on the greater canvas, its success, since its goal lies not in itself but beyond its limits. To this all the elements of our history summon us; this is the end that they yearn for.

6. [Art and 'Theurgy']*

Hierarchically speaking, art's standing is higher than that of economics, since its territory lies on the frontier between two worlds. It perceives a beauty that is not native to this world and reveals it to the world. It does not feel itself to be without ways of articulating this; it is aware that it is capable of taking wing. [...]

Beauty is only a pleasant illusion and poetry no more than fantasy if art itself is no more than a stimulus and an enticement towards the beautiful in the midst of an unbeautiful world, if it

---

* pp. 370–3, 381, 388–90.

entertains but does not transfigure. It is this recognition that gives birth to the 'cosmourgic' pathos and anguish of art, that prompts the thirst for effective actuality; if beauty once saved the world, then art must prove itself an instrument of this salvation. In every fresh creative act, the artist extends his embrace ever more widely; yet the goddess slips away from him, an alluring vision, leaving him dumb and despairing, ready to break in pieces his tuneful but impotent lyre. If the tragedy of economic action, when it understands its own limits, lies in the awareness of its own prosaic, subordinate and earthbound character, the tragedy of art lies in its awareness of its own impotence, in the appalling schism between what is revealed to it of the true splendour of the world and the concrete reality of its deformity and ugliness. Does art then not 'save', does it not alleviate the anguish of existence on this earth? Does it do no more than amuse? Must it and should it be no more than an entertainment that has no power to change anything? It is possible for the products of the arts to be admired and loved in their own right, but this only has the effect of making the chains of this 'vile existence' more palpable. And it is impossible to love these products with a living human affection: Galatea in her sculptured marble beauty is still deprived of the warmth of blood and muscle and remains only a counterfeit.

Every creative act strives to attain an absolute status, not only in regard to its origins (since in it the inexpressible core of personality, transcending all its manifestations, struggles to express itself), but also in regard to its goal. It longs to *create* a world of beauty, to triumph over chaos and convert it to order; but what does it actually save or convert? A lump of marble – or whatever else serves as its raw material. And the great waves of 'cosmourgic' energy sink down in powerlessness, in an atmosphere weighed down by the exhalations of the material world. So the artist, even if the greatest artistic attainments are granted him, has all the greater a sense of unsatisfactoriness or frustration as a creative personality to endure. Creativity is a stony path, where the weight of the cross is laid on the shoulders of Simon of Cyrene, whether he wills it or no. It is possible to break free from this tragic destiny, to cast aside the cross of Christ, to refuse the destiny it imposes of a self-crucifixion of the worldly, unenlightened ego, but only at the cost of a total spiritual paralysis of the personality. Instead of beauty, mere attractiveness will come to seem sufficient; and once the artist has fallen in love with this, he becomes deaf to the real imperatives of creativity. It is possible to construct one's own little world, with its quite demanding 'canons', out of the techniques of a strict and exacting artistic discipline – and to be content with this. Aestheticism, as an expression of this making terms with the world, this sufficiency to oneself, is the supremely refined seduction of spiritual *Bürgerlichkeit*. [. . .]

Art yearns to become transfigurative, not just pleasing or consoling; transfigurative in a real, not a symbolic, sense. This aspiration was recognised with particular force in the Russian soul, which gave it a prophetic articulation in Dostoevsky's inspired dictum, '*Beauty will save the world*'. The same conviction lies at the root of Soloviev's doctrine of efficacious artistic activity, to which he gave the designation of '*theurgy*' – a usage that has unfortunately become well established. Soloviev, by doing no more than providing a purely verbal definition of the task of art as 'theurgic', did a great deal to hinder a clear understanding of the essence of this problem; he obscures and even distorts the issue (as well as going against his own essential world-view). He set spiritual explorations of this question off on a false trail, so that now it is necessary to bring them back again to the starting point, and, above all, to pose the fundamental question of principle: is it possible to speak in relation to *human* creativity about 'theurgy', *theou ergon*, God's work? Consistency demands that we distinguish the *action of God* in the world, even though it is accomplished in and through man – which is 'theurgy' in the strict and proper sense of the word – from *human* action, accomplished by the power of divine Sophia present with it. This *anthrōpou ergon* is thus also a 'sophiurgy', *ergon ek sophias*. The former is the divine condescension, the latter is the human ascent; the one moves from heaven to earth, the other is directed from earth to heaven. Both possibilities, 'theurgy' and 'sophiurgy', must be definitively distinguished: to the extent that they are constantly mingled together, there is ambiguity and unclarity. What, then, in concrete terms, are we really talking about when we speak of the 'theurgic' task of art? In what sense is it possible to make any accurate assertions about this?

Theurgy is the action of God, the outpouring of his pardoning and saving grace upon humankind. As such, it depends not upon human beings but upon the will of God. In its essence, theurgy is inseparably connected with the incarnation, it is the incarnation itself extended in time and uninterruptedly in process of accomplishment, the unending action of Christ in humanity: 'And lo, I am with you always, to the close of the age' (Mt 28.20). Christ laid down the absolute and irreversible foundation for theurgy, and passed on to his Church a theurgic power through the inheritance of the grace communicated to his apostles: 'Jesus said to them again, "Peace be with you. As the Father has sent me, even so I send you". And when he had said this, he breathed on them, and said to them, "Receive the Holy Spirit"' (Jn 20.21–2). 'You shall receive power when the Holy Spirit has come upon you' (Acts 1.8). This is what is brought to completion at Pentecost, which is thus the ultimate foundation for Christian theurgy. It is realised in the liturgy, whose essential centre is the sacramental life of the Church, above all the Eucharist: and consequently, *all* liturgical action can be seen as sacramental in the broad sense, for the grace of God in sacramental action flows out in every direction. Theurgic power belongs to a priesthood, in association with the people of the Church – although grace finds its own chosen means, apart from these foreordained channels, in the lives of Spirit-bearing saints. In great saints and wonder-workers like St Sergius or St Seraphim there is no doubt that theurgy is at work in an essential and authentic sense. But the fundamental principle of Christian theurgy was solemnly established on Maundy Thursday [at the Last Supper], foreshadowing in itself the events of Golgotha.

However, a theurgic character was also present – though only to a certain degree – in the liturgy of the Old Testament era, to the extent that the Old Testament Church is indivisibly connected to Christendom and is full of symbols and fore-types of the incarnation. Nor is it alien even to pagan worship in its own measure, worship in which the vision of God and the grace of God become accessible to the pagan world in so far as its rites and mysteries possess religious authenticity. Cultic activity in general is, so to speak, the normal, but not the only, sphere of theurgy; and its central hearth-fire is the sacramental life of the Church. [...]

In an epoch of 'culture', i.e. secularisation of all sorts, the sphere of *cult* no longer receives artistic enrichment, experiences no new discoveries. Cult is very readily satisfied by the wealth accumulated in the past, which is certainly adequate to the task it faces. But for all its regular requirements, it is content to make use of the services of an 'art industry', with its more or less superficial aestheticism and stylisation – that is, essentially, its counterfeits and surrogacies; and that means that it has no art that is truly *its own*. The artist who combines artistic sensibility with religious awareness must now feel with particular keenness that the mystery of prayerful inspiration, of an art dedicated to the Church, has been obscured, never to be rediscovered; and in time he will be completely numbed by the burden of this painful sensation. In any event, the future of ecclesial art is bound up with nothing other than the destiny of art in general. [...]

So how should we define the immediate goals of an art that has become conscious of its own nature and meaning? When art develops this elevated awareness, it becomes vulnerable to dangers that are not to be met with along the paths of pure aestheticism. These consist primarily in a facility for the *ersatz*, connected with an exaggerated or mistaken estimate of art's goal and resources. For art, spiritual sobriety and self-awareness are of particular importance. And above all, it must remember that the sophiurgic task cannot be fulfilled by the powers of art and human will alone, but presupposes also the influence of God's grace. Neither technical artistic virtuosity nor aestheticist magic, but only Beauty itself, is the truly transfigurative, sophiurgic power. And art will fall into deliberate error if it seeks the accomplishment of its task only by its own processes, devising new tricks of the trade, new focuses in artistic technique. Along this route, it can easily go astray into the realm of magic and become open to the influence of dark forces. Art must always remain itself, never fading away in doubtful experiments. The boundaries fixed by a strict aesthetic, an exacting canonical discipline (which, of course, has nothing to do with simple stagnation), are dictated by the need for self-preservation; they are the asceticism of art, protecting it from dissolution and formlessness. Art must have hidden in its depths a prayer for the transfiguration of the created order, but it is not itself called to the daring enterprise of sophiurgic experiment. It must, patiently and hopefully, carry the cross of an insatiable yearning in its own passionate hunger, and await its hour. In this interior affliction, this hunger, a particular *tone* in symbolic art is undoubtedly generated and formed, adding a depth and mysteriousness to its romantic turbulence. It is able to awake in art new and unprecedented powers and to make fecund its creative potential. It may be that these possibilities are at first defined in mistaken ways, since it is impossible to guarantee in advance a successful invocation of creativity and inspiration. But one thing is hard to doubt, and that is that art is always destined to be kindled by the fires of religious vision. On this basis a new rapprochement between art and cult is possible, a renaissance of religious art – not a stylised virtuosity that is impotent in terms of creativity and inspiration, but a completely free, and thus ultimately honest, prayerfully inspired creativity, comparable to the great religious art of an earlier epoch. In any event, art will preserve the most profound acquisition that has accrued to it in the age of 'secularisation' – its growing freedom and autonomy: when it is brought to the altar, brought within the frontiers of the Church by the sacrificial offering of its inspiration, it does not become in any way heteronomous, it does not limit itself; it is not doomed to captivity within the realm of liturgy, but preserves the full range of its diapason, at least as a possibility.

However, there is no need to think of this possible religious renaissance in the arts – a possibility only, which might or might not come about – as if it would be a fulfilment of the sophiurgic hope: on the contrary, such a fulfilment *cannot* fail to be realised. The rebirth of religious art, should it happen, would not in any way be a response to these demands [for 'sophiurgic' transfiguration], and so it would still remain *within the limits* of art as such; whereas the idea of sophiurgy takes us beyond its frontiers. However, a prayerfully inspired religious art has, of course, the greatest possible potential for being the spark from which a global fire can be kindled, so that the first glimmers of the glory of Mount Tabor may be seen on earth.

So: is the sophiurgic task accessible for art and should art be striving towards it? Yes and no. It should nurture this ideal in its heart, conscious at the same time that it can in no way be fulfilled by artistic means; it must long for the unattainable and impossible, striving 'to transcend itself in the divine adventure'. But along with this, art must become the pledge and promise of Beauty: only so can it be itself the rumour, the good news, of a higher world. And its creative impulse, by God's good will, can appear as a starting point for sophiurgic action. There can be no return to 'pure' art, with its aesthetic complacency and limited horizons, without at least a spiritually stagnant and reactionary result.

7. [The Nature of Political Authority]*

In order to arrive at a vital understanding of the problem of what 'theocracy' means, it may be necessary to give a provisional delineation of how theocracy is visibly manifested, so that it has a clearly defined character to set against the character of authority in its purely human form, its naturally 'animal' or 'feral' quality. And in this we may see the positive dimension of 'secularisation'. The *heteronomy* of authority characteristic equally of pagan pseudo-theocracy and of the clericalism of the 'Christian state' has obscured the nature of authority in its proper *autonomy*, and has led to a serious confusion between Caesar and God. This has involved a doubtfulness and vacillation [over the nature of authority], resulting in counterfeits and frauds, despotism or pseudo-theocracy, i.e. in the triumph of precisely the 'animal' principle [of unregenerate human power], even when this is concealed by official phraseology of a quite different kind. This paved the way for the triumph of secularisation in external affairs, the 'legal state', with its human

* pp. 399–401.

rectitude, protecting by its integrity the 'public good' and the freedom of the populace.

But this atmosphere of a militant deification of 'the people', of the 'kingdom of this world', has resulted in a spiritual stifling of what had been nourished in the soul by the religious ideal of authority with its refusal to *worship* the 'animal' dimension of power and to receive its 'mark' [the 'mark of the Beast', Rev. 13.16ff.]. It is possible and necessary to maintain loyalty to and endure an unfavourable political order, even to value its highest practical achievements, seeing in it a relative this-worldly good, or at any rate a lesser evil, in preference to an old order of authority that has become degenerate and untruthful. But to *love* such an unfavourable system, to feel a religious *eros* towards it, can only be understood as a sharing in the cult of the democratic Caliban, 'offering sacrifice to the Beast'. We should understand public order, reduced to the terms of political utilitarianism, as concerned simply with the burden of economic concerns, and accept the integrity of this project, pursuing it in an ascetical spirit as a matter of vital 'obedience' [*poslushanie*]; but 'integrity', correctness, is only a religio-ethical minimum, whereas religious commitment looks for the maximum in all human acts. Nonetheless, this secular version of political order is in its own way already a *negative revelation* of true authority. This fractured and differentiated body that is secular authority is also the 'accursed ground' [of Gen. 3.17], broken and parched, thirsty for the goods of heaven. The 'legal state', with its guarantees of law and all its worldly prudence and man-related justice, will never do away with the pain caused by the reality of *another* kingdom, one not of cold legality alone, but of love, *another* kind of authority which is 'theocratic'. But of course this question has meaning only within the Church, where the discourse is not about politics in the usual sense of the word, but rather about the religious triumph over the 'political', the *transfiguration* of authority, which is also its manifestation in *New Testament* terms. Here, only expectations and confused anticipations are possible: the where, when and how, whether in the visible or the invisible world, we do not know. Only speculative hopes are possible, of which there is no room to speak here.

The Russian people, always aquiver with apocalyptic feeling, have preserved this anticipation in the form of their notion of a holy king, the 'White Tsar'; through the prism of this myth, they were able to understand and accept the reality of Russian autocracy. The same thing is touched upon in the prophetic vision of those who have given most profound expression to the Russian soul – the Slavophils, Dostoevsky, Soloviev, Fyodorov. Even Tolstoy's implacable hostility to the 'animal' principle of state authority, Tolstoy, whose every positive idea is so wrapped up in negations and always takes the form of saying no to something else, speaks of the same vision. It can also be found in the mystical revolutionary beliefs of the intelligentsia, with their quest for the invisible city that is to come – though here it is clothed in the alien and monstrous form of sociopolitical utopianism; and in a certain diffused apolitical spirit in the whole Russian people, rooted not only in the lack of discipline in individual and social life, but also in a general absence of any taste for the middle ground or the relative good.

And so: empirically speaking, there has been, on the face of things, a dissolution of the religious principle of authority; secularisation has triumphed. But in the mystical depths a new revelation of the nature of authority has been prepared and matured, a revelation of theocracy, announcing its ultimate victory on the threshold of this new age.

4

The Lamb of God: On the Divine Humanity (1933)

INTRODUCTION

Bulgakov was ordained to the priesthood in 1918. In his autobiography he makes it plain that he had been aspiring to this since his return to the practice of Orthodox Christianity ten years before; but what had held him back was the continuing association of the Church with the autocratic state.[1] In 1917 everything had changed, and the Church was both free and persecuted. (Bulgakov had, incidentally, been one of the lay representatives in the abortive Council of the Russian Church in 1917, which had restored the Patriarchate of Moscow as the supreme authority in the Church rather than the state-controlled Synod with its lay Procurator.[2]) He now felt it possible to offer himself for ordination, and, early in 1918, approached one of the Patriarch's suffragans in Moscow (Bishop Fyodor, who had also ordained Florensky); he was made deacon at Pentecost 1918 and priest the day after. There was some urgency to all this, as Bulgakov's family were in the Crimea, where the Civil War was becoming increasingly bloody, and he was impatient to go and find them (he had no news of them in

---

[1] *Avtobiograficheskiya zametki* (*Autobiographical Fragments*), ed. Lev Zander (Paris, 1946), p. 38. There is an English translation of Bulgakov's account of his ordination in *A Bulgakov Anthology*, eds. James Pain and Nicolas Zernov (London, 1976), pp. 3–9.

[2] A brief account in Nicolas Zernov, *The Russian Religious Renaissance of the Twentieth Century* (London, 1963), pp. 191–9, brings out very clearly the degree to which the 'liberalising' tendencies of members like Bulgakov in questions touching Church government were in the ascendant at the Council, and how this helped to guarantee the survival of the Church in the first years of persecution. For further details, see A. A. Bogolepov, *Church Reforms in Russia, 1905–1918* (Bridgeport, Conn., 1966).

the first months of 1918, and there was a strong likelihood that they had been killed). Two weeks after ordination, when news of the family's safety had at last reached Moscow, Bulgakov left to join them; he never returned to Moscow.[3] At the beginning of 1923, he was exiled from the Soviet Union, along with a large number of other non-Marxist intellectuals.

In the Crimea between 1918 and 1923, he had worked as a professor in the University of Simferopol,[4] and had completed a number of essays and other works, including a lengthy set of philosophical dialogues, 'Na piru bogov: Pro i contra' ('At the Feast of the Gods: Pro and contra'[5]). Understandably, these pieces are marked by a strong sense of tragedy and unclarity about the future. The dialogues do not give a clear indication of whether Bulgakov himself is identified with any one speaker, but it is obvious that he resists the simplistic rhetoric of White Russian conservatism. At the same time, there is an equally obvious fury at the ravages of Bolshevism, and some hard words about 'socialism' in general. As we shall see in the last two extracts in this book, the word and the concept of socialism meant for Bulgakov a bewildering variety of things, and at this point they signified something demonic.

Like other exiles, he found himself in Constantinople (where he visited the church of Hagia Sophia for the first time,[6] with no possessions and no clear future; but – again along with many others – he moved on to Prague, where the Russian émigrés were establishing a Russian Law Faculty (founded originally in 1922 as part of the 'Russian Academic Group in Czechoslovakia', incorporated in July 1922 within the structures of the Charles University in Prague). Bulgakov, with Struve and

[3] *Avtobiograficheskiya zametki*, pp. 42–3 (*A Bulgakov Anthology*, p. 9).

[4] N. Valentinov, *Encounters with Lenin* (London, 1968), has some reminiscences of Bulgakov's teaching in the Crimea and the scornful ferocity of his polemic against Lenin.

[5] An English translation, 'At the Feast of the Gods: Contemporary Dialogues', may be found in the *Slavonic and East European Review*, vols 1–3 (1922–3), pp. 172–83, 391–400, 604–22. The dialogues appeared as part of a collection, *Iz glubiny* (*Out of the Depths*), published by the periodical *Russkaya mysl'* in 1918; the entire volume has now been translated by William Woehrlin, with a preface by Bernice Glatzer Rosenthal, as *From the Depths* (Irvine, Calif., 1986); Bulgakov's dialogues are on pp. 65–118.

[6] *Avtobiograficheskiya zametki*, pp. 94–102 (an extract in *A Bulgakov Anthology*, pp. 13–15).

Florovsky, and other names celebrated in the past and the future of Russian philosophy, taught in the Faculty (publishing an essay on Orthodox canon law in 1924)[7] but his interests were very clearly now on the side of dogmatic theology rather than social or legal philosophy. When, in 1925, the Institut de Théologie Orthodoxe, otherwise the Institut Saint-Serge,[8] was founded in Paris, Bulgakov was invited to become its Professor of Dogmatic Theology and first Dean; this was to be the scene of the rest of his career, as teacher and pastor.

Before leaving Prague he had taken the opportunity of clarifying some of the concepts in *Svet nevechernii* in an essay written for Struve's Festschrift in 1925, under the almost untranslatable title, 'Ipostas i ipostasnost' (Scolia k *Svetu Neverchernemu*)' – 'Hypostasis and hypostaseity/hypostatic existence/hypostatic character (Scholia to *The Unfading Light*)'.[9] The difficult word *ipostasnost*' seems to mean the capacity for being hypostatised, being concretised in an active subject, as opposed to existing directly as an agent or subject or hypostasis. Thus this essay finally bids farewell to Florensky's vocabulary, and introduces a new element in Bulgakov's thought. The Palamite distinction between the transcendent divine essence and the immanent *energeia* plays a significant role here; Bulgakov claims that recognising this distinction is fundamental for theology.[10] It enables us to conceive Sophia neither as the divine nature in itself nor as a mythological individual, but as an aspect of the divine nature *in action*, in relation. And this is elucidated further by an analysis of what 'spirit' means. Spirit is the union of an act of self-awareness, conscious independent existence, with the 'nature' of which it is conscious; neither term in this union is real, concrete, without the other, so that there *is* no actually existing ego without the concrete 'what' that it thinks. But equally, there is no individual and isolated unit of ego-plus-nature, because the 'I' exists only

---

[7] 'Tserkovnoe pravo i krizis pravosoznaniya' ('Church Law and the Crisis of Legitimacy'), an inaugural lecture in the Russian Faculty, published in *Ucheniye zapiski (Academic Notes)*, 1 (1924), pp. 9–27.
[8] For its history, see D. A. Lowrie, *St Sergius in Paris* (London, 1954).
[9] In *Sbornik statei posvyashchennykh Petru Berngardovichu Struve* (*A Collection of Essays Dedicated to Peter Berngardovich Struve*, Prague, 1925), pp. 353–71.
[10] 'Ipostas', p. 353.

with another 'I'.[11] This complex relationship between ego and nature and Other is a clue to how we are to think of God as 'Spirit' in the absolute sense. God is wholly and simultaneously a co-existence of three moments of saying 'I', each manifest only through its 'others'; but the divine 'I' cannot be concrete without the divine 'what', the divine nature.[12] What the divine 'content' of being is *per se* we cannot determine; but the content of the life revealed to us is love and glory. God as personal (hypostatic) love, love in action, loves also the *fact* that self-emptying love is *what* God is. And that 'what', which is not simply conceptually identical with any or all of the trinitarian hypostases, that eternal object of divine love, is Sophia. As object of eternal love, it is the prototype of the created world, or, speaking boldly, the prototype of *humanity* – because humanity is the perfection of the world's being as object of divine love; what is loved is always love itself, but love cannot exist without loving *agents*, and so when God loves the world he cannot but love in it the capacity of the world to be 'hypostatic', a world of agents and subjects.[13] Thus what God loves is the directedness of the world towards the human; God loves the heavenly image or idea of humanity, the 'Heavenly Adam'.[14] And that reality is fully actualised when Christ, the divine person, brings created humanity to perfection because he introduces into humanity the action of the perfectly other-directed hypostatic life that belongs in the Holy Trinity.[15]

This almost breathlessly intricate scheme builds obviously on the idea in *Svet* of Sophia as the loving of love itself; but here it is more tightly interwoven with a particular understanding of the divine image in us (as spirit) and with Christology. 'No sort of augmentation can be admitted' in the Trinity,[16] and talk of Sophia as any kind of hypostasis is bound to be misleading. Sophia is certainly a *concrete* reality, but not as *a* subject in any sense at all.[17] If love always loves love (and how very

---

[11] 'Ipostas', p. 354.
[12] 'Ipostas', p. 354.
[13] 'Ipostas', pp. 360–4.
[14] 'Ipostas', pp. 364–5.
[15] 'Ipostas', pp. 355–6, 365 (Christ 'transcends created limitation in love, opening up his "I", pouring it into the ocean of tripersonality').
[16] 'Ipostas', p. 361.
[17] 'Ipostas', pp. 361–2.

THE LAMB OF GOD: ON THE DIVINE HUMANITY (1933)

Augustinian Bulgakov is in this respect!), the loving persons of the Trinity cannot love what they are if that nature is simply an abstract set of divine qualities; what they love is the capacity for love which is the foundation (though not the cause or origin, as if the abstract came before the concrete) of the eternal life they actually lead. And any other that is to be the object of divine love must be likewise grounded in the same capacity, the 'feminine', waiting, receiving potential for love.[18] Only in God is there absolute union and simultaneity between the active and the receptive, the possessor and the possessed;[19] but it is to this absolute spiritual reconciliation that we move in Christ and the communion of the Church. For our capacity to be hypostatic, to be reconciled spirit living in activated nature, is a capacity to live in the communion of the Trinity – which is what is made possible by living in Christ. The new concern with the analysis of what it is to be a spiritual 'I' and the connection of this with the trinitarian life was evidently something to which Bulgakov was giving much attention in the twenties, and we have some notes and sketches on trinitarian theology from the period which show how his mind was developing in this area.[20] But this very dense essay is perhaps the most important bridge between the earlier and the later Bulgakov, firmly laying the foundations on which he was to build the great edifice of his major trilogy in the thirties and forties.

In the later twenties, however, he concentrated on completing a less ambitious trilogy of books on Mary, John the Baptist and the angels;[21] the first two, whose composition is shaped by the iconographic tradition of having Our Lady and the Baptist depicted on either side of Christ in the icons where Christ is receiving the supplications of the saints, outline the distinct ('male' and 'female') types of relation to Christ in the Church,

---

[18] 'Ipostas', pp. 362–3; cf. pp. 365–7 on the motherhood of Mary as an image of the 'sophianic' Church.
[19] 'Ipostas', p. 363.
[20] 'Glavy o troichnosti' ('Chapters on the Trinitarian Life'), *Pravoslavnaya mysl'*, (1920), pp. 25–85, (1928), pp. 31–83. There is a German version, 'Capita de Trinitate', in the *Internationale Kirchliche Zeitschrift*, 26 (1936).
[21] *Kupina neopalimaya* (*The Burning Bush*), on the Virgin (Paris, 1927); *Drug Zhenikha* (*The Friend of the Bridegroom*), on the Baptist (Paris, 1927); *Lestvitsa Yakovlya: Ob angelakh* (*Jacob's Ladder: On the Angels*), (Paris, 1929). *A Bulgakov Anthology* has extracts of a few pages from these (pp. 86–99).

and elaborate the sophianic image of Mary *as* the Church; the third is a meditation on the angelic vocation of service as an image of the 'kenotic', self-emptying action of God, Sophia as *realised* in kenosis, a theme already well orchestrated in Bulgakov and a dominant feature of the later work. But it can fairly be said that these three books, though pretty substantial, do not add any new features to Bulgakov's system as such; they are almost marginal notes to the development of the theology of creation and incarnation that was coming to completion in the work published in 1933, *Agnets bozhii (The Lamb of God)*,[22] from which the extracts in this section are taken.

The subject matter and idiom of this book will already be familiar; but again there is a refinement of what had earlier been sketched, as Bulgakov tries to make sense of the notion that God is both Absolute and relational. He had already noted the paradox in *Svet*; here he attempts to spell it out in a less aggressively paradoxical way. God is in one sense not 'God' without creation – since 'God' is not the name of the divine essence (which cannot be named) but the name of the One who emerges from transcendence to be the God and maker of a universe.[23] If we say that God's absoluteness does not permit God to be in relation, we are making absoluteness a limiting characteristic of God, rather than a way of saying that there are no limiting characteristics in divine life. It is an interesting and sophisticated point: God as Absolute cannot mean God as separate, for that would be to treat the absolute God as *a* subject over against others. God, we are told, 'needs' the world, not to be what God is or to satisfy a lack (the divine life is self-sufficient in the mutuality of the Trinity) but to express the illimitability of the outreach of love. That God is self-sufficient tells us nothing important, because the language of need and sufficiency, the minimum conditions, as it were, for God to be God, is inappropriate to the force of the divine self-sharing. These pages are likely to drive a strict scholastic to drink, but they express something quite central to Bulgakov's theology –

---

[22] *Agnets bozhii: O bogochelovechestve (The Lamb of God: On Divine Humanity*, Paris, 1933). *Bogochelovechestvo*, literally 'Godmanhood', is a word that consciously looks back to Soloviev's usage.

[23] *Agnets*, pp. 141–5, esp. pp. 143–4.

THE LAMB OF GOD: ON THE DIVINE HUMANITY (1933)

the conviction that the thinking of God outside the relations God has in fact established is impossible, even blasphemous, and that those relations, taken in conjunction with what revelation shows us of the divine life, make it actively misleading to talk of creation as only arbitrarily or accidentally related to its maker. Bulgakov here stands closer to Hegel than he thinks – but, surprisingly, he stands closer to Barth than a casual reader might suppose.[24]

Sophia is a way of speaking about the non-arbitrariness of this relation; and Bulgakov explains how we might see the creation of the world as specifically a revelation of the *trinitarian* life, so that the world's life is shown to be established on the same (sophianic) foundation as God's. There is the sheer impulse of self-giving, the life of God as 'Father', emptying himself in letting the Other be, just as he does in the generation of the Son. But this in turn means that the Other always has the form of the Son for the Father; it cannot be but that he is at the heart of creation's otherness. And the Spirit, who is the joy that proceeds from the Father's giving and the Son's responding, is in the world as beauty, as that which urges forward and completes the world on its way to perfect relation with God. The world is thus that complex of relations that is God in eternity translated into process and temporality.[25] Worth noting at this point is the way in which aspects of creation's life that the earlier Bulgakov ascribed indiscriminately to Sophia are here reconceived in trinitarian plurality.

Humanity stands as the crown of creation because it is the place where the world becomes personal. Here again, Bulgakov employs language that seems designed to provoke the traditionalist: he ascribes to the human constitution an 'uncreated' element.[26] It is, I think, clear that he does not mean this in a

---

[24] There is a fleeting allusion to Hegel in *Agnets*, p. 131, n. 1: Sophia does the work in Bulgakov's system that thought or *Geist* does for Hegel, at least as far as God is concerned. Sophia is the perfect coincidence of thought and object in the divine life (as in 'Ipostas'). But the repudiation of an irrational or groundless element in God's relation to what is not God is a basic datum in Hegel. As for Barth, *Church Dogmatics* III/1 wrestles with the same problem of how to speak of a relation neither necessary nor arbitrary; and Barth consistently maintains that God *chooses* not to be God without the world.
[25] *Agnets*, pp. 151–2.
[26] *Agnets*, pp. 159–60.

Gnostic sense, as if there could be a 'portion' of God detached and imprisoned in the material world. He seems rather to be implying that the spirit in us is not a thing that is brought into being like material objects; it is a *relation*, to God and others and the natural, given environment, that can as such have no beginning in time, since God's side of the relation is eternal. Admittedly this is far from clear in what Bulgakov writes in these pages, but a reading in the light of the 1925 essay, 'Ipostas i ipostasnost', helps a little, since it provides a handle on what exactly Bulgakov meant by spirit. Another new element is the suggestion that the relation of the sexes in creation images the relation between Son and Spirit in the Trinity, though the human ensemble is also the image of *Christ*. A certain priority of Son over Spirit thus becomes the foundation for the authority of man over woman – though neither images God adequately in isolation, and the *formal* characteristics that manifest the image are common to both sexes – above all, freedom and creativity.[27]

Image and likeness are distinguished, in a way not unfamiliar in Eastern tradition, as potential and realisation; and the realisation – very much as in *Svet* and other earlier works – is seen in terms of the transfiguration and humanisation of the cosmos; here lies the risk implicit in freedom, and the Satanic temptation to return to the self-enclosure that grace sets us free from. In a very interesting passage,[28] Bulgakov suggests that the temptation offered by the serpent in Eden was the acquisition of 'magical' power over the world – power without cost or labour; the effect of this is in fact to give the world power over us. And the result of this inversion of proper order in the cosmos is that the world at large, the natural and material order, loses its focus and meaning; instead of humanity giving meaning to the environment, it takes its own meaning *from* the world around – which is disastrous, because without human meaning nature is directionless, 'subjected to futility'. This is what it means to speak of 'fallen Sophia'. There is no question of a myth of some heavenly power rebelling against God, let alone an element in the divine somehow becoming alienated from God. It is simply

---

[27] *Agnets*, p. 162.
[28] *Agnets*, p. 168.

that nature cut off from its true focus of meaning in humanity working with God for its transfiguration loses access to its divine prototype. It retains a coherence, but only at the mechanical level; but, more seriously, it becomes a source of spiritual corruption for humanity. Precisely because even the fallen world still possesses beauty and order (though not true spiritual cohesion and meaning), it can seduce and enslave humanity. And when Christ comes, uniting divine Sophia with the frustrated potential for sophianic life that is hidden in the world, it is nature and matter as well as humanity that is renewed and saved.[29]

Bulgakov goes on, in the sections following the extract printed here, to discuss in detail the person and work of Christ.[30] As in his doctrine of creation, the image of kenosis is all-important. Bulgakov's theory about the nature of spirit allows him to develop some very involved speculations about the character of the divine self-emptying in the incarnation, speculations which still await proper consideration by theologians. Briefly, the distinction between spirit and what it is conscious of, the distinction which is fundamental for Bulgakov's anthropology, is set to work to establish that it is possible to conceive of the divine subject yielding its self-knowledge *as* divine in order to know itself only through the medium of humanity: the divine 'I' has for its object or content the human 'me'. As in his anthropology generally, Bulgakov rather gives hostages to fortune by stressing the uncreated and timeless character of the divine 'I'. He is aware that this sounds like the ancient heresy of Apollinarianism (the denial of a human subjectivity to Christ); but he is unapologetic. The spirit is in any case not a created thing, as we have seen, so that Christ is not a special case; and there is no denial of a subjectivity like ours in Jesus, because the *formal* conditions for human subjective life are met – there is a union of spirit and nature, or hypostasis and substance.[31] The work of Christ completed in cross and resurrection enables us to be united, through the Holy Spirit, with his perfectly 'hypostasised' humanity, a humanity

---

[29] *Agnets*, pp. 178–9.
[30] The third part of the book is devoted to the incarnation; see esp. pp. 191–239.
[31] See in particular pp. 205–19 (pp. 212–14 on Apollinarianism).

without egotism and exclusion; when we have freely committed ourselves to this, we are caught up in Christ's *continuing* work in history.

There is much more to be said about this monumental essay. It has been recognised by some serious Western theologians as a major contribution to Christology,[32] but its density of expression and also (I suspect) its almost liturgically rhapsodic style in places have made it a minority enthusiasm. In its day and context, however, it proved explosive stuff. Within three years, Bulgakov's theology had been condemned by the Russian Church, and controversy over his teaching had provoked bitter splits in the émigré community in Paris. Tension between the Russian exarch in Paris, Metropolitan Evlogii, and the administration in Russia had already reached a critical point in 1930, when Metropolitan Sergii of Moscow, effectively the acting Patriarch, suspended Evlogii from office.[33] Most of the French parishes remained loyal to Evlogii, and were taken under the jurisdiction of the Ecumenical Patriarch in Constantinople. Some émigrés, however, were deeply unhappy about an open repudiation of the legitimate authority of Moscow (and about what might have seemed like a desertion of the mother church at a time of serious suffering and crisis), and continued to regard themselves as part of the Muscovite jurisdiction. The group around Bulgakov and the Institut Saint-Serge followed Evlogii; a small group of younger theologians, including Vladimir Lossky and the 'Brotherhood of Saint Photius', which he

---

[32] Donald MacKinnon notes it more than once as a significant contribution to modern debate (e.g. in 'Lenin and Theology', published in his *Explorations in Theology* (London, 1979), p. 26; Hans Urs von Balthasar refers to it a few times in his *Herrlichkeit* (*The Glory of the Lord*), esp. III.2 (ET, vol. 7, Edinburgh, 1989), and in *Theodramatik* (*Theodrama*), esp. III (ET, San Francisco, 1992). For both these writers, the most important point seems to be the notion of the cross as involving the whole Trinity and the definition of the divine life as such as kenotic.

[33] Relations had come to something of a crisis in the wake of Sergii's requirement in 1927 of a 'Declaration of Loyalty to the Soviet State' from the bishops of the Russian Church, within Russia and in the diaspora (background in D. Pospielovsky, *The Russian Church under the Soviet Regime 1917–82* (Crestwood, NY, 1984, vol 1). Matters were further complicated by the existence of a vocally conservative party in the Emigration headed by Metropolitan Antonii, formerly of Kiev, who were increasingly claiming the right for self-determination apart from Moscow, but were wholly unsympathetic to the ethos of the Parisian communities and the Institut Saint-Serge.

had been instrumental in founding, maintained their allegiance to Moscow.[34] One or two others, notably Georges Florovsky, found themselves at odds with all parties.[35]

In 1935, Metropolitan Sergii requested a report from Lossky's group on Bulgakov's theology; the report was highly critical, and the Russian bishops in communion with Sergii issued a condemnation of Bulgakov's sophiology (and other aspects of his teaching) in the same year. Bulgakov was accused of 'Gnosticism' and of confusing natural attributes with hypostatic existence in the divine life (we have seen how Bulgakov had already attempted to meet such a criticism in 'Ipostas i ipostasnost'); his anthropology was also condemned, and the ambiguous language about an 'uncreated' human spirit was, predictably, brought in evidence.[36] Bulgakov and Evlogii responded with a substantial pamphlet,[37] objecting not just to misrepresentations or misunderstandings of Bulgakov's views but to the procedure followed: there should be no condemnations pronounced from on high by hierarchical authority (this is stigmatised as a 'papal' tactic). The Orthodox Church works by

---

[34] The Brotherhood was established in 1928; also involved was Evgraf Kovalevsky, later to be heavily involved in the attempt to establish a 'Western Rite' group within Franco–Russian Orthodoxy.

[35] On Florovsky, see *Georges Florovsky: Russian Intellectual, Orthodox Churchman*, ed. Andrew Blane (Crestwood, NY, 1993); pp. 11–217 provide a very full and well-documented biography of this brilliant and combative polymath. At the period under review, he was teaching at Saint-Serge, having been encouraged to join the faculty by Bulgakov himself (in 1926). He, like Bulgakov, had been much involved with the Russian Student Christian Movement, in Prague and elsewhere. He was already, as we have noted (above, p. 125, n. 51), critical of sophiology, and had published an article in 1930 fiercely hostile to Florensky ('Tomlenie dukha' ('Vexation of Spirit'), *Put'*, no. 20 (1930), pp. 102–7). His later work was consistently and severely critical of the entire heritage of Russian religious philosophy, finding classical expression in his monumental *Puti russkago bogosloviya* (*The Paths of Russian Theology*, Paris, 1937; ET, *The Ways of Russian Theology*, 2 vols. (vol. 1, Belmont, Mass., 1979; vol. 2, Vaduz, Liechtenstein, 1987)).

[36] Sergii's text is to be found in *O Sofii, premudrosti bozhiei: Ukaz moskovskoi patriarkhii i dokladnaya zapiski prof. prot. S. Bulgakova i Mitropolita Evlogiya* (*On Sophia, the Wisdom of God: The Decree of the Moscow Patriarchate and the Statements of Professor the Archpriest S. Bulgakov and Metropolitan Evlogii*, Paris, 1935). On 'Gnosticism', see pp. 6–7; on confusing hypostatic and natural, pp. 7–9; on anthropology, pp. 9 and 12.

[37] The statements of clarification were published in *O Sofii*.

doctrinal consensus, not hierarchical decree.[38] The reply illustrates very clearly the gulf between the Russian bishops (few of them except Metropolitan Sergii theologians of any capacity) and the Christian intelligentsia, who had learned their theology not from textbooks but from the speculative and imaginative writers of the late nineteenth century, Khomyakov and Soloviev in particular – not to mention Dostoevsky, with his parable of the Grand Inquisitor, denouncing the mechanics of ecclesiastical authoritarianism. Yet it is not simply a case of young radicals and ageing reactionaries: for the circle around Vladimir Lossky, Bulgakov's generation were the theological establishment, and the atmosphere in which they lived was found stifling by younger souls. Lossky in particular was deeply impatient with the veneration paid to the literary-philosophical giants of the nineteenth century and to the mystique of the Russian soul that went with it: the Brotherhood of Saint Photius was quite consciously in revolt against Russian sentimentality and xenophobia, pleading for a more truly universal vision in Orthodoxy. For Lossky, this was to lead to a return to patristic sources in theological work. Florovsky was already moving decidedly in the same direction.

Much venom was expended on the Brotherhood, who were, not surprisingly, blamed for the condemnation.[39] Lossky was at first refused space to reply to his critics in the major organ of the emigration, the famous periodical *Put'* (an open letter was eventually published in 1936).[40] Reminiscences of the period record scenes of appropriately Dostoyevskian violence and drama in the Russian salons during the winter of 1935–6.[41] It must be said that Bulgakov's supporters do not emerge with much credit from these episodes, though Bulgakov himself behaved with an extraordinary dignity and generosity,

---

[38] *O Sofii*, pp. 25, 53.

[39] N. O. Lossky, *Vospominaniya: Zhizn' i filosofskii put'* (*Reminiscences: Life and Philosophical Development*, Munich, 1968), p. 267. This work, by Vladimir Lossky's father (who outlived him), is an invaluable source for reconstructing some of the details of the controversy.

[40] Lossky, *Vospominaniya*, pp. 267–8; the letter from Vladimir Lossky to Berdyaev, then editor of *Put'*, appeared in no. 50 (1936), pp. 27–32.

[41] Lossky, *Vospominaniya*, pp. 268–71, reproducing a letter from Vladimir to his father.

The Lamb of God: On the Divine Humanity (1933)

encouraging Lossky to devote more time to work on Orthodox dogmatics.[42] Equally, though, the publication in 1936 of Lossky's pamphlet, *Spor o Sofii* (*The Sophia Controversy*), developing and extending his critique of Bulgakov, did nothing to lower the temperature.[43] Matters were further complicated and embittered by Florovsky's involvement in the commission established by Evlogii himself to look into Bulgakov's theology in 1935 (while Evlogii was prepared to defend Bulgakov's right to theological speculation, he wished also to distinguish his teaching from what could properly be regarded as the official views of the Church). Florovsky was included because he had already emerged as a critic of Sophiology (though not directly of Bulgakov). For reasons that are not at all clear, the majority report of this commission, which was favourable to Bulgakov, was never submitted, while a paper by Florovsky and another of Bulgakov's critics, Sergii Chetverikov, was presented to Evlogii. Although they held back from declaring Bulgakov materially heretical they were sufficiently critical for Evlogii and his bishops to request a formal clarification from Bulgakov.[44] This was not a serious disruption and had no adverse effect whatever either on Bulgakov's reputation or upon his relationship with Evlogii; but it was read in a very sinister light by some of Bulgakov's allies, and Florovsky was made to feel distinctly unwelcome by many in the Paris community and at Saint-Serge in particular. The whole episode was a major contributory factor in Florovsky's decision to spend more time away from Paris in the immediate pre-war period.[45]

---

[42] Nikolai Lossky had worked for a reconciliation (see his letter to Bulgakov, *Vospominaniya*, p. 273); Boris Lossky, in a note to Nikolai's memoirs (*Vospominaniya*, p. 330), refers to the subsequent correspondence between Bulgakov and Vladimir. When Bulgakov died in 1944, Vladimir, who had escaped from Paris before the German occupation, returned, at some personal risk, to attend Bulgakov's requiem.

[43] *Spor o Sofii* (*The Sophia Controversy*, Paris, 1936), published by the Brotherhood of St Photius.

[44] Blane, *Georges Florovsky*, pp. 66–7. He does not make it plain whether this clarification was the explanatory essay published along with the text of the Muscovite condemnation (see above, n. 36). I am not aware of any other statement by Bulgakov at this time, and it is misleading to refer to this (as Blane does) as a retractation.

[45] Blane, *Georges Florovsky*, pp. 67–8; though Florovsky resumed his position at the Institut after the war for a couple of years before going to the USA.

The details of Lossky's critique of Bulgakov would take too much space to survey; but one or two salient points are worth noting. Lossky, like Bulgakov himself, regards the debate as being about procedures and canonical proprieties just as much as doctrine in the strict sense. Bulgakov's protest against the authoritarian style of the Muscovite decree shows, says Lossky a 'dilettante' attitude to the Church and its proper canonical requirements.[46] There is no question of the Russian Church pretending to issue an infallible definition; this is simply a disciplinary order, to which a priest of the Church should submit with proper humility. Anyone who understands canon law should appreciate this. If the hierarchy do not have the right to make disciplinary pronouncements, we are restricting them to a purely sacramental function. Tradition is something to be interpreted by a hierarchy who have a claim on the compliance of the clergy; by behaving as if he were still an independent lay theologian, Bulgakov shows that he has failed to grasp what tradition really is – as have most of his generation of convert intelligentsia.[47]

This is a disagreeably shrill attack (worse still if read in tandem with Bulgakov's account of what his ordination meant); but it does bring a significant issue into focus. Lossky's real *theological* worry is that if theology comes to be dominated by speculation of vaguely philosophical parentage, it will never truly be itself; and if it is to be itself, it requires the voice of the teaching office in the Church to remind it of its business. The rights of the hierarchy exist for the sake of theology's own integrity, and Bulgakov's thinking is uncomfortably hybrid. What is more (reflecting Lossky's abiding impatience with Slavophil romanticism), without such hierarchical controls, theology falls into a cultural or national captivity – crystallised for Lossky by the appeal to ecclesial 'consensus' and to the Slavonic word *sobornost'*, 'conciliarity' rather than to the historical self-determinations of the Church in cult and dogma.[48]

---

[46] *Spor*, pp. 9–10.
[47] *Spor*, pp. 6–7, 8–9, 12.
[48] *Spor*, pp. 9–10. Lossky's intellectual allergy to the language of *sobornost'*, so very popular with Slavophil theologians and their imitators, can be traced throughout his work; see for example his essay 'Concerning the Third Mark of the

THE LAMB OF GOD: ON THE DIVINE HUMANITY (1933)

In the 1930s, the protest against a cultural captivity for theology had a good deal of contemporary force for anyone aware of what was going on in Germany; Lossky should not be dismissed as a captious critic, and the question of how theology discovers and maintains its distinctive voice, free from the corruptions of localised and exclusivist cultural modes, is a fair one. The problem is that Lossky's critique does less than justice to the way in which a dominant theological metaphor can itself transform 'cultural' or philosophical material into something new. Tracing the evolution of Bulgakov's sophiology, what is striking is the way in which the language of kenosis more and more organises the sophiological scheme around itself; and, purely stylistically, the two theological trilogies are far more dominated by biblical and liturgical allusion than by any extraneous intellectualism. Perhaps the most basic disagreement between Bulgakov and his critics, especially Lossky, is, though, over whether the unifying metaphor of Sophia, however demythologised, is necessary or desirable. Lossky's pamphlet says, in effect, that sophiology is bound to end up in some sort of determinism and impersonalism, since it interposes between God and the created person an extra level of reality which is supposed somehow to absorb and channel as well as to shape and stimulate personal response. The gracious miracle of entry into communion with God is 'naturalised', reduced to the terms of a cosmic process;[49] the humanity of Christ is obscured and the work of the Holy Spirit loses its Christological focus and its necessary connection with personal transformation. For Lossky, this is not simply a matter of an unwelcome cultural colouring for theology: it undermines theology itself.[50]

Yet this misses much of what is most carefully delineated in Bulgakov's mature sophiology. As the *Philosophie de l'économie* had already made plain, the appeal to a transcendental subject of labour is in no way a denial of the freedom and

---

Church: Catholicity' (originally published in *Dieu vivant*, 10 (1948), pp. 78–89, as 'Du troisième attribut de l'Eglise'), reprinted in Lossky's *In the Image and Likeness of God* (Crestwood, NY, 1974), pp. 169–81, esp. p. 170, n. 1.
[49] *Spor*, p. 61.
[50] *Spor*, pp. 85–6. Bulgakov had claimed that sophiology was simply a 'theologoumenon' (a theory to elucidate or develop dogmatic statements rather than a novel doctrinal proposal in itself) in his response to the Muscovite decree.

concrete creativity of the particular labourer, any more than the Kantian appeal to a transcendent subject of knowledge dissolves the specificity of human acts of knowing. The question is how labour, like knowledge, possesses intelligibility; how the Good can be conceived as *one* in all the historical plurality of human action. As this becomes clearer, the residual mythology of something apparently like an active, subject-like World Soul is more and more qualified and eventually purged. Bulgakov might reasonably have said that, by the time of writing *Agnets bozhii*, he had made it as clear as he could that there was no sense in which Sophia stood 'between' God and the world. Rather, Sophia is now the divine capacity for love, eternally realised, mirrored in the created world and historically realised in redeemed humanity. The second volume of the larger trilogy, *Uteshitel'* (*The Comforter*), published in 1936 at the height of the Sophia debate, makes abundantly clear his opposition to any sort of spiritual determinism, and sets out in great detail a vision of the Church as holding the balance precisely between a false individualism and a bland or oppressive collectivism – a vision, in fact, notably close to what Lossky himself was to elaborate in the forties and fifties.[51]

The debate of 1935–6 is the sharpest illustration of how the religious concerns of the Russian diaspora were developing in different directions after the disruptions to Church life in the late twenties. The Hegelian inheritance combined with the mystique of the Slavonic consciousness had come to appear burdensome and anachronistic to younger theologians, who were increasingly mixing with both Protestant and Catholic thinkers for whom the idealist aesthetics and metaphysics of Bulgakov's generation made little sense. Lossky was close to the neo-Thomist revival through his contacts with Etienne Gilson, and he was later to be much involved in the circles from which the *nouvelle théologie* of the post-war period in France emerged – literate in the theology of the Fathers, alert to cultural trends and conscious of the need for a theology that could address people stirred by the existentialists, interested in

---

[51] The final section of *Uteshitel'* repays reading in tandem with Lossky's *Mystical Theology of the Eastern Church* (London, 1957), and the essays in *In the Image and Likeness of God*.

the simplification of some of the structures of Church and liturgy.[52] The paradox is that this could be an account of Bulgakov's own concerns, especially between 1908 and 1918. Florovsky was already heavily involved in the Ecumenical Movement and had met Barth in 1931; his philosophical roots were in any case different from Bulgakov's (he had no sympathy at all for Hegel), and he too was drawn towards the Fathers.[53] Ironically it was Bulgakov himself who had urged Florovsky to pursue his work in patristics.[54] Like Lossky, Florovsky was hostile to anything that looked like a cult of Russianness for its own sake; unlike Lossky, he reacted by adopting an extreme position on the absolute necessity of Greek forms and formulations in the expression of Orthodox theology. The paradox *here* is that Bulgakov, impatiently associated by both Lossky and Florovsky with Slavophil nostalgia, was probably, of all the Orthodox writers of the early part of this century, the most fully aware of Western European discussions of religio-philosophical and historical problems. He knew his Weber and Troeltsch, he had read Schweitzer, he retained a warm enthusiasm for Anglican Biblical scholarship; no-one could have accused him of xenophobic obscurantism.

But there was no-one in a position to offer helpful mediation in the thirties between the divergent schools (although personal relations between Bulgakov, Lossky and Florovsky did not suffer in the long run, a fact that says much for all of them). There is, as any reader of Dostoevsky or Turgenev will appreciate, a solid Russian tradition of sons attacking fathers; and that is at least part of this story. But beyond that, the parties to

[52] In the thirties, Lossky was working on medieval philosophy at the Sorbonne and was close to Gilson's circle; in 1945, he was one of the founders of the periodical *Dieu vivant*, which sustained a dialogue with contemporary philosophy and published work by the rising stars of the revival in patristic scholarship, including Jean Daniélou and Hans Urs von Balthasar.
[53] See Blane, *Georges Florovsky*, pp. 58ff. on Florovsky's early ecumenical contacts. For his philosophical influences, see G. H. Williams, 'Georges Vasilievich Florovsky', *Greek Orthodox Theological Review*, 11 (1965), pp. 7–107, esp. pp. 23–4. The meeting with Barth took place in Bonn, during the summer of 1931, when Florovsky participated in his seminar.
[54] See Williams, 'Georges Vasilievich Florovsky', on Florovsky's patristic revivalism; there is an abbreviated version of the same material in Blane, *Georges Florovsky*, pp. 287–340 ('The Neo-patristic Synthesis of Georges Florovsky'). On Bulgakov's encouragement, see Blane, *Georges Florovsky*, p. 49.

the dispute all had legitimate concerns: Bulgakov and his supporters feared that the cautious opening-up of religious thought that they had witnessed and fostered in the first decade of the century would be stifled again under a new ecclesiasticism, made still more unwelcome by its subservience to a Godless government. Lossky and Florovsky and their friends feared for the future of an Orthodoxy bound to a discredited philosophy and a narrow nationalism. The debate is instructive in the context of some of the problems currently facing the Orthodox churches in Eastern Europe, though the lines of division run differently; today the legacy of Bulgakov's generation seems radical again, though it has found ample common ground with a new and philosophically acute interest in the Greek Fathers. The real problem is how all of this relates to a new nationalism, often of an extreme and violent kind, which is not without friends in the hierarchy.[55] The Sophia dispute merits far fuller study than it has received, not least because of its character as a debate about theological integrity and the proper defence of a particular ecclesial tradition – for which both sides were concerned.

The last word on the sophiological controversy I leave to a British commentator, Arthur Dobbie Bateman, who published at the end of 1944 a highly perceptive and original memorial tribute to Bulgakov.[56] Having said that Bulgakov 'could have done for us what was done by Kierkegaard' (meaning presumably the provision of a new focus for reflection on the character of freedom and the nature of Christian identity), he goes on to say, 'When he named the existential problem Sophia, we behaved like Greeks who thought Anastasis was a goddess'.[57] The allusion is to Acts 17, Paul's speech to the Areopagus, where v. 18 implies that Paul's hearers thought he was proclaiming two 'foreign divinities', Jesus and 'Anastasis', 'Resurrection'. It is a well-turned point. The commonest and easiest

---

[55] On the present condition of theological education in the former Soviet Union, see Jonathan Sutton, *Traditions in a New Freedom: Christianity and Higher Education in Russia and Ukraine Today* (Nottingham, 1996), esp. pp. 82–7.

[56] 'Footnotes IX: In quos fines saeculorum' ('Upon Whom the Ends of the Ages [Have Come]'; see I Cor. 10.11), *Sobornost*, n. s., 30 (1944), pp. 6–8, byline 'A.F.D.B.'; Dobbie Bateman was active as a translator and interpreter of Russian Orthodox material.

[57] Bateman, 'Footnotes IX', p. 6.

The Lamb of God: On the Divine Humanity (1933)

misunderstanding of Bulgakov's language is precisely to take him as talking about a kind of heavenly individual rather than divine action and created process. His own laboured and over-rich idiom undoubtedly encourages some such misunderstanding; but by 1935, perhaps his readers should have been better attuned.

The Lamb of God: On the Divine Humanity

Wisdom in Creation*

I. *The Creation of the World*

The world as the work of God
God created the world out of nothing (*ex ouk ontōn*). How does this action relate to God's own life, to his eternity? God is a being possessed of total self-sufficiency and blessedness: God's eternity contains all the fulness of his life, and his hypostatic being is manifest in that eternity (in its trinitarian character), as well as his natural divinity in the divine Sophia. In his own life, God is absolute and divine, and does not experience in himself any need for the world. To create or not to create the world is not for him a hypostatic or a natural necessity for his self-completion, since his *hypostatic* self-definition is entirely exhausted by his threefold personal life – the circle is closed; while God's *nature* is the fulness that contains all things in itself. Consequently, the necessity of creation does not derive from the life of divinity in itself nor from its own self-positing. In divinity there can be no place for such necessity. And, in this sense, the creation of the world can be nothing but the *work* of God, arising not from his hypostatic nature but from his creative liberty. As far as the life of the Godhead *itself* is concerned, the world might not have existed.

However, this liberty, understood as the absence of natural or hypostatic necessity, does not mean that there would have to be some element of contingency or arbitrariness in the being of the world. Indeed, we could not conceive that the world could have

* pp. 39–80 (French); 141–79 (Russian).

been created by some sort of fantasy of omnipotence, without any foundation in, or any meaning for, the creator himself, but simply as a manifestation of his might. Such a view is impious; it corresponds to nothing so much as Schopenhauer's atheistic philosophy, according to which a divine 'Will' fortuitously, or by meaningless caprice, gave rise to the cosmos. God's freedom in the creation of the world signifies simply the absence of a *determinate necessity*, a need to perfect or develop himself (a conception by no means alien to the pantheism of Schelling or Hegel). But this in no way entails that the world is unnecessary to God in any *other* sense than that of being God's self-complement, nor that God could have failed to create the world – a humiliating position for God's majesty. God *does* 'need' the world, and the world could not have remained uncreated – although God needs it not for himself but for *its* sake. God is love, and the property of love is loving and extending oneself by loving. And it is proper for the divine love itself not merely to realise itself within the limits of divinity but to go beyond those limits. Were it otherwise, the Absolute itself would have become a frontier, a boundary, for the Absolute, limiting it in its love or in its affirmation of itself; and this would witness to a limitation of its own omnipotence as well as to a degree of powerlessness in the realm beyond itself. It is proper and natural for the ocean of divine love to spread out beyond its shores; it is proper and natural for the fulness of the life of divinity to transcend its frontiers. And *if*, in general, it is *possible* for God's omnipotence to create the world, it would not have been proper and natural for the love of God *not* to realise this possibility, since it is natural for love to love by exhausting *all* the possibilities of love. One of two choices: either the creation of the world is an impossibility for God, and this impossibility then imposes a restriction upon him, makes him limited; or if such a possibility exists, the love of God cannot but realise it in creating the world. Consequently, God-as-Love *needs* the creation of the world so as to *love* no longer only within his own life but beyond it, in creation. In the insatiability of his love (which is satisfied in *divine* terms within God himself, in his own life), God goes out from himself towards the creation so as to love outside himself, to love no longer only himself. It is this extra-divine existence that constitutes the world, the creation. God

The Lamb of God: On the Divine Humanity

created the world not for himself but for the world's sake, moved by a love which could not be restricted even by divinity itself, but which diffuses itself beyond God. In *this* sense it could not have been that the world would not be created. It is indispensable to God – although this is not at all by virtue of a natural necessity for self-completion, nor by any externally imposed necessity (since there is nothing 'external' for God). But it is by the *necessity* of love, which cannot not love, and which realises in itself *the identity and fusion of freedom and necessity*. For love is essentially *free*, but its freedom is not arbitrary. It is determined by an internal structure, a 'law' of love. *This is why creation and relatedness to creation are an integral part of the very idea of God.* They cannot be rejected as contingent, non-essential, as if they might or might not have existed. *It is impossible for them not to exist.* The Absolute, God in himself, unrelated to creation, as conceived by theology, is a conventional abstraction by which we examine the question of God's nature. Concretely, there is no such thing, because relation to the world, being for the world, belong to that nature and are inseparable from it. 'The Absolute' is God, and does not exist and cannot be understood except in relation to the world. God exists as creator, not as a frozen 'Absolute' closed upon itself. 'God' is a relative concept, containing in itself his relatedness to the world.

God and the world

It is not enough for God's greatness that he exist as Absolute, closed on itself and excluding all else, at least for the sake of the integrity of that absolute life in itself. His proper nature is to be *God*, i.e. the 'Absolute-Relative', the mystery that unveils itself, which the language of logic can express only by antinomy. The world is nothing, *ouk on*, in respect of its existence in itself before the face of God; but this nothingness is included in God's eternity, and God is not accessible outside his relation to the world. This inseparability of God and the world must in no way be understood in pantheist terms, as an identification of God and 'the All', or an abolition of the ontological boundaries between God and the world. The frontier between creator and creation must be preserved in fact, but the existence of such a frontier does not destroy the *relation*, the *bond* between God and the world, without which the life of God would be without its fulness. The world cannot transcend the abyss between creator and creation; God himself transcends it. If God had existed without the universe, abiding in himself, he would have existed as the Absolute – which exists for nothing outside itself (given that there is in any case no 'outside'); and this means he would not have existed at all, since existence means being *for* some other. But God is not the Absolute, that is not his primary self-definition; he is God, i.e. the Absolute existing for another, for the world.

Panentheism
In this way, the *other* is taken into the depths of the divine life (*panentheism*, everything *in* God or *for* God, as distinct from and as opposed to pantheism, God *as* the All, with the consequent disappearance of God). To diminish the meaning of the world for God, reducing it to pure contingency, without any internal connection with God, is to diminish divinity in the desire to exalt it at the world's expense; we impoverish the divine love, making it an abstraction; we may even be said to blaspheme. For nothing is either essential or contingent for love. If the divine love diffuses itself outside divinity, it still possesses undiminished all the nature and power of that love in this 'external' sphere. Even in God, love has many faces and forms, as we know; but all these faces and forms are *equally* divine in their origin, and God loves the world with the same divine love with which he loves his divinity. It is this that makes possible that wonderful equation of divine love: God so loved the world that for its sake he did not spare his son. What further affirmation do we need of the inseparability of God and the world?

God in creation
God, then, is the Absolute in himself, but the Absolute-in-Relation for the world, existing in himself but also beyond himself. For him to go out from himself in what is *other* to him, to posit himself in extra-divine being, to 'repeat' himself, so to speak, to reproduce himself beyond himself, this is the proper work of the divine Absolute, of *omnipotence*. This exteriorisation of God in what lies beyond himself, the 'extra-divine'

sphere, is *creation*, the eternal act of God's creative spirit – no longer a self-revelation [*to* the self], as in the inner life of the Godhead, but an external revelation. The act of creation is no less immanent to him than his own divinity. An Absolute that was not trinitarian, that was not love (if we can even imagine this product of mystical dreams and philosophical fantasies), might be able to remain 'one', in the limitlessness of its own egotism, rejoicing in itself (which would be more like the usual picture of Lucifer). It would be able, not from love, but to satisfy the despotic whim of its omnipotence, to create a world of playthings, if only to destroy them. But this nightmare image, full of contradictions, can only arise in a diseased mind. The trinitarian God-who-is-Love, is, in his Wisdom, creator in virtue of that very fact of his nature. In no sense does he become so at a given moment in time, when the creation of the world 'begins'. For God and in God, the condition of being creator is no less eternal than his very being, no less eternal than the Holy Trinity in its Wisdom. The world's creation has a beginning only from the world's point of view, not from God's. For God, it exists in his own eternity and in *this* sense is co-eternal with God. But what in God is eternal is only manifest for creation in time; and in this respect, a certain 'translation' from one language to another is in fact indispensable. Creation, *quâ* God's creative activity, is temporal to and for itself, eternal to God. God in his eternity creates the world for a temporal existence, and so also *in* time. In this there is a genuine *transcensus* of creative activity with respect to creation, of the action over the fact, eternity over time (and conversely): *coincidentia oppositorium*, an identity between distinct and contrary realities. The world that exists in time, like time itself, can only be understood *in relation* to the eternity that is the ground of both; and conversely, eternity has its image in time as if in a mirror.

The world as creation

The temporal world is created by the eternal God, it is his creation. That is the primal and fundamental intuition of the creature about itself and the conditions of its existence. This condition in its givenness, its createdness, is the *metaphysical fact* at which our consciousness and our being come to rest. It consists in the fact that our being, in ourselves and for ourselves, is yet not posited *by* ourselves. Knowing the place of the self in our being as *persons*, we are, in virtue of this, apt to think of the limit of the self as something on the far side of which begins the condition of givenness or createdness. In this awareness of contradiction and limitation, the creature carries in itself the metaphysical recollection of its created condition, its creation by that which has the *capacity* to create, God. But over and above this, the act itself, like the *fact* of the world's creation by God, is inaccessible to us: there is the frontier that *separates* us from the Absolute. This act only exists, from our point of view, in its irreducible facticity, which – again from our point of view – is a limit-concept (*Grenzbegriff*). This is why creation cannot be known by reflection, but only by faith: 'By faith we understand that the world was created by the word of God, so that what is seen was made out of things which do not appear' (Heb. 11.3). The very nature of creation is such that one can only *believe* (or not believe) in its created condition, with the same faith we have in God; for the origin of the world – that is to say, our own origins – cannot be *known*. The physical origin of the world, in its different parts and different epochs, can be explained by countless forms of knowledge, it can be taken to a generally acceptable point where it comes to a halt: but its metaphysical origin, its actual emergence into being, these are *beyond* knowledge, concealed – as far as human thought is concerned – by the iron gauntlet of the 'physical antinomy' (Kant), which we pursue in vain, losing ourselves in a *mauvais infini* as we press on further and further, into an illusory eternity, in our identification of causal agencies.

Nonetheless, as bearers of the divine image, we *do* know the creative act through our own experience. In the degree to which the light of an authentic act of creation shines through in our activity also, it is inexplicable and wonderful, the bringing into being of something new out of what did not exist. It is unknowable for us, as much in its character as an action as in its character as a fact – both in its 'how' and in its 'what'; and since we can only look at the finished fact, we provide a causal explanation for it, postulating a causal relation between creation and creator. But creative acts in themselves are the radiance of an *alien* light in the night of createdness. That is why even the creature's creative activity contains some witness to its inexplicable and wonderful character. However, although it bears the seal of its divine Prototype, the creature's creative activity is always limited by the *givenness* [of its environment]: it is the creativity of a *creature within a created order*. Absolute in form, it is always relative in fact. Absolutely speaking, it is not even a real creative act, if that means the creation of something new not just from what is given but from nothing, from what is absolutely non-existent. Creative activity works *in* the world, *for* the world, and starting *from* the world – which is for it the immediate presence of 'non-being', already created and containing *all* the possibilities for the further creations that take it as a starting point. The creative activity of human beings fashions its treasures only within the one great solid rock of the world; and the existence of this rock is not itself the *object* of created creativity but its *condition*. Thus the creation of the world by God is the proper *work* of the creator, and is in this sense an absolute miracle which we postulate in its metaphysical inaccessibility, but can only *assert* by faith. Nevertheless, even if we are not in a position to explicate anything further prior to this initial and fundamental fact, we can give ourselves some account of its content, its conditions and its results, if we take our bearings from revelation. The creative activity of the Godhead is an absolute activity which has nothing beyond itself to affect it: in this sense, the world is created *ex nihilo*.

The nothingness of the creature: becoming

However: does this *nihil* 'exist'? We must not think of the relation between God and this nothingness as if the latter were a *limit* for the Absolute, for God himself, a kind of emptiness, as it were, spatially containing the being of God. Such an idea is, of course, incoherent (though it is often enough tacitly presupposed). Nothingness does *not* 'exist' for God as something wholly over against his divine being. It is not even 'the Void', since that implies a containing reality, i.e. something concrete and limited. There is only God. Outside or beyond God there is simply nothing, since there is no 'outside' or 'beyond'. Furthermore, in order to *be*, 'nothingness' must *come* to be, posited by God who, according to Dionysius the Areopagite, is the creator even of nothingness. In other words, 'nothingness' is a *relative* notion, the correlative of a particular *quid*, i.e. of a being already in existence but incomplete in itself, non-absolute, in which nothingness finds its place. In this way, nothingness is not being but a *state* of being corresponding to its lack of fulness, its character as *becoming*. Nothingness belongs in being that is in process of becoming; indeed it *is* this process, as Plato testified. Having created the world as being in process of becoming, God, by that very act, gave a place for nothingness to exist. Creation *ex nihilo* is nothing other than a summons into life addressed to *temporal* being, being *in process of becoming*. This is why God 'creates' nothingness as temporality and becoming; and it is to the latter that the definitions of time are applied, beginning, continuation, end.

The revelation of Sophia in creation

The 'nothingness' from which the world was made is understood in mythological thought-forms as the raw material of creation, analogous to the Babylonian 'Tiamat' and other religious and philosophical images of primal matter. But the biblical idea of creation is, uniquely, that there is *no* primal matter: God does not create the world out of any *thing* since there is no such *quid* in existence, not even a quasi-substantial *nihil*. But from what, then, did God create the world? What constitutes the *quid* that is the world's ground? Here too, mythological thought-forms tend to picture God pouring out diverse things, 'forms' of being, invented expressly by the 'manifold wisdom of God', into the empty receptacle of 'nothingness'. In this fantasy, close to that of the *Timaeus*, the receptacle, which is itself at the same time the primal matter for the realisation of creatures, is as irreverent and incoherent an image as that of God realising his designs in this primal matter. We are envisaging God sitting in front of 'nothingness', turning over in his mind what forms of existence he can create out of it. Such a theory of creation, taking it in the sense of a specific new 'invention', must be rejected as irreligious, however elegantly it may be expressed. It involves no more and no less than a denial of God's eternity, a denial of the absolute and immutable character of divinity itself. It would imply that God, 'before' the creation of the world, did not have a clear idea of the content of his own being; that it was only at the creation of the world that

The Lamb of God: On the Divine Humanity

this appeared for the first time – not simply for the world, but for God himself. In this way God-as-creator would distinguish himself, so to speak, from God himself, in the sense that certain things are 'there' for God from the first and certain others appear in him only when the world is created. But neither the Bible nor the tradition of the Church contain any such impossibilities. In the Word of God, it is said that creation was made through the Logos – 'All things were made through him, and without him was not anything made that was made' (Jn 1.3) – or again, in the language of the Old Testament, made through the Wisdom of God: 'The Lord created me at the beginning of his work, the first of his acts of old' (Prov. 8.22); she was 'beside him, like a master workman' (Prov. 8.30). In the same way, the Fathers of the Church speak of the eternal *prototypes* of creation in God, bearing out the idea that the content of the world is determined by God's own thinking, and that it is one and the same plenitude or totality that is eternally expressed by the Logos in the bosom of the Godhead and expressed in the creation. In other words, the *totality* that exists in the divine world and the created world, divine Sophia and created Sophia, is identical in *content*, though not at all so in actual existence. *It is the one Sophia that reveals itself both in God and in creation.* This is why, if the negative definition, 'God created the world from nothing', rules out the hypothesis of some kind of non-divine or extra-divine principle in creation, the *positive* content of the doctrine is that God created the world from himself, from his own substance. And the idea that the world's content is invented ad hoc by God at the time of creation must be rejected on principle. The *positive* content of the world's being is no less divine than its ground in God, for there is no other ground or principle for it. But what is eternally in God, in his self-revelation, exists in the world only in becoming, as a divine life in process of formation. And the world's creation consists, metaphysically speaking, in God's establishing or positing his own divine world, not as a world eternally existing but as a world in *becoming*. In this sense he has blended it with 'nothingness', immersing it in the process of becoming understood as *another aspect* of one and the same divine world. This latter is the foundation, the content, the final cause and the meaning of the created world. Divine Wisdom becomes the

Wisdom of creation as well. God, so to speak, 'repeats himself' in creation, is reflected in non-being. Creation is the 'divine ecstasy' of love, which is the creative fiat addressed to what is beyond itself, to the extra-divine being which is thus constituted, summoned to life. The phenomenal appearance of this being, in its manifestation and process of becoming, naturally takes on a plurality of forms and levels; total unity becomes the total multiplicity of differentiated existence, and this is accomplished by the creator's Wisdom during the six days of creation which establish the hierarchy of being in its plurality and totality. Only when the fulness of the divine world has been exhausted in the created world, so far as the latter can contain it, does God rest from his labours.

The world in process of becoming

Nonetheless, this inclusion in the world at its creation of 'seeds' of divine life was naturally only a beginning, an incomplete, non-definitive fact. The seed is only a seed, not the full-grown plant. The world in process of becoming must traverse the long path of universal existence in order to reflect in itself the face of divine Sophia. This latter, being the *ground* of the world's existence, its entelechy, is there only *potentially*, and the world itself must actualise it in its own life. That God places his own divine world as a potential within extra-divine being is precisely a *creation from nothing*. Becoming is being immersed in non-being, modified in every part by the presence of non-being, yet liberating itself from it. The integrity of God's total unity is realised in total multiplicity, which is made coherent by it and transcended by it in its innermost reality. 'Nothingness', understood as the potentiality of becoming, is really – in this sense – the 'place' of the world's existence as this becomes accessible to the intelligence, the Platonic *ekmageion* [shadow or obscuring veil], the darkness that lies before and beyond being, of which it is said: 'The light shines in the darkness, and the darkness has not overcome it' (Jn 1.5). It is the cause of the multiplicity of the world and its principles; in this sense, it can even be called the 'primal matter' of the world, that *in* which (though not *out of* which) it is created. The initial and universal condition of potentiality is precisely what is meant by the *earth*, created by God even before the distinct acts (the 'six days') of creation: it is the potential for worldly existence which already contains in itself *all* the elements of the latter. 'The earth was without form and void, and darkness was upon the face of the deep' (Gen. 1.2). Nonetheless, this primordial substance of the formless and empty world, this most primary of all strata in the divine world as it is made from nothingness, already has a manifest plan laid up for it in heaven, outlined in the angelic world: 'In the beginning God created the *heavens* and the earth' (Gen. 1.1). The holy angels are the hypostatic prototype of creation; they are the 'ideas' of creation.

The creation of the world as the kenosis of the Godhead

The creation of the heavens and the earth – an act of the divine love transcending the limits of the divine life itself so as to diffuse itself in the world – is a voluntary self-diminution, a metaphysical 'kenosis' in respect of divinity itself: God establishes alongside his *absolute* being the *relative* being with which he then sets himself in relation as its God and its maker. The creative fiat, the command of divine omnipotence, expresses at the same time the sacrifice of divine love, God's love for the world, the absolute's for the relative, the love in virtue of which the Absolute itself becomes the Absolute-Relative.

Aware of being 'relatively absolute', the creature reflects the Absolute-Relative by the relation that defines its being, the twofold relation of originating-from (fiat) and being-towards ('in him we live and move and have our being' [Acts 17.28]). God is not diminished in his immanent divine being but he goes out beyond its limits into the world. In the divine self-positing, this is a secondary, not a primary, fact in the sense that God's love within the Holy Trinity and God's being in himself are the ground of the divine love outside the divine self, the creative act of kenosis. That is why the creation of the world is not the interior self-positing of the Godhead, which is God as Trinity, but a specific *work* of God, constituted by a series of works, creative acts, after finishing which God 'rested ... from all his work which he had done' (Gen. 2.2). God's own being belongs in eternity, where there is neither beginning nor end, where the reality and actuality of the divine self-positing is never exhausted: temporal categories here are wholly inappropriate. But the world as a process of becoming belongs in time, which is becoming. In consequence, granted that the act of creating the world belongs in eternity *to the extent that* it is God's self-definition, that act turned towards the world acquires a temporal dimension; it is finished in time, in 'six days' (however we interpret that), it has a beginning and an end, it exhausts itself. In short, we have here the passage from eternity to time, from the immobility of the Absolute to the process of the relative. This act, as a deliberate work of God, contains within itself the inspiration of love, God's 'self-inspiration' which, within his own being, is linked to the third hypostasis, the Holy Spirit who 'was moving over the face of the waters' (Gen. 1.2) at the beginning of creation, 'before' the Six Days.

The self-revelation of the Trinity in the creation of the world

The world is created by God in his being as Trinity, and each of the hypostases is revealed by the world's creation in a way appropriate to its own mode of being. In creation too, the Father is the principle, the primordial will, creating the world by his will. Because of the Father's personal *proprium*, which is ecstatic love, he is manifest in creation not as the generating Father, but as 'creator of heaven and earth, and of all things visible and invisible'. It is from the Father that the will to go forth from the divine self proceeds, to go forth in creation through the creative fiat. He is the creator in the strict sense, as the Creed has it. The Father's kenosis in creation consists in this expansion beyond self, the expansion whereby he becomes God for the world and enters into relation with it, as 'Absolute-Relative'. His *transcensus* towards the world is the Father's sacrifice of love; and in the divine life in the bosom of the Trinity, this has its analogy in the birth of the Son, when the Father generates the Son in an act of 'self-devastation'. The Father creates the world through the Word – 'And God said, "Let there be ..."' this is how the work of the Six Days is completed, through the six utterances of the Word by the Father. The Son is the content of the act of creation for the Father, he is all the aspects and forms of this act. As Word of God, he proceeds from the depths of Godhead towards the creation, so as to identify himself with it, in a certain sense, to become for it also the Word that is of all and in all.

The Lamb of God: On the Divine Humanity

Here already, then, in the creation of the world, the Son creates what the Father wills; he is sent by the Father into the world – not yet in hypostatic form, but only as the Word spoken 'about' the world and the utterances of the Word in this world. Now this coming forth of the Word from the depths of the Father and his coming into the world are already the kenosis of the Son, his eternal *exinanitio*, his humiliation in the creation of the world. The Son, the Lamb of God, is from all eternity 'sacrificed' in the creation of the world, as the hypostasis specifically 'cosmic' in nature, the demiurge in the Godhead. This image of the Son as the sacrificial lamb reveals a new aspect of the sacrifice of the Father manifest in the world's creation; for it is not only the outpouring of the Father's being, but also the sending of the Son, the beginning of the victim's oblation.

The participation of the third hypostasis in the creation of the world is the decisive or determinative factor. It gives *being* to the Father's fiat, it 'finishes' the making of 'the heavens and the earth ... and all the host of them' (Gen. 2.1). With his divine thought realised, his Word having become reality, God the Father sees what he has made in its finished beauty and 'sees that it is good'. The third hypostasis is what creates *kosmos*, clothing the structure and order of creation with beauty. The object of God's creativity, the world, is not only a universe but an artistic work, the *kosmos* in which the artist rejoices. The Holy Spirit, the crown of creation, is the *joy* of the creator over his creation: for the Father it is the joy of the Word's being made manifest; for the Son, it is the joy of the Father's self-revelation in the world. The Holy Spirit is what inspires the creative activity of God in his making of the world.

But the Spirit too has his kenosis. He is, in eternity, integrally dependent upon the Son as the hypostatic love of Father and Son; here he goes outside that eternity, as the Father's love for the Son *in and through creation*. Thus the Spirit himself is poured out in creation's process of becoming. The Spirit both rests and depends on the Son, who is the Logos of the world, to the extent that the world in its becoming is able to receive him. He becomes, so to speak, the becoming of the world, the process by which its content is realised, just as the Son is the *essential* being of the world. He is sent and received, in increasing measure, from the time when he moves 'over the face of the waters', until the final consummation when 'God shall be all in all' [I Cor. 15.28]. The very life of the world *is* the Spirit, 'the giver of life'. The joy and beauty of the world are identical with the Paraclete, the Comforter. But, in the process of its becoming, the world cannot contain the fulness of life or the fulness of transfiguration; and this movement out of lack into fulness is the Spirit's work, the Spirit's kenosis in the world.

God as love and God as creator
Thus the creation of the world is the *work* of God, the revelation of God's plenitude, his omnipotence, his wisdom, his inspiration. But it is also still the revelation of a divine love that seeks to embrace even what is not, beyond the limits of the Absolute itself. And this is not a gratuitous love, in the sense of being arbitrary or irresponsible because it has no necessity of existing, no necessity of nature; it is a love manifested in all its weightiness, its responsibility, its sacrificial and thus also tragic character: a love that sacrifices all it has in realising itself. The Absolute descends from the throne of its absoluteness towards the relative; God creates the world by his love. If we understand the act of creation thus, as the work and the revelation of divine love, we rule out any contingency in the existence of the world whereby the world that is outside God and other than God might not have existed, or (which comes to the same thing) God might have been other than creator of the world. In total contrast, we want to bring together in God the creator and the Absolute, in the most intimate and indissoluble way. If God is creator in so far as he is love and, if, consequently, he cannot *not* be creator in virtue of that love, then the object of that love, the world, exists for God precisely in virtue of the interior force of love. As a result, we cannot conceive of God without the world. The world's being is thus introduced into the very idea of God. To represent God, not only as a pre-mundane, but as a non-mundane, being, living in himself in all the fulness of his love, fails utterly to correspond to the idea of God *as* love. God is love and therefore is creator. And the world is bathed in the light of God's eternity. While it is creaturely *in itself*, not possessed of eternity, the world *in its relation to the Creator* is co-eternal with God. 'All things were created through him and

for him. He is before all things, and in him all things hold together' (Col. 1.16-17).

II. *Eternity and Time*

The relation between time and eternity
The process of becoming is the process in which temporality enters into eternity and finds its own ground there. Temporality stands in opposition to eternity in the same degree as is posited by it. Without and beyond the latter, there can be no temporality as a coherent process, no temporality that does not disintegrate into separate atoms. Time in its duration is not only discontinuous and atomistic, so that each one of its moments is squeezed out and annulled by the next; it is also continuous, so that its separate moments belong in a single whole, are part of one and the same general and unique content. Like a mosaic, it reflects the physiognomy of eternity. Even as temporal, the world is one. It does not fragment into the infinity of temporal atoms that make up its being, and its unity is objectively consolidated by the fact that it is not only a unity of temporal sequence but one of causal cohesion. Despite the canon of methodological analysis, *post hoc non propter hoc*, applicable to the distinction of particular causal sets, the principle *post hoc propter hoc* is firm and unshakeable as far as the ensemble of worldly causality is concerned. Time contains a law-like structure for the *logos* of things: in time, nothing can take place or bring itself into being that is not included in this *logos*. The world is ordered in time by a structure of law that defines time itself and which is therefore above it. The *deficiency* of worldly existence is there in every atom of real time, each one driven out by the next; but each is included in the unique cohesion of the whole ensemble which is above time, which defines time as an aspect of becoming and which exists prior to time. In a word, time is process as well as duration, it is the realisation of a particular content which is its ground and its project, its final cause, its entelechy. Time possesses within itself its plan and its synthesis, it has a content. This is the idea unconsciously expressed in the concept – absurd in itself – of the world's *evolution* out of empty space, a concept that flies in the face of the axiom about the world's existence) *ex nihilo nihil fit*: what 'evolution' presupposes is precisely the

appearing of a supra-temporal form of being within the temporal. This is why worldly causality is a teleological harmony, a purposive causality, within the being of the world. And the divine world, eternal Sophia, represents this aspect of the created world, as well as being the actual ground of the created world. But the unique, integral vision of total unity within the temporal order multiplies itself and fragments into the various aspects of temporal being which time itself gathers and reunites by its laws. In this way, eternity is the depth, the reality, the principle and the content of time; time is correlative to it, would not exist without it. Time is the created image of eternity, eternity-in-becoming. Time and eternity are created Sophia and divine Sophia. This means that time is not a void, the 'vanity of vanities' of the writer of Ecclesiastes, but is full of eternity. It approaches eternity asymptotically, realising its image ever more completely, yet without ever being identical, in its mode or type of existence, with eternity. This manifestation of eternity's image within time is, in this sense, the *end* of time – which, by the same token, must have a beginning as well. Thus the Angel of the Apocalypse (Rev. 10.6) swears by the creator of all things that 'there would be no more time' [RSV, 'there should be no more delay'] when 'the mystery of God' is to be 'fulfilled'. However, from the point of view of time as it moves along, manifesting eternity in itself, the distinction remains between eternity as such, which has no ground and has its principle within itself, so to speak, and the eternity of the creature, a temporal eternity which has its ground in God's eternity and is only the manifest image of the primordial Image (this is the classical distinction between *aeternitas* and *aeviternitas*). Consequently we are not to belittle the reality of time simply because it is in motion: time is real in virtue of the reality of its content, which is divine Sophia, its eternal entelechy, both content and limit. God, in creating the world, made time and temporality; precisely this is what the verb 'created' implies. Time is the most general form of created existence in its character as the 'becoming' of eternal existence. The multiplicity of total unity within creation appears in the multiplicity of time as if in a broken mirror. It multiplies, reproduces and distorts the forms of authentic existence, which is united with non-being through the limitations of its creative realisation.

THE LAMB OF GOD: ON THE DIVINE HUMANITY

Time from God's point of view

One question that is essential for all theology is: what is the relation between time and eternity, not in the created order, bound to time because it is in process of becoming, but in God himself, the eternal one? Does time of any sort exist from the point of view of eternity and how do the two relate? The most simple and widespread opinion (though it has not normally been followed through to its conclusion) is that, for God, time simply has no reality at all, since his eternity renders it wholly transparent and dissolves it. Time exists only for creation, as a sort of illusion, in virtue of its limited mode of being; but it does not exist for God, for whom eternity alone is real. However, this point of view raises great difficulties if pushed to its natural conclusion. Above all, the Bible, the divine record of God's relations with man, the divine economy, negates it absolutely. God's revelation to human beings and all of God's works in the world are presented as happening in time, no less in respect of God than in respect of man. If we look on this as no more than unavoidable anthropomorphism and strip if of any reality, we are weakening the entire content of our faith, transforming the creative and all-powerful God, loving, merciful and saving, into the static absolute of Hinduism, in which all concrete forms of existence are extinguished and the whole world becomes illusory. And from this standpoint it becomes supremely difficult to understand and accept the incarnation of God, with all the associated events of the Saviour's earthly life, such as the resurrection and ascension. The whole of the Christian religion presupposes, for its truth to be credible, the reality of time, not only for the world but for God; and the one is the condition of the other. It must be added that, in biblical imagery and in the Christian belief that is founded upon it, God lives in and with the world in correlativity. He does not simply act in the world, he is himself defined by the world: he 'repents' (of creating the world), he is angry, he rejoices ... And to reduce all this to anthropomorphism is to close our eyes to the divine reality and exchange the radiant utterances of the Word of God for a seminary scholasticism. In himself, God is eternal, with a divine eternity which is divine Wisdom, the plenitude, the immutability, the complete blessedness, of his own life. In himself God is eternal with a divine eternity in his tri-hypostatic being, which is the eternal act of reciprocal love between the three persons. *But God is also the creator who creates life outside himself, and himself lives in that life outside himself.* The whole reality of the world is determined by God; the reality of *time* in this world is significant for God, since it is his own work, and, in its entirety, his own act of self-definition. Coming out from itself in the creation of the world, the love of God, in its kenosis, establishes time as a reality for God himself, so that God lives also in time and, in this sense, shares in the world's life, its process of becoming: the world's history is the history of the incarnation; and what the apostle Paul sets out, in I Cor. 15.24–8, is precisely this process of God's 'becoming' all in all for the world.

God's 'becoming' in and for the world

The idea that God is in process of becoming, not for himself but for the world, along with the world's process of becoming, is an indispensable consequence of whole-heartedly accepting the Christian revelation. In no way is it a pantheistic doctrine, *identifying* God with the world, as if they were two different states of a single absolute principle, developing itself in the form of immanence. This is the thesis of the young Schelling (for whom the complete development of God is identical with the goal of the world process), or of Hegel (for whom 'logic' is God *before* the 'creation' of the world, revealing itself concretely along with the world), or of Böhme, with his notion of God developing out of some *Urgottheit*, or other similar theories. It is characteristic of pantheism to see in God only a higher level in the evolution of the world, and to see the world as the fundamental principle in the evolution of God. Between God and the world there is no *transcensus* in this scheme, no breach in continuity in the development of being from world to God; the world is only God in an imperfect stage of evolution. The very idea of creation is here ruled out, as postulating a frontier between the creator and the world. All this fundamentally parts company with Christian doctrine, which posits just such an ontological boundary between creator and creature, prototype and image, in the *act* of creation itself. In this doctrine, the world is not God's self-development, but a work of God, arising not out of the metaphysical necessity for self-revelation, but out of the creative inspiration of love in its freedom.

The Lamb of God: On the Divine Humanity

However, in this distinction and opposition between God and the world, we should not allow a dread of the spectre of pantheism to lead us to abolish the reality which the world has for God, transforming it into an ontological illusion, so that we fall into the docetism of the Hindus. The world is real in virtue of God's reality, not only for itself but for God as well, for whom it exists as the object of his divine love. Consequently we must also recognise that the temporal duration of the world, without which there would be no process of becoming, is real for God. Thus, in and with this world, God himself lives in time, although in *himself* he is timeless and eternal. This unity and identity between time and eternity pose a perennial problem to human thought, since they are a divine mystery no less unfathomable for the creature than the fact of its own creation. However, although we do not have the strength to attain to the fulness of this mystery, we can and we should trace its outlines. The correlativity between God's eternity and the temporal order depends upon the general relation between God and the world. Between eternity and time there is an irreducible opposition in formal logic, 'static' logic: eternity extinguishes time, time abolishes eternity, so that we seem to be faced with reconciling a simultaneous 'yes' and 'no' in trying to relate them. Eternity belongs to the Absolute, time is linked to the relativity of becoming; and there can be no equivalence between Absolute and relative. Nonetheless, this 'fleshly' representation of the question, as we might call it, does not correspond at all to the fundamental point at issue, if we examine the relationship between time and eternity from a dynamic and ontological point of view. In this context, eternity appears not as the negation but as the *ground* of temporality, its depths, the fulness of eternity unfolds its reality within time, and time draws the force of its own being from eternity. God as creator, God in relation to time, does not cease, for all that, to be the eternal God; on the contrary, it is precisely this eternal divinity, proper to his own being, that is the foundation of creation. Had he not been the Absolute in himself, God would not have been creator; and conversely, it is *as* the Absolute that God reveals himself in the relative by creating the world. Eternity and temporality are correlative, and the one does not intrude upon the other. There is no sense in which temporality can diminish or limit eternity, since it belongs to a *different* ontological level. We might say that eternity is the noumenal aspect of time and time the phenomenal aspect of eternity. They are linked by the relation that subsists between the ground of reality and its concrete being, but they are not to be confused or seen as limiting each other. That is why the seal of God's eternity rests upon all created beings, for the latter constitute the manifestation of the former. Time is 'the moving image of eternity'. But every aspect of time has its roots deep in the eternal, is nourished and pervaded by the eternal. Only if we stick to this principle of the indissoluble union and correlation between eternity and time can we make sense of the simultaneous affirmation of God's immutable eternity and the temporal character of all his works in the world, his reiterated and multiform revelation, without falling into a series of crude and fruitless contradictions. The mystery of this union between time and eternity is contained in the human person as image of God. Eternity for man is not time of a particular quality supervening *after* temporal life as if it were itself an event *in* time, but is something to be explored and experienced from the temporal point of view; it is the depth of human existence itself, constantly revealed, the rootedness of this existence in God. And this eternal life begins to come to fruition in temporal life. 'This is eternal life, that they know thee, the only true God, and Jesus Christ whom thou hast sent' (Jn 17.3).

III. *Humanity*

The humanity of the world

The human has a share in the world of the divine. This world is the heavenly Theanthropy of the God-man, the Logos. Humanity here means the form and prototype of a multiplicity of concrete beings, or principles, or 'ideas', or spiritual substances grasped in their unity, as the self-manifestation of the Logos. In *this* sense humanity is his spiritual 'body'. The Trinity is turned towards Sophia, the 'divine world', in the immediacy of the Logos who is in this sense identical with Sophia, the personal centre of Sophia, the demiurgic hypostasis – but who nonetheless completes his work only through the third hypostasis, the formative agency of the cosmos. The created world in its

The Lamb of God: On the Divine Humanity

character as created Sophia exists in conformity to its heavenly prototype; and this is why it is also a *human* world, centred upon and by humanity. The human being is 'the universe in sum' (microcosm); and the imprint of the human marks the whole universe (macrocosm). The world reaches its fulness and its summit in man, who is its 'logos', and there is in principle nothing in the world that cannot be 'humanised', nothing that man cannot attain by his knowledge, his feeling or his will. Man is created to 'fill the earth and subdue it', to 'have dominion over every living thing' (Gen. 1.28). The whole world is created for man, and the story of the six days of creation is the story of the world's preparation for man, his progressive and gradual upraising; it is overall the story of the creation of the world as the story of the humanity of man. The relation of man to nature reproduces essentially the relation of Logos to Sophia, though in the mode appropriate for creatures; i.e. the All, which exists in its integrity in Sophia, here appears in process of becoming, in plurality, in a creaturely hierarchy, as the inorganic, vegetable and animal worlds are brought before man in this primordial hour of universal being so that they may be humanised by him and in him, and so realise what they are predestined for. Furthermore, created humanity expresses itself in the various levels of the inorganic world and then the vegetable and animal worlds, all the levels of *pre*-human existence, in distinction from its eternal prototype, with whom everything exists in the fulness and unity of the divine life without particularising itself in separate, multiple and variable, centres of life. The natural world is united with man through his *body*, in its completeness. At the very beginning, the human body is created 'from the dust of the earth' (Gen. 2.7), from the earth which is the primordial matter containing the totality of the creature's life. But then man is created at the same time as the vegetable and animal worlds, in so far as he represents the 'totality' of vegetable and animal worlds, in so far as he represents the totality of vegetable and animal life on the biological ladder; he knows the animal world *from within*, and is able to find names for it. The bodily unity between the human and nature is reinforced by the taking of food (expressly enjoined by God: Gen. 1.29–30, 9.3). And finally man is united to the entire created world by the animal principle of life, the animal soul residing in the blood ('Only you shall not eat flesh with its life, that is, its blood', Gen. 9.4; 'for the life of the flesh is in the blood', Lev. 17.11, Deut. 12.23) – in the blood of human beings as in that of animals. The animal soul is an integral part of the created world, its proper creaturely mode of living. But it is precisely what constitutes the principle which gives the spiritual life the place and the possibility of revealing and developing itself; so that it must be obedient to the spirit in what affects the particular character of the latter. The animal soul 'in the blood', in man as in animals, is multiform and exists at different levels. It is diverse within the limits of the different states that exist in the animal world, where there is place for some notion of animal individuality. But where it has no share in the spiritual principle it is spiritually blind and has no *personal* existence (even if it is familiar with *individual* particularity). Even of man, when immersed in the life of the flesh and forgetful of the soul, the wrath of God can say, 'He is flesh' (Gen. 6.3). The animal soul is created, like all other things; which is why *personal* immortality does not belong to it, for it is essentially *impersonal*.

The human constitution

Man, however, is distinguished from all the rest of the created world, whose master, in consequence, he is, by the fact that he, like the angels, possesses in himself an *uncreated* principle, a spark of divine life: 'God ... breathed into his nostrils the breath of life' (Gen. 2.7).

If we compare these words with the eternal deliberation of God about the creation of humanity, 'in our image, after our likeness' (Gen. 1.26), their meaning becomes clear: the human spirit (the 'soul') has an origin that is divine, not created; man in his very *raison d'être* is a created God. There is no need for us to examine here the question whether the structure of human existence is trichotomous or dichotomous; this distinction is, in large part, the effect of a misunderstanding. What concerns us here is that there is a real ontological duality in the human, that there is this uncreated, divine principle in human beings, the spirit (or soul), as well as a created body, the flesh, animated by the soul. Consequently, man's ontological structure is complex, more so than that of the angels, who have no bodies, or of the animal world, devoid of spirit. The whole of created nature, the

Sophia of creaturehood, belongs to the human spirit, which is its hypostatic focus. Man is already 'divine' man in virtue of the 'image' in which he is created, in all its complexity. The first Adam is created in the image of the second, he receives the image of Christ and so is 'theanthropic' in his primordial structure. He is created in such a way that it is possible for Christ to be incarnate in him – not only as regards the body of Adam, in which, according to Tertullian, God already foresaw the future Body of Christ, but as regards the whole of his complex structure. Man, as the world's spiritual hypostasis, possesses within the natural order the image of the heavenly God-man, Logos within Sophia. The prototype and the image, despite all the unbridgeable distance that separates creator from creation, are united by a certain identity that establishes a positive correlation between them and looks forward to the future incarnation. The hypostatic spirit of man, despite its divine origin, does not belong to the hypostatic life of the threefold God in which the divine 'hypostaseity' is entirely and exhaustively grounded. It is created, called into being by an act of God's creative love that is beyond all creaturely life. God multiplies and reproduces the hypostatic dimension of his life in the angelic and the human worlds, and these [created] hypostases, in virtue of their very origin, exist in communion with the divine nature. This is the ontological foundation of the divinisation of human beings ('I say, "You are gods, sons of the Most High, all of you"', Ps. 82.6; cf. Jn 10.34). This cannot mean that the children of God possess the divine nature as God possesses it, i.e. in an eternal and personal actuality, but that in virtue of their origin they can possess this participation in God's nature, that they have in themselves the possibility of being 'born of God', i.e. of becoming the children of God, sharing in the divine life. 'That which is born of the flesh is flesh, and that which is born of the spirit is spirit' (Jn. 3.6). For the angels, this participation in the nature of God is life itself.

Man as the image of Christ

Now for human beings there exists both a proper, natural, creaturely life and a life of grace, in virtue of their participation in the divine nature. What matters here is that the human spirit by its origin becomes in itself a sharing in the life of God, even if only as a possibility; but this possibility is already ontological reality. At the same time, this spirit is immersed in the createdness of human nature – though this too is already both divine and human from its first conception, since it has a unique hypostatic life and holds together divine and created nature. In other words, the first Adam, as God-man, is already the image of Christ, in his waiting upon Christ's integral revelation and consummation of original humanity. That man is created in the image of God means precisely that he is made in the image of *Christ*; for man, Christ is the revelation and the perfection of the image. The image of the coming Christ is included in the first man, not only in his body (the image of the sophianic world), not only in his spirit (which is, in a sense, sent from heaven), but in his very structure, in the fusion of two natures, spirit on the one hand, soul and body on the other, in one hypostasis. The created condition of the human spirit can be spoken of only in relation to the divine fulness, in which no created spirits as such have part, since as created, they remain outside the divine essence. Nonetheless, in virtue of their nature, which proceeds from God and is in communion with him, these spirits cannot be considered only as created spirits, because their divine nature is co-eternal with God. By the same token they do not appear as created *in* time (as the naive form of the doctrine of creation would have it – God, as soon as he sees a natural process of generation coming to fruition, creates at the same time and sends into the world a new soul). The human spirit is not created in time but in eternity by God, 'before time',* on the very edge of time, although it is predestined for temporal existence when it embarks on a fixed term of life. The fulness of the human condition, like that of the angelic, is eternal in the divine life and is only *revealed*, not brought into being, with the creation of the angels and the temporal duration of the human world. However, in Adam all human plenitude is already contained and formed in advance, to realise itself by being fruitful and multiplying. But this eternal existence in God does not mean that created spirits have another 'pre-existent'

---

* This does *not* mean an Origenistic pre-existence of souls within world time, before or after the creation of the terrestrial order. We are not dealing with an opposition between two temporal states, before and after, but with the difference between eternity and time. [SB]

life which is replaced by life on earth and can be represented as an episode related to that life. The human world has no pre-existent reality 'in heaven' as in some other world, but finds in heaven its proper and sufficient *foundation*: in its nature it is grounded in the primary images of the divine world, and its hypostases are rooted in the life of God. Creaturely hypostases are images of the uncreated divine persons. As single hypostases they cannot in *any* way reflect the tripersonality of God, only the distinct hypostases of the Trinity. But can the hypostasis of the Father be the prototype of creaturely hypostases, since it reveals itself in the Wisdom of the divine world not by showing its own face but only through Son and Spirit? If it is not wholly wrong to think of the existence of the angels as responding to the divine Fatherhood, always immersed in the shared life of God, in mystery and silence, then it is no more wrong to think, where man is concerned, that the image of his hypostasis can only derive from the hypostases that *reveal* the Father, as much in his own divine world as in the created order.

The prototype of human persons
Above all, it is the hypostasis of the *Word* that performs this revelatory task, and so is the primal image of the created human persons that radiate from its light: 'The true light was that which enlightens every man coming into the world' (Jn. 1.9). The spiritual physiognomies of human beings are images of the Word, the heavenly man. In the degree to which the Word, as Christ, reunites these images in his Body, the Church, it can be said that 'there is neither male nor female' in him (Gal. 3.28). And the primary image for human hypostases is also, at the same time as the Word, the *third* person of the Trinity, since the Spirit rests upon the Son and, together with the Son, reveals the Father in the heavenly form of the humanity (and, in the incarnation, the Spirit responds to the divine Motherhood manifest in the Virgin, the Spirit-bearer). In other words, human hypostases have a dual prototype in the two aspects of heavenly humanity, Word and Spirit. We can connect this with the fact that man is created in the image of God as male and female. What is more, the context of Gen. 1.26–7 obliges us to see the fulness of the image of God precisely *in* this unity-in-duality. In humanity a precise distinction is established between

the male and the female, marked by the fact that woman is created from man's side, not directly from the dust of the earth, and that, in general, it is the man, as possessing the image of the 'demiurgic' hypostasis of the Logos, who has the dominant role. The two sexes, different images of humanity, bear in their unity the fulness of human nature, and, in so doing, the fulness of God's image. They are sealed with the dyad of Son and Spirit, revealing the Father. In their capacity to 'be fruitful and multiply' they contain the image of that pluriform unity inscribed in the whole human race. Thus, man is a created and an uncreated being, divine and cosmic, 'theanthropic' in structure from his first beginnings; he is the living image of the three-personed God in his Wisdom.

IV. *Image and Likeness*

Man and animal

Man has in himself the image of God as the ontological basis of his existence; and this image is not limited to any one particular facet or faculty but permeates the whole of human life. Man possesses the divine image just as much in his spirit as in his nature and his relation to the world. But this image is not the same thing as the primal image; despite their measure of identity, they are necessarily different. Their *mode* of identity is in no way a reversible relation.

Liberty is a property of spirit that cannot be lost or destroyed. Liberty, like knowledge and self-determination, is, in general terms, proper to any and every living thing. Life is, in the first instance, a movement which has its source within itself, a certain primary 'self-positing'. Now this spontaneity has multiple degrees. There is in it a level of sufficiency for the attainment of particular ends, a kind of interior law of being, an 'instinct'. There is also the capacity to sense organic needs and react to impressions received. Animal consciousness can raise itself to the point of some manifestations of intention and understanding, while animal affectivity has some aptitude for sensibility and emotion – maternal feeling, anger, joy, sadness, fear, the instinct for self-preservation and, finally, attachment to human beings. This last trait, although not at the moment universal, still witnesses to the fact that man is the master of the animal world in virtue of his creation. The 'soul' of an animal contains diverse possibilities of life, i.e. of spontaneous reaction to the outside world which is for it a given, unshakeable fact. The animal soul is limited by this 'givenness' in its environment; it has no creative relation to it, any more than there is any creative dimension to mutual relations in the animal kingdom. There is no reason to be amazed at the extraordinary manifestations of teleological convergence that can be observed in the animal kingdom, the sign of something that seems to transcend human reason: the mysterious wisdom of instinct. It is a 'sophianic' wisdom, built into animal life as an interior law; but it is not the achievement of reason, which the animal soul does not possess in any exact sense. We should not be amazed at the incredible practical wisdom shown in the work of bees, spiders or ants, for it is a wisdom belonging to species and instinct, which never evolves but is immutably repeated. Animals are given both for themselves and for man, who attains this wisdom by reasoning, and so attains to the wisdom underlying the whole creation. That is why animals exist 'according to their *kinds*' (Gen. 1.21, 24, 25): they repeat themselves, but they have no *history*. That belongs only to man's spiritual being. The spontaneity of life created by God still falls short of being a reasoning liberty in its own right; but this animal life, in the extended sense of the word, the life of the *anima* or soul, is no less included in human life, and unites itself to the spiritual freedom of this life.

Freedom of spirit: the creation of self
The spirit's freedom is the faculty of creative self-determination by which it possesses its own life, from and for itself, as a 'self-positing' reality. Such absolute freedom strictly belongs to absolute spirit alone, for which there is no aspect of its life that is 'given'; it is wholly its own self-positing. That is its nature. Here nature and freedom are identical, nature is spiritual and thus is free. In absolute spirit there is no room for any kind of distinction between freedom, considered as self-positing, and what is given, understood as necessity or nature. Freedom and necessity overlap in the principle of divine existence, i.e. tri-hypostatic spirit, which is love. Love is a free necessity, a necessity of freedom. God, who, as Spirit, is free, transcends in

his self-positing the correlation of freedom with natural necessity. What is more, liberty is to be found not only in the life of spirit as the correlation between personality and nature, the self-posited and the given; it is also present in the personal awareness of self as such, as pure ego. 'I' carries within it an act of self-positing; it is a pure act of freedom, effected in a pre-natural and extra-natural mode. Personal awareness bears in it the breath of freedom; it contains that freedom which is the essential theme of spiritual life. 'I' as 'I' is free, i.e. self-legislating will. We can apply this freedom to the absolute 'I' of God as pure self-positing, but we can also apply it to the 'I' of the creature, image of the divine 'I'. Nevertheless, this pure self-positing can never be appropriated to the 'I' of the creature, belonging as it does to the divine 'I' alone. The creaturely self remains, in spite of everything, *created*, called into being by God. However, this calling into being involves not only the divine act of creation but also, as it were, a divine question addressed to creation – will it now posit itself? – since not even God himself can posit the personal 'I' by his creative act alone without the creature making its contribution. This is not a limitation on divine omnipotence, which is fully manifest in the calling into being of the creature's consciousness. On the contrary, the creative act which establishes the 'I' of the creature is the greatest of all the works of divine omnipotence manifest in the making of the world. But omnipotence does not work arbitrarily across the grain of the creation's meaning. Spirit is not a thing, and cannot be created as a thing, in the same way as the natural world, by the creator's fiat. The 'I' as 'I' can only be posited by itself; that is why, when the 'I' is created, the imperative fiat of creation is addressed to this created self, positing itself, in *interrogative* form. Thus, although the fact of creaturely selfhood is posited by God, it must join in that positing when it is created. Properly speaking, the creative act establishes only the *possibility* of the self-positing effected by the 'I' itself, saying its 'yes'. This liberty of the self-positing 'I' is what contains the divine image in created spirits, human and angelic. The whole of the animal creation, established as 'living being', is what it is directly through the action of divine omnipotence, a *thing* that derives solely from God's command to the earth: 'Let the earth bring forth living creatures according to their kinds' (Gen. 1.24), and similarly, 'Let the waters bring forth swarms of living creatures' (Gen. 1.20). The earth, primal matter, is also the mother of all terrestrial things. However, this immediate creation does not apply to man: here divine deliberation intervenes: '"Let us make man in our image" ... So God created man in his own image' (Gen. 1.26–7). Creation in the image of God is something different from the creation of the rest of the world; it implies the creature's self-positing, for the angelic as for the human self. This non-created condition, if we may call it that, of the self of the creature already carries in it the possibility of a fall in the direction of self-divinisation. To the extent that man sees God as his prototype, he has a conception of his condition as a creature, his lack of 'metaphysical originality'. He knows himself as the reflection of the divine sun in a droplet of existence. At the same time, it is in the free acknowledgement that he is only the *image* of an other, of the Primal Image, that love for the other comes to birth, love for God, a love which is, as it were, the seal of the Logos, of the divine sonship. The Son loves the Father; and man, loving God, sees himself only as the image of his creator from whom he derives and holds his being. In freely positing himself as *image*, man accomplishes the kenotic act of love. But in turning from the sun, refusing kenosis, he remains alone with himself, aware only of his Luciferian self-positing. He recognises his own source and primary image only in himself, making himself god; and thus he transforms his creaturely self into a pseudo-divine self. This is the way of Satan, extinguishing love to fall into a solitary selfhood; in general terms, this is the way of self-divinisation, and this too is ontologically open to man, precisely in virtue of his character as a self-positing 'I'.

Thus the image of God – and specifically that of the Son – in the personal awareness of the creaturely ego consists in its knowing itself, in a free act of love, to be an image of the primary Image; i.e. it possesses its personal being, as if it were in no sense its own, in the act of giving it back to God. In this sense the divine sonship is immanent in the human ego as an ontological postulate as well as a datum for its freedom. In the human capacity to say 'I', the divine selfhood is imparted to man, and he is called upon to grasp and understand this divine 'I' which is also for him a divine 'Thou'. His created selfhood prayerfully looks upon itself as it exists within the absolute 'I' of God.

Man in nature

The image of God in man finds expression in man's relation to the natural world, which is also the nature that properly belongs to him. *Man possesses nature*, which belongs to him as his own *human world*; he is linked to it by his soul, which has affinity with the whole animal world, and by his body, which makes him a citizen of the world of material things. It is in this connection between man and the world that we find the image of God in his nature, the divine Sophia. The world is creaturely Sophia, created humanity which has heavenly Sophia as its foundation. This world is given to man so that he may be its master and make of it a garden for God. The world, potentially human, belonging to man, must be completely humanised by him, must become transparent to him. Man's possession of the created order means that the image of God is more completely revealed in man than in the bodiless nature of the angels, who do not have a *world* of their own, a natural order of their own, but are there to 'serve' humanity and the human world. Man is the *logos* of the world, the one who realises it, as cosmos, as a work of art.

Nonetheless, the relation of man, the 'god' of creation, to the world is only the image of God in his Wisdom, an image grounded in the Primal Image but distinct in essence from its prototype. In the first place, divine Sophia, as the self-revelation of the true God, is entirely hypostatised [in the Trinity] and wholly transparent to the divine personal life, as it is the very life of God. In it, therefore, there is no condition of potentiality, no 'givenness' to be worked on; it is the absolute life of God, God himself (*theos*). However, the natural world, in and beyond man, is precisely an order of 'givenness' for man, and an order of coercive necessity; it is the natural order which first, empirically, 'possesses' man, not the other way around. For his spiritual liberty it is a prison (not only in Plato's *Phaedo*, but in St Paul too: 'Wretched man that I am! Who will deliver me from this body of death?' – Rom. 7.24). Of course, this refers to the state of the fallen world, weighed down with the curse of human sin. But even before the Fall, nature was for man a matter of givenness and necessity, from which God's power expressly set him

The Lamb of God: On the Divine Humanity

free in some measure – 'And the Lord God planted a garden in Eden, in the east; and there he put the man whom he had formed' (Gen. 2.8) – while beyond this paradise lay the universe, still in darkness, where our first parents were driven on account of their sin. Man was not yet made free for his possession of the world, and the world, though sophianic in its being, was not yet disclosed to man in its sophianic quality. And after the expulsion from Paradise this sophianic quality is more deeply hidden and closed off, since paradise had shown to man a kind of image and promise of such a quality. If Adam was unable, in spite of this, to enter into possession of the world in its sophianic quality, this is because the world was not given to one man alone, in his solitary hypostatic existence, not even to the first Adam, but to the whole human race in its multiple hypostatic life, its totality which is the image of the Holy Trinity. So the world, raised up before man as fact, as 'givenness', is *given* as a proposal, a 'project', the potential of Paradise, so that man can genuinely make his home there and manifest his humanness. In other words, the proper relation between humanity and nature is not a stable one from the human side, from the viewpoint of created spirit seeking to define itself in relation to its nature. God's nature, divine Sophia, is spiritual in virtue of God's spiritual essence. God is spirit both in hypostasis and nature, which constitute his life. But the nature of the world is not spiritual in itself; it is only body and soul, 'flesh', i.e. a being that is alive and a life that is a *process* of living, organised on the different levels of its natural scale. It can (and must) become spiritual by associating itself with the voluntary motions of spirit, spiritualising itself by shedding its 'fleshly autonomy'. But in its psychic condition, nature begins to penetrate the life of spirit, in so far as man is incarnate spirit, and a *stable* equilibrium between spirit and flesh can only be worked out in its own *active* life. In respect of this task of self-definition, Adam was like a newborn infant who needed to experience and exercise his latest spiritual powers; which is why God gave man a law which symbolised this summons to self-realisation.

The Fall
Although man had received the fulness of the power and assistance of grace in his very creation, he was no less obliged to manifest his participation in his own creation by freely defining

himself. Possessing – as it were – two centres of his being, spiritual and creaturely, he made his choice: he turned aside towards the flesh, subordinating his spirit to its demands, rather than subjecting them to the spirit. This is the ontological event which is symbolised in the Bible by the breaking of God's command, the Fall. Adam, the potential Godman, had at the heart of his spiritual life the possibility of being in communion with the divine life, living in and by the nature of God, and deploying the powers of this divine life to make the world 'sapiential', to reveal the Sophia of the created order. Instead of this, he closes off the path to divine life, dies spiritually and in effect ceases to be a potential Godman; he becomes a 'natural' man. And nature now appears to him purely under its aspect as created, no longer as sophianic, as 'fallen' or 'darkened' Sophia, an image of non-being, of sheer materiality in a condition of nakedness, abnormality and falsehood: an earth accursed for humanity and all other creatures, lamenting together with the one who had once subdued it. A different life begins for man in the land of his exile. Christ is eclipsed in Adam, the Christ who was prefigured in the image of man, made in the image of God, i.e. in the image of Christ. Man takes an illicit step towards the natural, the animal world; he puts fleshly satisfaction – eating the forbidden fruit – above the nourishment already given him: fulfilling the Father's will and doing his works. We learn of this through the example of the new Adam, Christ (Jn 4.34). In place of the nourishment that comes from the tree of life, foreshadowing the food of heaven, the bread of life (Jn 6.51), man develops a taste for earthly food, for 'the knowledge of good and evil', and so sets out on the road towards a 'magical' mode of possessing the world, natural rather than spiritual, not a Christlike mode. This is how man comes to be invaded by the sensuality of the 'flesh', which stands in opposition to 'spirit', rather than being filled with the innocent sensations of the *body*; and that sensuality already bears within it its own condemnation in the form of shame. Before the Fall, our first parents were naked and not ashamed of their nakedness; after the Fall, they saw this nakedness with the eyes of concupiscence, and themselves experienced shame. Though not being simply an animal, man allied himself with the animal world; but this very fact means that he sinks *below* the animal level, since there is still in the animal world a kind of innocence proper to the animal soul. Animals know nothing of depravity or perversity, which are possibilities for man alone: the higher the summit, the further the fall. What is natural for the animal, the animal norm, is a debasement and a fall in the human. Instead of reigning over the animal world, guiding it towards that degree of spirituality practicable for it, leading it Godwards, instead of being its king, its prophet and its priest, man degrades himself by assimilating himself to it; and in so doing, he diminishes his own spiritual power and his dominion in the world.

Image and likeness

The image of God, given to man from the first moment of his creation, is indissolubly linked with the *likeness* to God: 'Let us make man in our image, after our likeness' (Gen. 1.26). Image and likeness are, as it were, the *gift* bestowed by God which is the 'sophianic' image of man, and the *project* which is the distinctive work through which man must realise this image in creative liberty, by conforming both himself and the whole created order to Sophia. The image of God is the ontological foundation that can never be lost, the initial *impetus* in man for life and creative action. It is capable of being both developed and diminished in man, of shining forth and of being obscured, because of the *liberty* of man. The likeness of God is the image of the creativity of God and the eternal actuality of spirit. The likeness of God in us is our free realisation of the image. In the divine plan, man is created *for creative work*, in his own being and in the world – as the Godman himself testifies, the one in whom image and likeness are identified: 'My Father is working still, and I am working' (Jn 5.17). This path of action as an imitation of God is, for man, a difficult path, surrounded by temptations, in which our efforts are limited by an unstable equilibrium. But it is at the same time the royal road of assimilation to God, the way of freedom. Man belongs to himself, but also discovers himself in the world, which belongs to him, just as he belongs to it. At first he does not fully know himself, and the world is still for him an unexplored territory just as is the breadth and depth of his own existence. To what degree can temptation intervene here? It is a *possibility*, since it is placed as something immanent in the very nature of what is created, in the creature's liberty. The creature in its original state, before this has been explored or transcended, is ontologically unstable, and, in this sense, carries in itself a risk of failure which is precisely what the love of God takes to itself in its sacrificial kenosis. Initially a creature lives in its 'minority', or even, so to speak, in the condition of a newborn baby – that is, without experience, with no awareness or knowledge of itself; whereas infancy, though it is innocent, finds itself defenceless when faced with temptation. God, preserving the reality of created freedom, gives man into his own hands (and the serpent takes advantage of this). So created freedom, limited as it is, is a place where different possibilities exist – and the need to choose between them (the divine freedom has no such need). It must begin by liberating itself from this defective freedom which belongs to the pre-adult phase, before it can establish itself in the *one* possibility that is truly natural to it, the possibility that corresponds to the initial inner norm of its being. Hidden in the metaphysical nature of the creature, which rests upon nothingness, the void, the great abyss, is the danger that this nothingness may be activated by human freedom, so that the abyss opens up. Nothingness is simply the texture of things – what lies between the threads in the weave of reality, the limitation of being as becoming. To the extent that becoming remains incomplete and the likeness has not attained full identity with the image, this limitation may be the source of an illegitimate self-assertion, a creaturely egoism (already expressed in our reciprocal impenetrability in space); it can represent the force of disintegration that belongs to the chaos 'waiting' and 'stirring' within it. Finally (but *primarily*, in ontological terms), the created spirit carries in itself the satanic temptation of putting its own selfhood in the place of the Primary Image.

The indestructibility of creation

In consequence of what has just been said, we can state that image and likeness between them are the foundation and the goal, the given and the project, the Alpha and the Omega, the beginning and the end. Furthermore, the world, after whose creation God was able to rest from all his works, was created only as a 'foundation'; its coming to full actualisation can only be attained with the participation of man (just as the creation of the creature's ego does not consist solely in being established by God, but also involves an act of *self*-positing). The world's creation is realised through man, and it is the long and difficult path of freedom involved in this that, in the abstract, contains the danger that the world may not 'succeed', may destroy itself, or at least corrupt itself in some definitive way, becoming the realm of 'the prince of this world', reigning with his angels over a human race possessed. Nonetheless, the world evades this first danger of destruction and ruin, of a collapse into nothing, the complete failure of creation, because it was created as creaturely Sophia, containing the divine conceptions of being, so that it still retains uncreated sparks of divinity – angelic and human spirits – and *cannot* turn itself back into nothingness, destroy itself metaphysically. It is indestructible in virtue both of the image according to which it is made and of its real content. Furthermore, it is held providentially in the hand of God and protected by that hand. The notion of the world's destruction must in general be rejected as an ontological paradox. The 'suicide' of the world which has deluded various pessimistic philosophers like Schopenhauer, Hartmann or the Kantian Renouvier, with its echoes of the nirvana of the Buddhists, is ontologically impossible, since the world contains imperishable elements within itself. Furthermore, personal conscious spiritual being is possible only in the effective presence of a metaphysical will to life which leaves no room for metaphysical suicide. This is why Satan, who bears in himself the principle of personality, like other spirits, is so far removed from the idea of suicide that, on the contrary, he seeks to establish his kingship in the whole of this world. The world is indefectible, and the ways of God in accomplishing his works are past searching out. This long and arduous process through which God pursues the goal of perfecting the world in company with man is what we call divine providence, the 'economy' of God's work; at its centre is the incarnation.

The cause of the fall
All that we have said leads us naturally to ask where we should see the ultimate cause of the Fall as lying. Is it in the serpent's tempting words, without which the Fall would not have

happened, or in the very essence of Adam? It is surely in the latter that we must look for it. God's commandment was addressed to Adam himself, to his freedom. It contained a question to which the answer might have been yes or no; which it was to be depended on man. We have no reason to think that man, at this or that stage of his development, in Adam or Adam's children, would not have fallen even without the serpent's suggestion, which did no more than realise the possibility already inherent in man. Adam's proper culpability, which takes its origin precisely from his liberty, and thus from his responsibility, is confirmed by the fact that God (Gen. 3.11) first asks Adam himself whether he has eaten the forbidden fruit, and only then enquires of Eve, who had dealt directly with the serpent, and that he condemns them as persons fully answerable for their actions. However, man's central position in the world is not qualified by the Fall and the expulsion from Paradise: if of Paradise it is said that man is placed there 'to till it and keep it' (Gen. 2.15), man is expelled from Eden 'to till the ground from which he was taken' (Gen. 3.23). What is meant here is surely not just the soil as something literally cultivated for food, but more generally the primordial 'earth' from which God made the human body.

It is still true, though, that the fall of man followed on the heels of a temptation coming from the spiritual world, in which a fall had already taken place. But this is no accident for man, because his link with the spiritual world belongs to the plenitude of his humanity and derives from the 'co-humanity' of the angels. To forbid man access to the world of spirits on the argument that there is a danger of satanic temptation would be to diminish his humanity and to contradict the nature of the world's foundation in the beginning as 'heaven and earth' together.

The nature of temptation
What method does Satan adopt in tempting us? He does not proceed openly as he did in inducing the angels to rebel directly against God, to fight against God in the name of their own 'divinity', refusing decisively to realise the image of God in a creaturely likeness. Though the possibility of such temptation lay within man's spiritual nature, Satan did not resort to it,

perhaps saving it up for the future 'man of lawlessness' (II Thess. 2.3–10) and the 'beast' with his false prophet (Rev. 13). This is why original sin is not a satanic but a human affair; man is led into it by means of a *lie* (for Satan 'is a liar and the father of lies', Jn 8.44). Satan's temptation starts from man's defined place in nature, it is addressed to man as a *natural* being who has the sophianic reality as the basis for his relation to the world, as an immanent norm. This norm appears in the form of divine commandment for man so long as he has not yet reached adulthood. It is in the name of God that man must define himself in relation to the world, not by some arbitrary action that would effectively be a submission to the flesh. Satan deceives Eve in her innocence, and through her deceives the innocent Adam also, by obscuring their self-awareness, suggesting to them the thought that they were called to be gods in this world not through obedience to God, not through spiritual advancement, but by tasting the fruits of this world – a *magical* means of acquiring power over the world, although in fact it is the world which thus acquires a magical power over man. 'The knowledge of good and evil' is not proper to God, for God does not 'know' an evil which he has not created. But the knowledge of good and evil becomes proper to created existence in its relativity and limitation, to the extent to which it immerses itself in this relativity by its own concentration on its selfhood its 'independent' divinity; thus it becomes, not a god by grace, but a god 'knowing good and evil' in the arbitrariness of its creaturely decisions.

However, our first parents, even when they were tempted, did not actively desire evil and set themselves up against God, even though they turned aside from God by their disobedience. Being mistaken about themselves and their relation to the world, even involuntarily, they turned away from God towards the world and the impotence of their creaturely status appeared immediately, precisely in their relation to the world. The judgement of God by which man was given over to *dependence* upon nature, sickness, poverty, toil and mortality, was only the manifestation of what had already been accomplished in man when he offended against the norm of his existence, so making himself abnormal.

The final stage of the development of the power of sin in man is twofold, both spiritual and fleshly. On the one hand, humanity becomes 'flesh', in the sense that in man nature now has supremacy over spirit. On the other, the satanic ideology of struggle against God, against the very idea of God, works itself out in practical atheism. Man, when possessed by the devil, wants to destroy the image of God in himself, to abolish the notion of God completely. The image of God is imperishable; but, overshadowed and corrupted, it must be re-established and manifested. This is the task of the divine economy, the 'saving' of the world, which God promised to our first parents even as he banished them from Paradise.

If man had not been a *species*, realising itself as a human species in time, and thus possessed of a history, the fall of man would have seemed irreparable in humanity as such – as indeed was the case, in a certain sense, for Satan, within the limits of the spiritual world. But man still had a future, and it is in a prophetic vision of this future that Adam calls his wife Eve, 'Life', just after the expulsion from Paradise; and, as God passes sentence, the promise is already made concerning the 'seed' of the woman, as if in a proto-gospel. The malady of sin in the history of the human race was found not only to broaden and deepen its effect, but to be the very stuff of life experience so long as the Woman, the Virgin, had not yet brought to birth the new 'seed': the Son of Man.

The power of sin in the world

The fall of man was decisive not only for himself but also for nature in general. Man was called to be the master of nature, to humanise it by becoming its *spiritual* centre. For nature in itself (the 'World-Soul') is not spiritual but only 'psychic', to the extent that it is a living being, and able, through this life, to associate itself with the life of spirit, in and through man, by becoming a *spiritual* body (as distinct from that embodiment of 'soul' which is intrinsic to its own life). As it has within itself, as its natural foundation, the seeds of the heavenly Sophia, reflecting and realising Sophia within creaturely existence, nature possesses within itself the witness to its own authenticity, its rationality and beauty. However, in hierarchical terms, 'psychic' existence is an inferior and inadequate aspect of being, which spirit must penetrate without in any way annihilating, lifting it to a level of higher fulfilment. Nature must be set free from itself, its natural psychic condition; and it is man who was called to be its liberator, it is to him that nature must belong. And since he failed to rise to the heights of his mission, but bowed down before nature instead of overcoming it and setting it free, 'the whole creation has been groaning in travail together until now' (Rom. 8.22); it has become a land under a curse, instead of being the Eden of God, the body and the dwelling-place of divinised man. Nevertheless, it still preserves the hope of an *apokatastasis* [restoration, reconstitution], the hope that 'the creation itself will be set free from its bondage to decay and obtain the glorious liberty of the children of God' (Rom. 8.21), the hope of a transfiguration to be accomplished at the end of the world, when there will be 'a new heaven and a new earth' [Rev. 21.1]. What is more, this re-establishing of nature in its full dignity is at the same time the re-establishing of man, as the apostle says: 'and not only the creation, but we ourselves, who have the first fruits of the Spirit, groan inwardly as we wait for adoption as sons, *the redemption of our bodies*' (Rom. 8.23).

'The creation was subjected to futility' (Rom. 8.20), i.e. its life became empty, it was deprived of its highest satisfaction, remaining in the realm of an unlimited and contentless becoming: so it was that the Preacher of Ecclesiastes experienced the vanity of life, to which he is an inspired witness. Vanity is vacuity; and a dehumanised nature, torn away from its higher meaning, deprived of its spirit, is precisely vacuity. But it *suffers* in this condition, it thirsts to be fulfilled and led back to spiritual reality. By the purpose of God, nature is protected by the angels of the natural world; but they act on the natural order only 'from outside', so to speak, being immaterial spirits, without any access to the interior life of nature. Man alone is the soul of the world, linking its interiority to the angelic realm; just as, conversely, he can distance the natural order from the angelic realm by his fall. Nature is ontologically bound to man, predestined to be humanised by the penetration of spirit; but if the human spirit, weakened by sin, submits to nature and thus as it were reduces itself to non-being, nature too will be 'subjected to futility', abandoned to the fate of its own vacuity. 'What has been is what will be, and what has been done is what will be done' (Eccl. 1.9): an 'indifferent' nature whose appearances can sometimes so chill the human spirit. In the Fall, an abnormal rupture between nature and man opens up, after which man becomes the captive and slave of a nature which bears the curse occasioned by human sin. The natural relation between man and nature was wholly changed: no longer was man the high priest of nature, dominating it and leading it Godwards. It was nature that vanquished man, taking him far from God, terrifying him by its power, enchanting him with its charms, subduing him with its rich abundance. Nature made man 'flesh' and enslaved him by making him dependent on nature for the maintenance of life – Prometheus in chains, Orpheus forgetting the way to bring back Eurydice from the dead. The fall of man was also that of nature. Nature lost its centre and its meaning. It became simply a being-for-itself, a *fact*, whose coherence is a matter of causal necessity. This multiform necessity is the world's law-governed aspect; as the world ceases to be cosmos, it becomes mechanism.

The limits of the Fall

In the Fall, man did not destroy the image of God in himself; he could do no more than obscure and weaken it. Likewise, nature, alienated from man, does not lose its sophianic basis and content, even though its face may be in shadow. The world is still God's creation, and the eternal fiat, the word spoken over creation, does not cease to echo in the world. That is why, even after the Fall, divine Wisdom still diffuses its light in the world as the revelation of God, and 'The heavens are telling the glory of God, and the firmament proclaims his handiwork. Day to day pours forth speech, and night to night declares knowledge. There is no speech, nor are there words; their voice is not heard; yet their voice goes out through all the earth, and their words to the end of the world' (Ps. 19.1–4). The inspired poet here bears witness to 'the glory of God', i.e. the divine Wisdom which still reveals itself up to the present day in the natural order; and what kind of creature must man be if he is deaf to this! Not only the faithful, for whom nature is an unwritten version of Genesis, but unbelievers too, who, in the blindness of their hearts, have no knowledge of God, still love 'nature' in its splendour and glory. The apostle testifies to this enduring sophianic aspect to the world: 'Ever since the creation of the world his invisible nature, namely, his eternal power and deity, has been clearly perceived in the things that have been made' (Rom. 1.20). 'Deity', *theotēs*, is here equivalent to 'glory', and signifies the divine Sophia as revealed in nature (cf. Job 12.7–9, and, more especially, 28.23–7). This Sophia which belongs to God, manifested in the world, is the inexhaustible source of inspiration for life in the natural order, elevating, purifying and strengthening even the life of fallen man. This sophianic character of the world is the basis of what is in fact the proper life of the natural order, even at its impersonal level: that is, the *hypostatic* quality of nature, which has no hypostatisation in itself, but is capable of becoming hypostatised and of living its life for man, the angels and God. This natural life, the life of stones, minerals, liquids, vegetables, is something of which man is conscious only in a confused way – although in some measure the life of the animal world is still accessible to him. This life, God's glory in creation, itself sings the praise of the creator's glory: the heavens are indeed 'telling the glory of God'. There is witness to this to be found also in the wonderful Song of the Three Children in the non-canonical third chapter of Daniel, where the three young men summon the whole creation to join in blessing God. This is the luminous face of created Sophia, turned towards heaven. However, nature has another face, nocturnal and shadowed: the 'dark face' of fallen Sophia (to borrow the expression of Fr Vasilii Zenkovsky).

'Fallen Sophia'

Nature is 'sophianic' in its positive base and content, but it too receives through the fall of man a mode of being alien to it. Being extra-divine, a creation out of non-being, nature is predestined to be divinised in and through man; but when man falls, nature is doomed to the illegitimate independence of existence outside God. It becomes a Godless world, sufficient to itself – the 'great Pan', endowed with all the plenitude of life in itself. The world, when it had become 'fallen Sophia', was split off from divine Sophia as far as the pattern of its existence was concerned, though not divided from it in its deepest foundations. Even in its chaotic and disintegrated condition, nature preserves all its fulness as 'total unity' (*vseedinstvo*); but this unity-in-multiplicity is now no more than the external and mechanical coherence of natural laws. It has clothed itself in an outer husk. And meanwhile the animal world, deprived of direction from humankind, is condemned to the struggle for survival, to mutual destruction. The life of nature, in certain of its manifestations, is subject to the cycle of decay and rebirth. Parasitic forms of plant and animal life appear, a kind of evil presence created in the midst of nature's turbulence. Nature, when not subject to man, acquires a peculiar power over man, a sort of inhuman *magical* influence. The forces of nature, with their elemental life, become receptacles of demonic activity: the demons identify themselves with the forces of nature. The life of the natural world acquires that mystique which hypnotises the human imagination and enslaves the will in pagan religion, especially in orgiastic cults. Nature presents itself to man as a goddess demanding veneration. Instead of nature being humanised, man is dehumanised, becoming a merely natural being.

In his weakened state, nature comes to seem more powerful than man. Man is called to become the 'soul' of nature, its spiritual centre, organising and spiritualising the life of nature. But in the Fall man ceases to be the *actual* soul of nature, though he still has the potentiality for it. Nature thus finds a 'soul' *apart* from man, a *false* centre for its life whose reality is accentuated by the absence of the true centre. This soul of nature, the living cohesion of the world, becomes demonic when it no longer belongs to man; it turns into a false Sophia, an 'anti-Sophia', Achamoth. Although it can never completely belong to the demons, since it is a sophianic creation, it becomes their habitat and their tool. When it has lost its 'orbit' and its spiritual focus, the soul of the world becomes ambivalent in its meaning, knowing nothing of good and evil, deceitful, untruthful. It is dangerous for the human spirit to mingle unreservedly with nature, trusting itself to nature's sovereign power. It must love nature, but also combat it, affirming its spiritual essence by asceticism. For man is above nature, he is not a mollusc or a plant or an animal. For him to live a life that is no more than natural, an animal life – this is precisely what the Fall means for man.

Thus man's relation to nature takes on, in a certain sense, a *tragic* character. Nature is for man the revelation of the glory of God, of wisdom and of beauty; but when it ceases to be the exterior form of human spirit, it becomes ambivalent and deceitful, driving man to become inferior to himself, to deny himself. This tragedy is intensified at the point where man's fusion with nature is most intimate: in beauty, and in art, which is the creative serving of beauty. Nature as 'reason', as a law-governed reality, is revealed to man as *logos* of the world, and this knowledge does not in and of itself have any poisonous content: it is only in relation to human freedom that it acquires an illegitimate application, in relation to the human will's liability to sin. But beauty, which is immediately seductive, may contain poison, may deceive, because the beauty of nature or natural beauty is independent of the Spirit, indifferent to good or evil – to which man cannot and must not remain indifferent. The enchantments of Achamoth, the malignity of fallen Sophia, are most dangerous when they wear the mask of beauty. But the beauty of nature is not only a mask. It is what the Holy Spirit breathes upon the world; beauty is immanent in the creation which it clothes. It is the remains of Paradise in the natural order, conserving the vestiges of Eden as a mirror of the heavens – even though, in the fallen world, beauty is separated from holiness. This natural beauty manifests itself to human beings, who are called to receive this revelation not only naturally but spiritually, in the fulness of their spiritual existence oriented towards God. This is why beauty for man is inseparable from holiness, a 'rational' as well as a natural quality. Beauty has its own immanent laws, it is independent of morality considered as a norm or a law, but in its inner life it is not independent of the integral wholeness of the human spirit. 'Rational beauty' is neither one particular aspect of beauty nor something to be found elsewhere in this world. On the contrary, it is the spirit's vision penetrating and judging the spiritual content of beauty. This is a matter solely of internal, not external, criteria. So far as spiritual or rational beauty is concerned, sin and beauty are not compatible: the sinful appropriation of beauty or the appropriation of sinful content wrapped in natural beauty is contradictory. This latter is generally what is going on in the abstract aestheticism that has sometimes found a home in the Orthodox world, as in the case of Leontiev.

Beauty contains the most powerful and the most dangerous seductions that nature holds for man. To reject, to blaspheme against, beauty is to close one's soul to the spirit's breath in nature. But to abandon oneself blindly to beauty in a way that denies its spirituality is to pursue a phantom, since authentic beauty is spiritual, even though it reveals itself in the natural order. Herein is the tragedy not of art but of the artist, who is called to journey heavenwards through his creativity, treading the path between aestheticism and demonism.

So nature as fallen Sophia is for man a force that is terrifying in its power, seductive in its beauty and strong in its life and vitality; a force that deafens, overwhelms and enslaves him, makes him a *pagan*, that is, a natural and not a spiritual being. Man lives with nature; from the moment of creation he is linked with it. Yet at the same time, face to face with nature, he finds himself spiritually on the defensive. Nature besieges and overcomes man. In the Old Testament, the chosen people were like an island in the middle of the ocean of paganism; they were chosen by the grace of God to struggle against the natural in the name of the true, supernatural God. With the coming of Christ, the purely natural, the 'great Pan', is brought to nothing at the deepest level, for the New Adam conquers nature and subjects it to man. In respect of the natural spirits of the 'great Pan', the incarnation is a kind of exorcism. Great Pan is dead; nature is shown to consist only of 'weak and beggarly elemental spirits'. However, in as much as the demons still return, more wicked than before, to the places from which they were expelled, nature, in Christian history, continues to represent the place where Christ and Antichrist join battle. The prince of this world is driven out, his dominion is broken, but he continues to be active in the world. Nature as an autonomous reality ('Pan') has already perished but the whole of its lifeless mechanism now rises up before man's eyes, so that man longs to master this – thereby turning himself into a mechanism (this is called 'rationalisation'). A new and distinctive aspect of 'psychic' as opposed to 'spiritualist' life appears when man comes to consider himself as no more than a natural phenomenon, one link in the chain of nature. In essence, *this* is the temptation now offered by nature; but in religious terms, it is already over and done with, and it survives only by the force of inertia and religious weakness. The new paganism is an incomparably poorer affair than the old; great Pan now seeks a hiding place in the inner life of man. But it is Christ who dwells there and this attempt is only the final dying spasm of 'cosmism'. Man himself has great creative tasks to accomplish in nature, the making of 'cosmos' in the natural order. The broken bond between spirit and nature must be re-established.

5

'The Soul of Socialism' (1932–3)

INTRODUCTION

Bulgakov never abandoned his early commitment to social justice as a properly Christian ideal;[1] but whether one could possibly call him a 'Christian socialist' after 1907 is doubtful. Certainly he would himself have repudiated the name; his substantial pamphlet on *Christianity and Socialism*, published in 1917,[2] like the dialogues published in the following year in *Iz glubiny*, reflect the basic assumption that socialism is inevitably an authoritarian collectivism, disfigured by its pseudo-religious or apocalyptic aspirations. Because socialism struggles against the world's problems with the weapons of the world, it represents a capitulation to Christ's first temptation in the desert, turning stones into bread. Socialist government, as it was developing in the early days of the Revolution, simply replaced one Leviathan, tsarist tyranny, with another, state collectivism, even more ideologically intolerant.

During the twenties Bulgakov published nothing directly on political or social issues. It is not clear exactly why he returned to this area in the early thirties; but, from 1929 onwards, he published a number of pieces, some quite substantial, reviewing the question of Christianity and socialism once again[3].

---

[1] For an anecdote illustrating this, see Nicolas Zernov, *The Russian Religious Renaissance* (London, 1963), p. 143, n. 15; cf. A. M. Choufrine, 'Sergei Bulgakov: His Life and his Reflections on it. A Case Study for the Churching of the Russian Intelligentsia', in *The Emancipation of Russian Christianity*, ed. Natalia A. Pecherskaya (Lewiston/Queenston/Lampeter, 1995), pp. 1–16.

[2] *Khristianstvo i sotsializm* (Moscow, 1917), published by an educational commission of the Provisional Government. A new edition of a section of this was published as *Khristianskii sotsializm* (Novosibirsk, 1991).

[3] An essay on Church and world in the Paris *Vestnik* (*Messenger*) 1929; a further piece on Church and city in the same periodical 1931; an essay published in Stockholm in 1931 on 'L'Orthodoxie et la vie économique'; a brief note on Christianity and contemporary social activism in *Put'* 1932; and the long piece

Although he had been involved, in Prague and Paris, with the Russian Student Christian Movement, he had had less direct contact with its social work among émigrés since his move to Paris. But part of the impulse to engage afresh with the social question may well have come from his deepening friendship with one of the most remarkable figures of the Paris Russian community, Elizaveta Skobtsova, a travelling secretary for the Russian Student Christian Movement, who had already, by 1930, made her mark as a champion of the most destitute among the refugees.[4] Bulgakov had become, effectively, her spiritual director. In 1932, after an ecclesiastical divorce from her estranged husband, and a year after the death of her daughter, Elizaveta took monastic vows as Mother Maria. Bulgakov and Metropolitan Evlogii had supported her in this decision and defended her liberty even as a nun to continue her work with the destitute – a novel and disturbing phenomenon in the context of early twentieth-century Orthodoxy, which was unused to nuns living outside enclosure and undertaking individual pastoral or social work. In 1935, she was instrumental in founding 'Orthodox Action', a group devoted to the practical support of refugees, especially migrant workers and the unemployed.[5] Initially concerned mostly with Russian exiles, its work soon expanded to take in the needs of Jewish refugees from Germany and Eastern Europe. It was this work that brought the attention of the occupying German administration upon Mother Maria in the war years and led to her imprisonment and execution (on Easter Eve, 1945).[6]

---

here translated, 'Dusha sotsializma', published in *Novyi grad*, 1932: 1, pp. 49–58, 1932: 3, pp. 33–45, and 1933: 7, pp. 35–43. This and the 1917 piece are included in *Sozialismus in Christentum?*, a collection of Bulgakov's more substantial writings on socialism, ed. and trans. Hans Jürgen Ruppert (Gottingen, 1977). *Novyi grad* was a significant organ of the circles in Paris sympathetic to Orthodox Action (see later in the Introduction); for an introduction to its concerns, see Marc Raeff, 'L'émigration et la "Cité nouvelle"', CMRS, 29 (1988), pp. 543–52.

[4] There is a vivid introduction to her life in Sergei Hackel, *Pearl of Great Price: The Life of Mother Maria Skobtsova, 1891–1945* (London and Crestwood, NY, 1981); see ch. 2 on her early involvement with destitute exiles.

[5] See ibid., pp. 64–8 on the beginnings of Orthodox Action.

[6] See ibid., ch. 8 on her wartime work and the refusal of many Orthodox leaders and activists to co-operate in the issuing of separate identity cards to Russian Jews in occupied Paris; see pp. 146–9 on her martyrdom.

'The Soul of Socialism' (1932–3)

Bulgakov was from the first a patron of Orthodox Action, along with Berdyaev and other luminaries of the Paris diaspora, and he was a regular participant in Mother Maria's seminars on social and religious issues.[7] It is not too much to suppose that the stimulus of her work and ideals was a factor in promoting new reflections on the old themes; and one notable feature of his writing in the early thirties on these matters is a clear impatience with the traditional Orthodox lack of enthusiasm for social witness. What he saw himself doing was providing some of the building blocks for a realisation of the potential in Orthodox theology for a coherent and radical social programme – though he is as vague as ever about *specific* projects. What is also notable in the text that follows, first published in 1932–3, is the refusal simply to repeat the denunciations of socialism that he had proclaimed in the immediate aftermath of the Revolution. Here, socialism is not a neutral or even beneficent possibility, as it seemed to him in 1903 or 1904, nor is it the diabolical and destructive force of 1917. It is addressed as a spiritual problem; as a phenomenon that is already spiritually 'charged' and is therefore not neutral but dangerously ambiguous in its possibilities. It must be admitted that Bulgakov's language is not very clear; socialism is indeed identified early on in this essay with social and economic determinism; yet later on what seems to be the threat is identified specifically as 'soulless' socialism, as if Christianity can leaven or transform the socialist enterprise.[8] It is not obvious whether he regards *all* socialist practice and theory as flawed by economic determinism. But what *is* plain is that he regards secular socialism as an impossibility. Because socialism has so powerful a 'utopian' component, so strong a commitment to a social order that does not yet exist, a history that has not yet begun, it is never a neutral or scientific thing. It will always be on the edge of apocalypse. These are ideas that Bulgakov had already been airing in the first decade of the

---

[7] Ibid., pp. 69–70.
[8] The essay's title can be read in two ways, either as signalling an analysis of what socialism's inner spiritual character truly is, or as intimating the possibility of discovering or realising in socialism a positive spiritual potential. The ambiguity runs through much of the text.

century, but the political experience of the Revolution and its aftermath had amply confirmed his analyses.[9]

Perhaps Bulgakov comes nearest to clarifying his vocabulary when he calls would-be secular socialism a *heresy*.[10] Christian doctrinal understandings of the nature of transformative labour and the discovery of freedom in community are twisted into an elevation of labour above freedom, the consequent definition of groups of persons solely or dominantly in terms of their class interest, and the final erosion of the very concept of the person. But heresy in the Church's history, says Bulgakov, is always a stimulus to theology, forcing it to develop fresh insights from the deposit it has been given. Because the Church has failed to understand its own vision and has settled down to a passive collusion with whatever order exists at any time (with a marked preference for autocracy, however), it fails to attract those who have a dynamic and creative understanding of history. In this context, the appeal and the moral plausibility of socialism have less to do with social justice as an ideal in itself than with a particular view of history as a purposive movement that involves creative risk – a view of the social order as something other than a simple 'given'. We have irreversibly moved beyond a patriarchal and 'organic' order, says Bulgakov. St Paul could accept the institution of slavery because it was part of an unquestioned and not completely inhuman order which gave to all a secure sense of belonging. This has gone for ever in Europe, and what is left is what he calls social 'rationalism' – the functional combination of human atoms. This is a phenomenon common to capitalism and communism; but it combines dangerously with the longing of human subjects for solidarity, so that new group identities emerge, freighted with more meaning than they ought to carry, class and national identities that undermine the distinctively human because they absolutise certain given features of a person's constitution. This 'pagan naturalism' produces pseudo-churches – collectivities which are, understandably, likely to be at odds with the actual

---

[9] Compare the long articles on 'Pervokhristianstvo i noveishii sotsializm' ('Early Christianity and Modern Socialism') and 'Apokaliptika i sotsializm' ('Apocalyptic and Socialism'), originally published in 1909 and 1910, and reprinted in the second volume of *Dva grada* (*Two Cities*, Moscow, 1911), pp. 1–50, 51–127.
[10] See below, pp. 238, 261.

'THE SOUL OF SOCIALISM' (1932-3)

Church, or which, at least, judge the Church by standards drawn from the supposedly natural data that ground their corporate identity.

Hence the impossibility of secular socialism – and implicitly, I think, the impossibility of secular politics overall for Bulgakov.[11] Outside the Church is an ideological chaos: determinism in theory combines with functionalism in practice; corporate rationalism denies the person in its fullest sense and favours the rootless 'anomic' individual, worker, investor and consumer; but this situation is subjectively intolerable, and is coloured by the search for new forms of belonging with a pseudo-religious character. Not for nothing does Bulgakov mention fascism at this point.[12] Were he commenting on the nineties, he might well note the ways in which group identity in a fragmented, rationalised or bureaucratised society increasingly fosters a model of society entirely dominated by the conflicting claims of interest groups. These pages can be read with profit by anyone looking to understand the Balkanisation of interest groups in the USA and its satellites and the erosion of a lively understanding of common good.

The Church is commonly prepared to settle for a tolerated status, as an institution among others – though there are societies where this is not allowed it. Bulgakov is naturally aware of the persecution of the Church in his homeland, but his remarks are prescient of the situation of 'Confessing' Christians in Germany a few years after the publication of this essay. But this is not enough. Bulgakov, in a tantalisingly brief paragraph, sketches how theology must sail between the Scylla of social utopianism, the Church identifying itself with a confident progressivism, and the Charybdis of clericalism, the Church seeking to control the social process. What is needed is for the Church to be what it is meant to be, a living model of renewed social relationships depending upon renewed relation with

---

[11] In his analysis of purportedly secular politics as concealing a drift towards sacralised violence, Bulgakov could well be read in tandem with John Milbank, *Theology and Social Theory: Beyond Secular Reason* (Oxford, 1990), which similarly argues against the possibility of a genuinely secular politics or sociology.

[12] He was a consistent critic of fascism and of racial suprematist ideology. For some of the ambiguities of his attitude to Judaism, see the Appendix.

God.[13] It has to work at inner transformation before it works for the abolition of structures: the latter can only come from the former. What prevents this being only a commendation of interiority and withdrawal is Bulgakov's reiterated conviction that the structures *need* abolition or radical reconstruction – and also his insistence that the Church has an obligation to undertake the active transformation of at least its own corporate life. Unless there is a Christian activism of some kind, people will be drawn away to the counter-religion of socialism. Just as much as in the first essay in the present collection, he acclaims the ending of economic captivity, slavery to natural processes and the unremitting struggle to avert the effects of scarcity; but he notes with increased urgency the need to fill the vacuum that results from unaccustomed leisure, if we are not to produce a new kind of slavery, the 'spiritual repression' of the entertainment culture. Once again, it is Christian faith as active and creative that alone can meet such a need. Without a coherent anthropology, the human itself is steadily eroded by the secularism that moves inexorably towards pseudo-religion.

In a way, by the time we reach the end of this long and dense reflection, it no longer matters so much whether Bulgakov is precise about the meaning of 'socialism'. The real argument is about the possibility of an intelligible and humane social order, and also – once again taking up themes from Bulgakov's earliest days – about the Christian understanding of history. There is, Bulgakov observes, a familiar Christian tendency to deny (in effect) that there is any history as such ahead of us; once the redemption is accomplished, we are simply filling in time until the Second Coming. It is tempting to react by looking for the realisation of God's kingdom on earth through human projects. What we need is a way between a Christian indifference to the present, grounded in the conviction that history is over, and a Marxist indifference to the present, grounded in the conviction that history has not yet begun. Both can justify present barbarism – the one because no external circumstances can now affect the fate of the elect, the other because historical, creative

---

[13] See below, pp. 254 ff., 265 ff. His vision in this respect can be compared not only with Milbank's but with those of Stanley Hauerwas or William Stringfellow in their very diverse idioms.

humanity does not yet exist, so that the present can properly be sacrificed in the eschatological interest of the humanity that is to be. In contrast, authentic Christian witness begins with labour *in the present*, with the risks and frustrations involved (this echoes the sombre 'bourgeois' ethic of Bulgakov's *Vekhi* essay); but what makes it more than an ethic of duty is the faith that present labour can be caught up into a movement or energy that is other than the sum of human effort, yet not an external supernatural system of guarantees or supplements. This essay does not discuss Sophia as such, but this is where the sophianic ideal comes into play. Part of the interest of the essay, indeed, is to see how the sophianic problematic emerges independently of the metaphysical and metaphorical complexities of other works: here it is plain that Sophia is no mystical agent entering history from beyond, but the capacity within the world of time for *sense to be made* of it. From the theological and philosophical work Bulgakov was involved in at the same time as the composition of this piece, we know exactly what he would have wanted to add: that this capacity is the necessary corollary of the world being the work of a God whose character is self-dispossessing love, personal relatedness. There could not be a world without such a character, since God neither makes nor loves what is alien to what the divine life is. Thus we know that the world is oriented in a certain way – not determined, so that an historical outcome can be foreknown, but indestructibly pressing towards the reality of communion and beauty. We can frustrate this but not eliminate it from the world. The story of our frustrations of it and our liberations of it is *history*, which is never simply 'over': faith tells us that history is a succession of incompletions, non-closures. In one sense, Marx's insistence that all our history so far is 'prehistory' has a point, to the extent that no story is rounded off tidily as a unit to be consigned to a definitive past. And this preserves for the Christian the vivid sense of *tragic* possibilities, and prevents us from lying about the cost or the risk of historical action.

'The Soul of Socialism' in fact draws together a remarkable range of Bulgakov's ideas, and displays some of the deepest continuities in his thought. It is not a carefully constructed piece or a manifesto for political renewal (Bulgakov is clear about the sense in which the Church is *properly apolitical* in the sense the world gives to 'political', while being itself inescapably a political reality). It is worth reading not least because it helps to explain how the abstruse disputes in which Bulgakov was involved in the mid-1930s about Sophia related to what he believed could concretely be done and hoped for in the lives of people like those Mother Maria was feeding and housing not very far from Saint-Serge in the same years, with his guidance and blessing.

The Soul of Socialism

I

The life of the nations at the present time is lived under the sign of socialism. Its red star stands in the skies of history like a threatening portent, a sign of judgement or prophecy – but in any case an unavoidable historical reality. We may or may not be in favour of it, we may be crying out for it or cringing before it, we may welcome it or hide ourselves from its presence, but there is no escaping it; it is a sort of fate decreed for the next generation, if not for ourselves. It confronts us like the riddle of the Sphinx, ready to devour anyone who does not give it an answer. And while it stands before the whole world as a threat or at least a sign of crisis, it also contains, as far as the Church is concerned, a question about its religious value and significance. Does it lie under a curse or a blessing, does it belong to the *civitas Dei* or to the *civitas diabolica*, with the Babylon brought low by an angelic hand (Rev. 17–18) or with the City of God coming down from heaven? For the Church is responsible for the life of the humanity to which it belongs, and cannot hold aloof from the spiritual struggles and sufferings of that humanity. The Church's answers will not be offered as dogmatic oracles; they evolve in the process of searching, in the restless struggles of thought and of disturbed conscience, as the agitation of the Spirit of God in human hearts: 'Seek and ye shall find' (Mt 7.7) is a word applicable even to the conciliar harmony [*sobornost'*] of the Church. History causes new shoots to spring out from the evergreen tree of the Church in the self-renewing creativity of its life, a life firmly anchored in ecclesial doctrine and tradition.

Today, then, the ecclesial consciousness faces a fact that poses a religious and dogmatic problem for the Church. For a long time it has been treated with caution and so not perceived in its full particularity, in that it has remained in the sphere of personal ethics or asceticism – which is how social questions have presented themselves in the awareness of the Church from time immemorial. In my opinion, socialism does not represent any problem at all, considered as an ethical issue; rather is it – from time immemorial, indeed – a natural postulate, so to speak, of Christianity's social ethic. Labour must be protected from illicit exploitation, and justice demands that it be rewarded with the fruits of its work, and that these should not be sacrificed to the power of capital. In recent times churchmen of various denominations have attempted to come to terms with socialism, in that they have adopted it from motives of Christian philanthropy (as in the diverse forms of 'Christian socialism' in our day); and they have sometimes joined forces with political parties (such as the Social Democrats) very much at odds with Christianity, without attempting to deal dogmatically with all the questions raised. But we must reckon with socialism as a fundamental and all-embracing fact in contemporary human history, a specific *spiritual* outlook, and we shall do so in so far as we take our stand on firm *dogmatic* and not merely ethical ground – in living communion with the Church, without trying to simplify the question. Just as, in the history of doctrinal definitions that express some distinct experience, any new step forward in the dogmatic awareness of the Church is preceded by a more or less protracted period of 'fermentation' for the questions at issue, so, in relation to socialism, we are still in that period of ferment, of questing, of individual interpretations ('heresies'). This cannot be forgotten or unspoken; but one cannot take any precipitate personal speculations for a comprehensive ecumenical achievement. First there must be a testing of the conformity of such speculations with the spirit of the Church, by connecting them up with the entire ecclesial tradition. But in this process we must never lose sight of the fact that the ecclesial and dogmatic evaluation of socialism and the social question, especially in the Orthodox world, is still at an absolutely elementary stage.

Socialism is not only a socio-economic movement, although it is most directly expressed in such terms. It is also a world-view, a *Weltanschauung*, or, more precisely, a *Lebensgefühl*, a sense and style of life in which different aspects of human nature find expression. It could be said that socialism possesses not only an historical 'body', but also a 'soul' or spirit; and in this sense it can

The Soul of Socialism

have the significance of a pseudo-religion for its adherents – a world-view with total claims, which is practical as well as theoretical. The *body* of socialism is there for all to see, in the social problems of our day – industrialism, the tyranny of the banks, class hostility, crises in industry and finance, unemployment, the emergence of socialist political parties, communism and the dictatorship of the proletariat – all those subterranean shocks and tremors that constantly threaten the stability of the old world and have already partly destroyed it. Lasalle's defiant motto, *nequeo si superos Acheronta movebo*, has already become reality, as have Carlyle's angry prophecies about Enkelados in chains, or Marx's vengeful foretelling of the dictatorship of the proletariat with its threat of 'expropriating the expropriators'. The 'body' of socialism is like Proteus; it has many forms, always changing. While yesterday it led an illegal, underground existence, today it has become a powerful and sometimes even a dominant reality, above all in my own homeland. But it is now generally true that the human race is dressing itself in more or less socialist garments, and is turning into a socialist anthill; its spread seems to be unstoppable. Economists may have different judgements about the limitations and the non-viability of socialism; and yet it is already impossible to deny or ignore it completely as a characteristic phenomenon of our life today. We can only discuss the different degrees in which the influence of non-socialist factors is manifest in a life fundamentally marked by socialism. Anyone now coming into the world finds him- or herself in a period in which socialism is continually widening its frontiers. Understood simply as a question about poverty and wealth, socialism has always been present in human history, though only as a fact which has hardly ever been historically notable or clearly defined. But now it has become a fact of our inner as well as our outer life, for socialism has a *soul* of its own – a soul that is admittedly wholly pagan – and a *spirit* which has so far been decidedly hostile to God. So let us first spend some time on this question of the 'soul' of socialism.

It is defined by the *anthropology* that is peculiar to socialism. There are two characteristic fundamentals in this doctrine of human nature, sociologism and economism. Both are based on a specific lived experience or vision that is particularly accessible and congenial to our times. *Sociologism* begins from the *collective* character of human existence: already in the Old Testament we encounter the personification of collective 'totalities' – Israel, Amalek, Assur, Ishmael and others, or the beasts of Danielic apocalypse, which also crop up in the New Testament Apocalypse. Today these beasts have imperceptibly transformed themselves into groups or classes, the mythical abstractions of sociology. The telescope and microscope of modern social thought, dictated by statistics and the social sciences in general, bring before everyone's eyes the reality and autonomy of the social corpus, although they have yet to recognise any comparable reality in personal existence; on the contrary, this is swallowed up in the totality of society and even denied in the name of society. In this way, belief in human personhood and its reality comes to be lost; yet it is precisely this that is the first and fundamental datum for religion. More of this later on.

The second fundamental, *economism*, is the general recognition of the dependence of human personhood upon nature – a dependence that is both realised in and overcome by labour, which produces value or wealth – but also, in and with these, the whole of human culture. Economism has its most extreme expression in Marxism, with its so-called 'economic materialism' – better designated as 'materialist economism', in opposition to a *spiritual* (or even spiritualistic) economism. Our age is entirely saturated with this – the development of economic knowledge with its particular, conventional, one-sided and stylised account of human life, the economic trend in historical science, in the press, in society at large. 'The world as economy' and man as *oikonomos* – that is the basic vision of this anthropology. This kind of economism generally sees itself not only as materialistic but as zoological. The economic struggle here becomes a special case of the general struggle for existence which is going on in the whole of the animal world; and furthermore, this social Darwinism is complemented by a crassly materialist perception (or rather misperception) of the economic process. There is no recognition that economy is not only the slavery of mankind under the yoke of elemental nature, but is also a continuing revelation of the human spirit, the triumphant revealing of humanity itself.

In man's economic relation to the world both the greatness of his vocation and the depth of his fall are revealed. It is a *practical* relation to the world, in which man governs and directs nature by humanising it, by making it a 'peripheral body' for himself. Man is a microcosm in the sense that he is the *logos* and the soul of the world. In the economics of labour the fulness of human activity is realised, not simply as the action of a physical worker ('hammer and sickle'), as materialist economism conceives it, but also as the operation of rational will in the world. Natural science and technology display the world to man as a limitless field of possibilities. Matter – dumb, sluggish and formless – becomes transparent and spiritual, a vehicle for human meaning; it becomes 'body' so to speak. It is thus that the cosmic nature of man, his vocation to lordship in the world, appears. In economics the unity of the human species is also graphically displayed and preserved at the external level, since man's labour as an economic agent (a 'transcendental subject of economics') is shaped in history into a unified form, uninterruptedly consistent and integrated. In economic activity the world is dematerialised and becomes a totality of spiritual energies. This is why, incidentally, even the advance of materialist economism is devoted to the process of a wider economic development which increasingly restricts the domain of matter as such by transforming it into *human* energy; the world becomes an 'anthropocosmos'. Yet it is also in the economic relation to the world that the fallenness of man finds expression; his life is mortal, and economics becomes also labour 'in the sweat of his brow' [Gen. 3.19] for the sake of sustaining life and the incessant struggle against death. Human dependence on economic activity is the captivity of death; it is indeed, in a sense, death itself. Economic activity is slavery to death, and so it is both forced and self-interested; it is in relation to this fact that Marxism has its truth, as a kind of halting philosophical recapitulation of the second chapter of Genesis, where God's sentence is passed on man. And yet even in fallenness man still possesses his 'sophianic' nature; his economic life is not characterised only by self-interest but also by the creative and artistic calling of human beings, the service of an ideal, and – like all human enterprise – by the struggle to *grow beyond the self*. This creative, world-embracing impulse in economics is something peculiar to our own age, in which the world has come to be seen as the *work* of man. 'Philosophers have sought long enough to interpret the world, but now it is time to change it'; 'the world is not there to be contemplated, everything must be worked for, nothing is without price' – these are the sayings of two almost contemporary philosophers of economics, expressing the same thought at opposite ends of Europe and in very different ways, Karl Marx and Nikolai Fyodorov. This massive fact of world history, the fact of the economic subjugation, humanising and, in this sense, transformation (if not yet exactly transfiguration) of the world, has already emerged on the historical stage, though it has yet to reach its consummation. It confronts our religious consciousness and demands a spiritual, even 'dogmatic', understanding of economics. So far this latter has known no dogma other than the pagan one of Epicureanism: any increase in need or demand is a good, the sole criterion in economic life is self-love and the struggle for wealth and so forth. Such is the ingenuous ethic of economic empiricism. Even the wisdom which the Church's consciousness possesses in respect of economics has not wholly escaped the influence of this unprincipled empiricism. As far as personal restraint is concerned, the Church has always had a clearly defined stock of ascetical ideas, firmly rooted in its spiritual tradition. Wealth is here related to in purely negative terms; it is treated as one of the lusts of the flesh in which the power of sin and death is manifested. This introduces an ascetical corrective into economic existence, which controls all economic activity by bringing it before the bar of conscience. But it is still inadequate as a response. According to scripture, work is in itself a religious obligation for human beings, such that the institution of labour is not just a matter of personal self-determination, in so far as economic life is a *social* process. In a certain sense, the sphere of economic work, with its distinctive possibilities, is a kind of destiny for human beings; and this 'destiny' consists in the fact that a complete economic cosmos for us to live in is being constructed out of all our individual economic activities, with all their heterogeneous goals. As far as this destiny and this cosmos are concerned, personal asceticism has no ideas to guide it; it relates to it in a purely empirical way, as to a brute fact. But this unawareness at the level of principle leads to changes at the level of practice – leads, in fact, to the *secularising* of interior and exterior life. A monastery which, spiritually speaking, rests on the foundations of ascetical renunciation of the world and on disinterestedness will still make use of all the achievements of technology and the economic process in meeting its own needs, and will take this quite for granted, since 'there's no stink to money'. Thus the Church ends up sanctifying in principle anything that the world brings out of its treasure-store, though the latter has long since passed beyond its control. It could be said that there has never yet been an epoch in the world's history in which economic life has been secularised and left to itself to such an extent as at the present time. In the pagan world, just as in the Christian Middle Ages, no such secularisation of economic life existed as prevails among Christian nations today (indeed the life of non-Christian peoples – Indian, Chinese, Japanese, Turkish and others – seems at first sight to be a good deal richer than that of Christians). This secularisation finds its ideological expression in materialist economism, which has a certain degree of accuracy where the economic life of our times is concerned, since it is carried on not in the presence but in the absence of God. So the struggle against this materialism cannot remain at the purely apologetic level; we can demonstrate its inadequacy and contradictoriness, but must also react positively, restoring Christian significance to the economic process and ecclesial significance to the elements of economic life. Meanwhile the prevailing attitude to economics is one of pragmatic and unprincipled acceptance of what was for a long time regarded only as one of the 'miracles of Antichrist'.

Where is economic development actually leading us? Does economics have a kind of prophetic office in and of itself, as socialism would have it? Is it perhaps the final and all-embracing time of trial for the whole of history, in the face of which the elect must take refuge in the caves and clefts of the earth (if there are any left)? Is it simply the Christian's fate to be tempted by it without ever understanding it, or is it rather a *necessity*, because the unavoidable road of history towards that eschatological fulfilment that lies beyond history leads through it? History and eschatology, temporal fulfilment and its final end, have for a long time been separated and set in opposition to each other, so that any sort of link between them has been, for all practical purposes, denied: the one must come to an end for the other, like a *deus ex machina*, to begin. In this eschatological transcendentalism, all earthly illumination is quenched and all earthly values destroyed: all that remains is personal merit and personal sin, with their equivalents of reward or punishment, which each individual receives for himself alone, without any regard to the collective work of humanity in history. From such historical and sociological nihilism in the realm of eschatology arises a corresponding nihilism in history. But history has its own *inner* apocalypse, which makes history itself already eschatology fulfilling itself in time: the Lord's Second Coming, of whose day and hour (in the transcendent sense) no-one knows save the heavenly Father, also has times and seasons in the immanent process of historical maturation; and even economics with its achievements must be allowed a place in this historical eschatology. In any event, we are faced with the question: must man's labour and toil under the sun be somehow included in the life of eternity which eschatology opens up, or should it be excluded from it? If the former, how and in what sense? If the latter, why so (since this has yet to be shown)?

History is the self-definition and self-revelation of the *human* – both in Christ and against Christ (since anthropology is also Christology and vice versa). But human life does not exist in some realm beyond that of human economic creativity, which is thus caught up in the ways of God in history. It is only natural that, in this age of economism, the question of the eschatological horizon of economics arises, at the two opposite poles of human thought – the Christian and the anti-Christian, the atheistic. Two names can be mentioned as standing for these two religious tendencies, two names which are in this sense symbols of the age with its two ways, the road to Babylon and the road to the Kingdom of God: they are the names of Karl Marx and Nikolai Fyodorov.

In Marx, the spirit of anti-Christian enmity to God finds a voice of exceptional power; but this spirit is nonetheless bound up with an authentic social pathos and an authentic orientation to the future. There is something in Marx of that outpouring of the Spirit that we find in Israel's prophets, for all the atheistic trappings, the outpouring of the Spirit that conquers the heart. Marx thought of man as a demiurge who, because he was capable of changing the economic and social world, transcended the limits of history ('prehistory' for Marx) and succeeded in passing (by 'a great leap forward') into eschatology ('history'). He transposed the ancient prophecies of the City of God in the messianic kingdom into the atheistic idiom of his materialist economism. Atheism, of course, has and can have no eschatology: eschatology consists, by definition, in God's encounter with the world, the manifestation of the face of God before the whole creation, while Marx's eschatology without God ('history') is generally a great void. 'Prehistory' (i.e. our history), with its dramatic quality and its fulness of content, far exceeds the void that is to come, which remains, as before, the sphere of death and temporality (in this connection Marx must be reckoned, along with other atheistic progressivists, among those who 'deify death', to borrow an expression from some contemporary followers of Fyodorov).

Fyodorov, with his 'project' for transforming the world and triumphing over death by means of the 'regulating of nature', was the first to attempt a religious interpretation of economics, by giving it a place in his eschatology. For him too, man is a demiurge, a builder of the cosmos; but he is also a 'son of man', a 'species being', who has forebears and lives in a universal human 'creation of brethren'. To the extent that he fulfils the will of God, he becomes also a child of God who brings Christ's work to perfection in the world and declares war upon the 'last enemy', death, seeking to achieve, by his own powers, the resurrection of the ancestors. The kingdom of the age to come will be perfected by man through the regulation of nature: history will become eschatology. None of the great thinkers who were Fyodorov's contemporaries and who were personally close to him (Dostoevsky, Soloviev, Tolstoy, Fet, Kozhevnikov) were able to say a decisive 'yes' to his project, despite their personal veneration for him; and the same is true among thinkers of our own time (except for Peterson and certain younger 'Fyodorovians'). But – which is no less remarkable – none of them wanted to say a direct 'no' to it either. It must be admitted that the time has not yet come for a living reception of his system: it is the prophet's fate to be ahead of his time. But in this 'teacher and pastor' there is worked out a real 'movement in Christian thought' (Soloviev); in him we find, for the first time, the Christian consciousness asking the same questions as the whole epoch, asking what God is saying in the revelation of history. Fyodorov understood the 'regulation of nature' as the *common task* of the human race, the sons of men who are called to become sons of God, and as the fulfilment of the destiny prescribed by God. Precisely in this insight, he points to a positive way of overcoming materialist economism, by applying the fundamental dogmas of Christianity to economics in a unique fashion. Materialist economism *can* be conquered by Christian thought. The Church today can still save individual souls from spiritual death, but it will only be strong enough to win this living victory when it makes plain the truth it has to tell about economism, and so cuts the ground from under all the familiar slanders and distortions. But this cannot remain at the level of personal opinion alone: it must become a task for the whole Church, which is 'the pillar and ground of truth' [I Tim. 3.15] because 'the gates of hell shall not prevail against it [Mt. 16.18]'.

II

Logically, materialist economism is bound to lead to fatalism, since what it sees as defining the movement of history is not personality, with its creative struggles, but the impersonal economic process. There is no room here for good or evil or, generally speaking, any notion of ideal value. Yet in practice, quite inconsistently with its doctrine, socialism has, in the modern age, developed an enormous historical dynamic, a 'revolutionary' attitude. The spirit of revolution has been brooding over Europe since 1789, and its pressure is more and more deeply felt as it absorbs more and more social material, so that society in our times is beginning to define itself in relation to revolution, as being for it or against.

Revolution is both a fact and a principle. As *fact*, revolutions are brought about by elemental forces of nature; they are like a volcanic eruption, throwing out lava and ash, or an earthquake that mixes together the different strata under the earth's surface, pushing down one continent and lifting up another. Such elemental forces are evil only in their irrationality; but they are far more evil when man himself becomes a 'natural element'. Animality and madness are aroused, and the memories of ancient injuries stir in the masses, vengeful rage and accumulated hatred – alongside the heroic enthusiasm of particular persons, leaders or groups, of course. The floods of Acheron break through – no limpid stream, but a torrent of water fouled with dirt and mud. The upheavals of history are never a moral idyll such as would satisfy a schoolmaster; Hegel had already remarked as much. As the flood of revolution bursts in, all the vileness in human nature that usually hides itself in shame comes to the fore; the worst elements in humanity surge up – and perhaps the best can manifest themselves as well. The violence and despotism of an oligarchy, the red terror that is always accompanied by such hypocrisy on the part of revolutionaries, demagogy and careerism, all these are a mirror of the wild frenzy that overtakes both the masses and their 'leaders'.

Revolution as a *principle* is the programmatic breaking of the threads of historical tradition, the desire to generate history out of itself. The passion for destruction is here identified with the passion for construction. The consequent barbarisation results not only from the mixing of different social strata but also from the general hostility of revolution towards the culture of the past, even when it actually serves the culture of the future. So it is no accident that the nihilistic revolt against historical tradition is directed equally against faith, and turns into 'militant atheism'. This cannot be explained only by reference to the sins of the ecclesiastical institution, which are unmasked and punished in the revolution. Revolution brings with it a nihilistic hatred for what has been valued, what has been held sacred, and it would be incomprehensible if earthly rebellion were not also revolt against heaven, passing over into enmity towards God.

But granted all this, is not revolution also a normal state of the soul? Cannot a sickness often be welcome, a catastrophe opportune? A sickness, what is more, has its own sufficient causes, usually reaching back broadly and deeply into the past. The executioners too are the victims of history, and all those actively or passively involved in revolution must take responsibility for them and their acts. Revolutions are certainly not made by revolutionaries themselves: in this respect they are overtaken by a quite fallacious historical arrogance. It is more true to say that they – as much as the counter-revolutionaries – are the product of the revolution. Yet it can rightly be said that revolution does have an *idée-force*, an energy deriving from ideas, the explosive material which impels inert matter into movement; and this is not only hatred: it is also *faith* and *passion*. In the idea of revolution the human yearning and striving for the future finds supreme expression, longing for the future, faith in the future: *amor futuri*. It contains a definite ideal of the future and on top of this a specific vision, a projection from the present on to the future. In this sense the soul of revolution is *utopian* (*ou-topos*) – something that does not yet exist in any identifiable place but which *will* come to exist (the word was coined by Thomas More, the Catholic confessor and martyr of the sixteenth century). There are many different kinds of utopia, but utopia in general is an object of social faith, hope and love, 'the assurance of things hoped for, the conviction of things not seen' (Heb. 11.1). Utopianism is not the direct opposite of realism; it can and must be united with it. Here we have a distinction between means and ends, the task and its fulfilment. Utopia is, in this sense, 'an ideal with a changing content', so that the end belongs to the realm of what will be, and the means to the order of historical teleology. Only when the necessary balance between the two is destroyed does utopianism invade the territory that belongs to realism, and feverish dreams result; or else realism loses its striving for the ideal and becomes an untheoretical pragmatism. The Christian ideal of the Kingdom of God is realised historically in a whole series of alternating historical tasks: at the present time, one of these is the attainment of social justice *along with* personal liberty. These tasks all have corresponding practical means for their attainment; and in this area there may be practical differences of opinion. This is why Christianity, which is called to realise unity in the spirit, cannot identify itself with any particular programme or party. Utopianism is in its essence as much a part of Old Testament messianism as of Christianity itself; but in more recent times it has in practice been monopolised by revolutionary socialism. Although it is fashionable in Marxist circles to dismiss 'utopian socialism' in favour of 'scientific' or realistic socialism, this latter is in no way less utopian than any other vision of utopia. Utopia is always a matter of fable, a story about the future which is still as yet invisible; but it is also a prophecy of the future, since the future is already contained in the present, which offers a foretaste of it. Utopia is the inner nerve in the dynamic of history. 'The heart lives in the future; the present is full of misery' (Pushkin) – that is the law and the dream of the human heart. There may be at times a weakening of this essential dreaming of the heart, but without such a dream man cannot live. History is made by dreamers, not by the hollow men who live by prose; by people of faith, prophets, 'utopians'. For them the present age of 'misery' is only 'prehistory', a prologue to true dialectical history, in which 'contradiction is what leads us forward' as it realises the rational pattern, the *Vernunft*, of history. This is Hegel's 'cunning of reason'. And this dialectic manifests itself, in the nature of things, as revolution in respect of the present which it refuses to accept; it is prepared to sacrifice itself for the future's sake – to sacrifice love of the neighbour for the sake of love for the most remote.

But a faith that has lost its spiritual balance turns into superstition or fanatical fantasy, which is inspired no longer by the vision of the city that is to come but by deceptive mirages. As soon as the utopianism that forms the soul of revolution has lost its religious roots, it ceases to have any spiritual balance. Its social idealism finds itself at odds with the tired positivism with which it has been yoked in the name of an imaginary 'scientific' perspective. Marx's utopianism – like that of other positivists – is wholly irrational, full of contradictions and religiously vacuous. Its conception of history goes no further than 'prehistory' – the epoch of class struggle; Marx's 'history' lacks all real content. Non-religious utopianism within revolutionary socialism (to the extent that it is more than just demagogy) is transmuted into a feverish dream, the *fata morgana* of a fever-stricken soul in the waterless desert. Yet in the name of that love which 'rejoices not in unrighteousness but rejoices in the truth' (I Cor. 13.6), we should recognise here too the expression of an authentic desire, unable to see or to find any religious means for its satisfaction and so failing to understand itself, to be aware of its own inner truth. And so the breach between social idealism, 'progress' and Christianity (especially any kind of faith in a personal God), the sharp reversion to paganism [in modern revolutionary movements], can appear definitive and inevitable. The hysterical blasphemies of the Russian regime, the suffocation of a whole people's religious faith and the development of an anti-religious Inquisition are almost more of a testimony to this than even the bacchanalia of the French Revolution. Social utopians – wild and hysterical in Russia, dim and chilly in other countries – make a religious idol of social revolution. And the other side of the coin is that the Church's representatives see in this only an excellent reason for sitting in judgement on the Revolution, washing their hands in innocence and denying all responsibility. So there develops a total mutual alienation, deafness and incomprehension. The gulf between Christianity and neo-paganism (which thinks it is atheism) certainly does not run along the line of a discernible 'scientific' method. On such grounds, we ought rather to be talking about a reversal of the positions of faith and knowledge; materialism [as a theory] is currently as much obscurantism as nonsense, on the whole. No, the gulf follows the line of an historical dynamic, of diverse relations to social praxis. Of course, it is impossible to minimise the evil will, the familiar and notorious hatred for what is holy in 'militant atheism', especially in its leaders, the generalissimos of the Revolution and their crack troops, who have built their careers on the betrayal of Christ and the spiritual massacre of the innocents. But Satan can assume the guise of an angel of light, in addition to his real and terrible appearance, in the sense that he can wrap himself in the garment of social justice; the atheistic movement is inspired by the deceptions of the Father of Lies, who sets up the pseudo-utopia of a world purged of God, a world that has him as its ruler. Spiritual integrity and simple truthfulness, however, both alike require a careful and patient examination of a situation as it has concretely developed before one makes a final judgement and (so to speak) refers the facts to a higher court. And where there are many people inclined to see this in terms of a spiritual struggle in which the guilt does not lie all on one side, is there perhaps less risk of the misunderstanding that arises not just from spiritual narrowness and evil will [on the part of one side in the struggle] but also through the presence of guilt on the other side as well?

The Soul of Socialism

'Repent – *metanoeite* (change your mind, examine yourselves), for the Kingdom of God is at hand' – these words of John the Baptist's, which then become Christ's words as well, have the most comprehensive sense imaginable, especially in the social-historical context. Is this *metanoia* not a summons to new kinds of action, and, above all, to the testing and rethinking of what we imagine to be self-evident, the foundations on which we rest? And do the Church's representatives seek social justice for their age, do they pursue the social utopia that lies at hand in their epoch, in a dynamic way? Or are they happy with a purely static conservatism to which fidelity to tradition can finally be reduced? Is there an historical future, with new tasks to perform, from the Church's point of view, or is the whole Christian philosophy of history exhausted in a simple waiting for the end of the world, in which all that can be looked for is the cancellation of all historical values – 'alles, was entsteht, ist wert, dass es zu Grunde geht' ('The worth of all things now and past/Is that they come to dust at last')? For there is such a thing as a spiritual 'abhorrence of the vacuum'; and we can hardly be surprised if men who can find here no easing of the questions of their conscience set out to seek it in a 'far country'.

Yet it was not always so. No-one could say that the Old Testament lacked an historical sensibility, an awareness of the 'pathos' of history – it is itself a sacred history, striving towards the coming messianic kingdom. But there is still more: the Old Testament takes in the whole of universal history in its pattern (already in Genesis, but equally in the prophets, especially in Daniel, the prototype of later apocalypses). The prophets give us such a sweeping utopian vision (in the positive sense of 'utopian', of course) that there is nothing comparable to them in boldness. What we have here is not just a religious philosophy of history, but also a set of ideal tasks, which lead us beyond our present historical reality. So the preaching of the prophets (Amos, Isaiah, Hosea) has a social aspect as well as all its other features. Is the New Testament any different? Does it leave behind the prophecies of the Old? This cannot be granted either dogmatically or historically. And yet there is a radical shift of sensibility in the New Testament: 'antinomism', the suspicion of law, comes on the scene, with its wisdom and its attendant problematic. The naivety of Old Testament man gives no place at all to this. And the Kingdom of God is 'at hand' *in* the world, it is 'coming', yet it is not *of* this world. It is *entos hēmōn* – that is to say, first of all, 'within us', but also 'among us'. In relation to the world, there is a tragic polarisation between love for it and (simultaneously) enmity towards it; and because of the complexity of this relationship, Christianity has no room either for the messianic paradise of Jewish apocalyptic or for the earthly paradise of socialism.

The question may thus arise of whether *history* really does exist for Christianity or whether there is only the *empty* time of an indefinite duration, in which there is nothing to be consummated, no 'last times'. This conception of the *last* times means that, if we take seriously the effects of God's incarnation, everything is indeed completed from God's point of view; but for Christian humanity, these 'last times' create their own epoch, with its own consummations and revelations. The New Testament Apocalypse is a revelation about *history*, not only about the end of time, as people so often assume. Here we have the struggle between two opposing principles laid bare in symbolic terms (partly shared with the generality of apocalyptic literature), the two principles that constitute the tragic quality in the pattern of history, with its alternation of victories and defeats. We read here not only of the triumph of the Beast and its false prophets but also of the appearance of the thousand-year reign of Christ on earth. The essential lines of this are filled out in other places in the New Testament; the preaching of the gospel to all nations (Mt 24.14) in connection with various other events, the conversion of Israel, 'life from the dead' [Rom. 11.15], the appearance of the 'adversary' [II Thess. 2.4] – all these mark the boundaries of particular historical epochs. The future is already in essence made clear by the Holy Spirit (Jn 16.13), even though its particularities are still shrouded in ignorance, since it is also the work of human creativity. Thus even in the 'last times' there is a real history; it is not an 'evil infinity', perpetuating for eternity a mixture of good and evil, as in the conceptuality of modern paganism, but has an immanent end or goal, serving as a transition to a higher level, but realised only through the power of God. The end itself, of course, is no longer an historical event, since it transcends history, it does not have a place in the sequence of historical time ('and the angel swore that time should be no more', Rev. 10.6). Although history is internally dependent upon eschatology, it cannot be externally oriented towards it, towards an historical apocalypse, since the end does not lie within but beyond history, outside its horizons, beyond its frontiers. This shift of perspective is often misused: people try to save themselves from historical panic by taking flight into the eschatological realm. Reflection on the end must be constantly echoing in the inner life of man (as must meditation on death and judgement), but it is forbidden for us to determine times and seasons, to utter false prophecies. It is not for this that revelation about the end of history (and about the general resurrection) is given to us; rather it is to reinforce our watchfulness ('Watch, therefore'; Mt 24.42) as a sort of guarantee of the victory of the good, of the positive outcome of history. As experienced in religious terms, history is the apocalypse coming to fruition – apocalypse understood *not* as eschatology but as 'historiosophy', which is something linked with the sense of an orientation towards the future, with the consciousness of obligatory tasks to be performed and of continuing historical labour. Time is measured not in years but in *acts*, and, in view of these obligatory tasks and historical possibilities, only someone for whom the whole of history is nothing but the gradual triumph of Antichrist, who is preparing the way for his personal appearance, can think about the end of history in a purely passive way. In contrast, Christianity demands courage, work and inspiration. Church praises the 'good and faithful servant' who makes use of his talent, and condemns the 'wicked and slothful servant' who buries it. Christian historiosophy reveals the apocalyptic breadth and scale that lies within the struggle to move from the city that now is to the one that is to come, for 'the form of this world is passing away' [I Cor. 7.31]. Thus the revolutionary dynamic that remains blind and unorganised in an atheist context is here acknowledged in its true form. The authentic concept of 'progress', i.e. movement towards a [determinate] goal, towards the Kingdom of God, is to be found only in Christian historiosophy, with its irreconcilable opposition to all that is limited and particularist, to the whole of the bourgeois mentality in history. This is very clear in the springtime of the early Church, when the 'little flock' opposed its heroic detachment to the entire world, and thus (according to Celsus) undermined the foundations of the ancient world and its fundamental values – state and culture. Yet this non-acceptance of the world was closely bound up with an expectation of the imminent end, and with the indifference to history and its concerns that sprang from such an expectation. And of course social quietism followed in its wake. ('Everyone should remain in the state in which he was called' – I Cor. 7.20), along with a distinctive note of conservatism ('There is no authority except from God' – Rom. 13.1); but this is combined with the menacing tones of the Apocalypse. What this amounted to was a peculiar kind of apolitical vision, which accorded significance only to the inner attitude of a man (hence the apparent indifference of Christianity to slavery; yet, historically speaking, it is Christianity that is responsible for exploding slavery from within). The primacy of the inner over the outer is not in dispute here: it forms the spiritual basis of social order. But this *primacy* does not mean social indifferentism or the absence of any value [in the historical world]. The kind of spiritual absenteeism that was not only wise in practical terms but really the sole possible option for early Christianity looked like weakness as soon as Christianity gained any influence in state and society.

In practice, Christianity turned out to be the spiritual leaven of the new social order; it brought to birth a new mode of personal existence, and its practical influence naturally extended far beyond the concrete boundaries of the ecclesiastical organisation itself. Of course, alongside this, it cannot be denied that church communities, like human communities in general, are far from living always on the heights to which they are called. Thus they commonly become a bulwark of conservatism, or at least of the status quo, externally as well as internally. Internal resistance to revolutionism, at least in its nihilistic forms, arises in the Church from its loyalty to *tradition*, by which its entire life is penetrated. This is the living *memory* of the Church, which stands over against the historical amnesia of the children of the Revolution, for whom history begins with themselves. This is a simple human *dignity* that will be constantly dissatisfied with the spiritual bad taste of such a nihilism; there is a more purely historical awareness that will sense this abolition of history to be a wild aberration; and there is, finally, an *ecclesial* awareness for which breaking with tradition as a matter of principle is an intolerable heresy. But at the same time, loyalty to tradition is not loyalty to immobility, to what is outdated or antiquated. Such an understanding is not loyalty to tradition but straightforward secular conservatism; the distinction between them has never yet been adequately drawn. Because of human weakness, alas, there is plenty of unchurchly contraband sailing under the Church's flag; many things that are alien and essentially destructive [to the Church] have gone on adhering to the hull of the ecclesial vessel in its voyage through the centuries, calling forth the *Schadenfreude* of atheists, who are skilled in exhibiting such things in displays and museums. Here the fire of the Revolution turns out to be also a purifying fire for the ecclesial community, however painful its impact may still be.

In any event, the relation of Christianity to the world and its values can never be purely immanent, as in neo-paganism. When the eyes are raised to heaven, they become blind to the immediate environment, and the summons of eternity creates a certain indifference to 'the tedious songs of earth'. There is a proper Christian freedom from the world, which (especially in earlier ages) sought expression in literal external flight from the world around. But such a flight, with its indifference to the question of earthly values, can only be fully realised in the eremitical life; and even there, there is either an aspiration to exercise influence upon the world or a summons to the world to move in the direction of the cloister. It is precisely in the monastic environment that Christian utopian visions have so often been developed, visions that would later become potent forces in the movement of history (the 'third Rome', the sacred empire, the theocratic state). One could even say that the more pure and incandescent in the spiritual struggle in the cloister, the more effective it is in the world (St Francis and his friars, Luther and the Reformation). Not infrequently, however, this world-denying impulse goes with an excessive conservatism in respect of the world, with a conservatism that is itself anything but world-denying. But generally speaking, one could say that in Christianity there is always a fulfilment of the quest for the leading idea within the historical development of the current epoch, and that a conservatism consisting simply in traditional styles of living cannot be considered to be the normal or distinctive mode of Christian social awareness. Between atheistic revolution and a Christian ordering of society there is, of course, a gulf. But does this mean that Christianity, because of its supernatural dimension, knows only a conservative and static vision? Or can it and must it not also acknowledge a practical dynamic? Is a *Christian reformism* possible, inspired by the idea of the Kingdom of God and finding its historical utopia, or, more precisely, utopias, not in any utopian vision of an 'earthly paradise', of course, but in the vision of the triumph of the good in and through the tragic processes of universal history, which lead towards the definitive separation between good and evil?

Here we come up against the fundamental question of Christian life in our times: that of the 'churching' of culture, as it is now expressed. Once again, the sphinx of history puts the question to our understanding, our heart and our freedom – yes or no? Today this question represents an historical watershed, from which the streams flow in divergent directions. The simplest thing is to evade the question under the pretext of a distinction between what belongs to Caesar and what belongs to God (in the individual spirit). That has been the answer of Protestantism, which has put in train the secularisation that is now suffocating the world. Perhaps there was an historical justification for this in the attempt to be free of papal hierocracy; yet the same distinction is not infrequently made in the name of Orthodoxy. Ascetic renunciation of the world, personal pietism, are here treated as a sufficient response – in the spirit of a world renouncing 'apoliticism', in which the dominant structures of society or 'political' passions pure and simple begin to occupy the whole expanse of the battlefield.

Now the Church *is* in fact 'apolitical' – in this sense, that it can never identify its eternal values with any relative or contingent tasks, or any historical institutions (as was once the case in Russia, where only the party supporting unrestricted autocracy counted as truly Orthodox). The Church cannot be a party; it must be *the conscience of a society*, never using humility as an excuse for compromise or indifferentism. But it cannot go along with the secularist disintegration of social order; rather must its spiritual domination struggle towards

The Soul of Socialism

victory *from within*. This was the ideal of a 'free theocracy' found in the early Soloviev and the later Dostoevsky.

We have lately seen diverse Christian confessions, each in their own way, taking some steps (though as yet still irresolute ones), jointly and for themselves individually, towards a Christian social order. This movement is associated on the worldwide scale with the name of the Stockholm Conference of 1925 (though the Catholic Church, sadly, was not included in this). Representatives of the various Orthodox churches deliberately involved themselves, and thus took on responsibility for educating the nations in the spirit of social Christianity. One of the weaknesses of this movement is what is, to say the least, an inadequate level of clarification of the ideological, or rather the dogmatic, foundations of a movement for the religious conquest of secularisation. The Church is taking on the burden of the ordering of society, in a conscious and principled way, not only *de facto*, as was formerly the case; but for this one needs faith, enthusiasm and a sense of vocation. We must begin to understand God's revelation in history as the apocalyptic reality fulfilling itself, that reality which leads to the full consummation of historical processes and, *in that sense*, to the end of history; and this is something more than a simple cataloguing of events according to their pragmatic significance. A further dimension needs to be in view – a living sense of the incompleteness of history (history as 'prehistory'), which still leaves room for 'utopia', for what *is* not yet but is to come, for the ideal, for hope. Christianity, in its idea of the Kingdom of God, possesses just such a comprehensive and inexhaustible ideal, including in itself all good human goals and achievements. But it also still has its promise, signified in the symbolic language of the Apocalypse as the inauguration of the thousand-year reign of Christ on earth (Rev. 20). This symbol, which is the guiding star of history, was for a long time locked in by a one-sided interpretation, so that the rejection without remainder of this dominant interpretation was immediately reckoned as heresy. But this ultimate manifestation of the Kingdom of God on earth, symbolically rendered in this way, cannot remain a purely passively understood prophecy (worthy of ideological rejection on account of this passivity): it must become an active utopian ideal, a hope. Naturally this symbol in itself is abstract;

but it is constantly being filled out with concrete content, in terms of actual advances or achievements in history, of the summons directed by the future towards the present. Pseudo-eschatologism is an expression of panic, spiritual corruption of fatigue, freed from historical responsibility, although as a matter of bare fact (i.e. in a pagan fashion) it does participate in history. But if there is indeed no way of avoiding society, if it is a kind of destiny, then the social order must incorporate into itself the quest for the Christian righteousness associated with the Kingdom of God, for 'Seek, and ye shall find' [Mt. 7.7]. What the Church has to offer cannot be taken away, even when we distance ourselves from it and bury this talent in the earth. But those things that find no adequate response in the Church life of the present day will imperceptibly fall prey to the forces of corruption. Who knows how many 'Sauls' are still trapped in the atheist camp, seduced by its dynamism, because they cannot find among us either attention or response to their questioning? Strength and truth are what will be victorious – not a weakened and compromising apologetic. The tragic experience of our homeland, together with the threats of the storm-clouds now gathering over our world, call us to new ways of living and thinking, '... So that your youth is renewed like the eagle's' (Ps. 103.5): constant renewal is the law and the condition of the spiritual life, as is loyalty to a *living tradition*.

III

Along with economism, *sociologism* is the other determining element of the modern self-consciousness. Man has always had a collective life and a collective consciousness, for example in the immediate organic unity of nation, tribe, family, and so on. Within these limits, the tormenting problems of our own day concerning the relation of personality to society did not arise: the personal and the social were organically bound up with each other, and in the context of this bond, the naive – but prophetic – wisdom of unmediated experience could find expression. Today we have so far lost sight of all this that the independent reality of the two competing elements has come to be doubted and even denied. The idea of the autonomy of society, developed from the work of the social sciences, seems to be something that has no room for the personal principle. Personality dissolves into the social totality and appears as no more than a 'reflex', an ontological illusion, a ripple on the wave of society. Ketle, as he spells out in this 'social physics' the scientific validity of statistical tabulation, objects to any raising of the question about the place of personality, with its free and creative originality, within the framework of this impersonal or suprapersonal system of validation. In general though, it is true that social science is frustrated and baffled by its own developments, and attempts to avoid posing the question of personality, in that it capitulates immediately to the principle of a supra-personal rule-governed structure and in practice absorbs personality into the social whole. Popular 'elementary education in politics' (*Polit-gramota*) is no less confident in taking the dismissal of any 'freedom' of personal existence as scientific dogma. In this world of social determinism, the palm must go to Marxism, which declares that the only human reality is that of classes, or groups involved in production. Thus a new social mythology is constructed, in which abstract generalisations are accorded a more significant level of existence than is the concreteness of personal life. In this form, sociologism as an attitude to life and a *Weltanschauung*, lacking any regard for the particularity of its own modes of expression, is fundamentally and essentially a non-Christian, even anti-Christian, worldview, which at the present time is appearing more and more clearly as a rival to Christianity in its negation of personality as a spiritual and creative principle in the name of an impersonal social automatism. The devastation that this superstition causes in souls is not hard to assess (although its effects are limited by practical inconsistencies in its application). It is a distinctive *social atheism*, and the first article of this atheistic creed proclaims that there is no such thing as personal being; from which it follows (incontrovertibly, in its own way) that there is no soul and no God, but only, ultimately, the social Leviathan.

Now Christianity too recognises that there is a real human unity-in-plurality – the *Body of Christ*, which consists of distinct, individual living members (I Cor. 12.12–27) – i.e. personalities; and in this dogma concerning the Church there is sufficient basis for developing the principles of a Christian sociology. Yet for so long, Christian dogmatics has hidden itself in passive silence when faced with pagan sociologism; without taking notice of it, without even once attempting to resist it and set matters to right again. Of course there is no need to fight against the *factual* obviousness of many sociological generalisations. This is as unnecessary as, for example, battling against the factual content of the natural sciences simply on the grounds that arbitrary and ill-thought-out pseudo-philosophical consequences are often inferred from such data. But, up to the present, social problems have been treated in theology only from an ethical point of view, not a sociological one. However, the existence, as a matter of fact, of such regularities in human life as a social body, even if this does not have a fully formative effect on human life, now thoroughly merits a place in theology as well. Christian theology is called to a *broader* view. It must provide an answer for the question before which the resources of sociology fail: how, in life and in thought, can we hold together the equal reality and the equal independence of personality on the one hand and of society as a whole on the other? *De facto* the reality of personality can hardly be contested, even if it is denied in theory: sociology suffers from this impersonalism, and Christian anthropology must be applied to it at this point. But there is also a *de facto* dominance in Christian dogma of an individualistic understanding of society, which is seen as predominantly an aggregate of mutually unconnected personalities – even though this notion does not correspond to its own doctrine of humanity as an organic whole 'in Adam', which is then assumed as a whole in the humanity of Christ. In Christ the whole of humanity exists as a generic reality as well as an ensemble of personalities, as a real unity-in-plurality. The idea of *sobornost'*, which lies at the root of the doctrine of the Church, can also acquire a sociological application, by means of which the lethal doctrine of godless sociologism may be overcome. 'You will know the truth and the truth will make you free' [Jn 8.32]. The entire biblical revelation turns upon the notion of a 'Son of Man' who can contain both the personal and the generic principle. And if theology itself has not up to now applied this principle with sufficient seriousness, it is now compelled to do so by the spread of a sociological heresy that violates in the most extreme way the dogma of the Divine

Humanity. The history of doctrine shows that the various heresies were in fact *questions* posed to theology, to broaden its awareness of its problematic; and something of this kind is going on today with this heresy of sociologism.

A soulless socialism is of concern to modern life not only in its character as a world-view – an ecclesiological heresy, relating to the sphere of doctrine – but as a heresy in *living* which expresses itself in the processes of secularisation, external socialisation, forced collectivisation, the transformation of the human into a herd or an ant-heap. At the present time, personality (at least in the countries of civilised Europe) is surrounded for the forces of compulsory collectivism and the standardisation of human life. We are talking not only of the Bolshevists, who herd men into the *kolkhoz*, the collective, by physical and economic violence and who in practice transform a godless and godforsaken, impersonal and depersonalised socialism into the militant shape of communism. The entire organisation of modern life is directed towards exactly the same end, even though less open and barbaric compulsion is involved. In a patriarchally ordered style of life, man existed in an *organic* form of sociality, in which his place in life was determined and rendered transparently obvious by a logic that seemed quite sufficient for the existing situation. Even the apostle Paul's injunction, 'Everyone should remain in the state in which he was called ... there let him remain with God' (I Cor. 7.20, 24), which to us sounds conservative and quietist, simply presupposes, historically speaking, and apart from its abiding ascetical significance, a patriarchal-organic form of life. For Paul, even so appalling a social institution as slavery had some relative justification, and as such is not condemned by him (Eph. 6.5–9). But this organic style of living has been completely destroyed; and on its ruins has arisen an artificial and rationalised form of life, grounded in technical and economic teleology. There are two aspects to this rationalisation: the revolutionising of life in terms of an atomising of society – so that the process actually leads to greater individualism, in contradiction to the sociologism that negates the reality of personality – and at the same time the forcible uniting of these human atoms in the process of economic and national life – in the factory (industrialisation), in cities (urbanisation), in national institutions (statist centralism), and in general the collectivisation of human life on the basis of the 'general good'. This is what can be designated as the socialism of concrete life, independently of its economic form (so that in this sense the supremely rationalised society of capitalism is perhaps no less 'socialistic' than the coercive regime of communism). Man is by nature incapable of continuing in an atomised condition, and so creates new forms of association; his life is socialised anew – but how, and on the basis of what principles? As a rule, on utilitarian grounds, on the grounds of the *de facto* commonalities of life, practical needs and interests. Hence the development of classes and organisations with their diverse modes of solidarity, governed by the principles of a militant sociologism. Thus the rationalistic form of life sets its seal even on these relationships.

Yet even in the midst of this spiritual decline and fall, man cannot be content simply with the given facts of the situation; he takes up an evaluative stance in respect of these facts and gives them an ideal clothing. He begins to see even forced collectivisation as a peculiar kind of *sobornost'*, which is actually striving towards the true ecclesial form of society. An *active* sociologism develops, something that is already an act of free self-determination: the man who belongs to this or that particular class, in this or that particular condition, begins to assert himself as a generic being with his own distinctive generic life. Modern society represents the ensemble of such vertical group identities, separated from one another, each one constituted as self-sufficient. They move forward in a mutual association, while at the same time, in their reciprocal relations, subordinating themselves to a particular overall standard in assessing their hierarchy of values (the proletarian International, Italian or German fascism, and so on). The general basis for these alliances is the pagan naturalism they share, so that, in this sense, what they share is their 'animality'. This means that what is placed in the highest rank of values or standards is not what has an elevated and autonomous axiological character, but only a subordinate kind of value; and this destroys the entire spiritual hierarchy of values. Of course the unity or solidarity of a class, at least within certain limits, has spiritual worth; likewise national identity as a fundamental principle has a value of its own, though not the supreme value and not an autonomous value that could serve as an ultimate criterion; and the same is true of the state. If any of them lay claim to an absolute status, these principles produce forms of association that really represent a kind of pseudo-Church. They can allow some room within their frontiers even for the Church as a national and historical institution, though one that is always judged by other and higher values than its own. But this kind of relationship to the Church serves only to underline the socio-cultural atheism which, however veiled, is not in any way different from militant atheism. Social life thus offers today a prospect of spiritual desolation and practical atheism. While the Church itself often fell under the state's influence, in the days when the two were united, what we see so clearly today is the 'Beast', the power of social self-legitimation with its automatism and forced collectivism, setting up its own values, causing all men 'to be marked on the right hand or the forehead, so that no-one can buy or sell unless he has the mark' (Rev. 13.16, 17). And 'the number of the Beast ... is a human number' (Rev. 13.18). What we are talking about is the combination of human collectivity at the natural level with the practical atheism of social life. This also introduces into the life of the Church's representative a state of spiritually divided loyalty to two kinds of authority; and the passive retreat into a supposed eremitical reclusion leads in practical terms to enslavement by precisely this lordship of the Beast.

Is the present relation between Church and society the only one possible? Or is it really a matter of handing over to Belial without a struggle what does not belong to him and what therefore cannot be yielded to him? Is there any possibility of a victory from within over this godless social automatism, this cult of the Beast, this 'animality' (in which of course a real *bestiality* is concealed)? *Dogmatically* speaking, this is not only possible but necessary. The Christian doctrine of man as a generically personal being contains also the true conception of what commonality in life might be – a social order in which the personal principle is affirmed as something inseparable from collective or generic life. Thus an individualistic seclusion from the world, an eremitism that cannot distinguish the wilderness [of asceticism = *pustyn*] from the void [*pustota*], is unmasked as a sinfully egotistical self-assertion. Incidentally, monastic solitude and even the hermit life are in fact only an aspect of Christian *service* under particular conditions, whereas egocentricity recognises no call to service, and, in this perspective, is on no higher level than the blatant and deliberate self-love of the Benthamite 'economic man'. Christianity has two commandments on which 'depend all the law and the prophets' – love for God, and in second place, 'like it', love for the neighbour, whereby each and every individual may be such a neighbour. Thus a 'Christian sociology' is possible as an aspect of dogmatic and practical ('moral') theology, which must provide a careful working-out of its problems and goals. This is the task that ecclesial reflection now faces. The ordering of society that rests on natural instinct or on rationalisation and automation must be overcome and dissolved in *ecclesial* life.

Humanity is running out of breath and losing its strength in this hopeless conflict between the egocentricity of individualism and the sadism of communism, between the soullessness of statism and the snarlings of racism. But the Church has thus far had no answer to give; under the pressure of threatened persecution, it has settled for carrying on as one tolerated or licensed state institution among others – or else it has endured, in the communist world, a truly bestial persecution at the hands of the Beast of pagan polity. Yet it is only the Church that possesses the principle of true social order, in which the personal and the collective, freedom and social service can be given equal weight and unified harmoniously. It is itself this very principle – living *sobornost'*. That is also the dogmatic foundation of an ecclesial polity. But to this end there must be an upsurge of fresh inspiration in the members of the Church themselves, a spring of living water which satisfies the thirst of contemporary humanity, for the sake of a new relationship between nations, a new mission to the darkness of social paganism, for the awakening of a new *spirit*. This is not the misplaced utopianism of a 'rose-tinted' Christianity that consigns the tragic character of history, with its necessary schism between good and evil, to oblivion, believing that before the ultimate separation the forces of good are bound to become fully manifest. Still less is this a belated renaissance of clericalism on the Catholic model, which struggle to possess both of the 'two swords', and wants to put the direction of all life into the hands of the ecclesiastical organisation: a life that develops in an ecclesial way, moving outwards from within, has no longer any need of external submission to authority.

No, what we are speaking of is belief in the Church and in its own distinctive living power, activated by the Holy Spirit's life within it. The proclamation of the Kingdom of God, which has never been silenced in the Church, must now make itself heard in those areas of life in which up to now, it has been propounded only in inadequate ways; the dry bones must be vitalised with a new spirit. Even the class struggle in our society of class divisions must not be defined by hatred; it can be defined in terms of class-*conscience* and the awareness of mutual duties. Is this not what the apostle Paul preached even in relation to slaves and slave-owners, in exhorting slaves to be submissive for the sake of Christ, their master, but also reminding slave-owners of their Christian duties towards their slaves? This is the kind of class-conscience that Carlyle devoted his time to developing, calling the 'captains of industry' to be mindful of their service to society. Of course, the class structure of society is, in itself, *not* a phenomenon that sits easily with the Christian conscience, and so is something that has to be overcome; but this overcoming must be something that proceeds from within, not only something that happens at the external level.

The great *sin* of the modern Christian community is its uncreative relationship to social life, a failure which is not made any the less serious by being concealed under the mask of an apparent asceticism. Indifference is not victory, and spiritual absenteeism is not asceticism. In its search for meaning, society is exhausting its powers: it still has no guidance from the Church and has itself lost direction. But in the meantime new projects emerge in the life of society, not only negative ones – the overcoming of that animal principle which has taken the place belonging to holiness – but positive as well, such as the provision of new meaning and motivation for economic work. There is the question, among others, of how rationalised and mechanised labour can have meaning, when, for the worker, it has lost the natural attraction of earlier days, and in a certain sense, lost its aesthetic dimension. Just as Marx's theory has it, such labour has become 'abstract', has drained away working energy. It has no inspiration left and no more delight in *personal* creativity; it has become a mechanical slavery, as much in capitalism as in socialism. There is a curious attempt at rousing some enthusiasm for work in the Soviet idea of *udarnichestvo* [the 'strike troops' or 'forward movement' of industrial construction], in so far as this movement really exists and is not simply cried up for propaganda purposes. Its main significance is that here there is still an attempt being made to give meaning to personal labour in that this is integrated into the common work of 'building socialism'. But it is clear that what is presented here is a pagan substitute for the Kingdom of God as the highest service to which men can dedicate their lives. So we must move away from a passive-quietist, conservative-assimilationist relationship to the work of society, in a direction that is active and practically innovative, and thus take forward the work of Christ. Otherwise the result will be a vacuum; and the spirit's abhorrence of a vacuum will fill it up with evil forces.

There is still one fresh difficulty, one new problematic, which will soon be rearing its head for mankind; a problem which this time arises from the opposite side, not from the burden of labour but from the burden of idleness and leisure. If the view is right which claims that, through 'technocracy', man is approaching a condition in which labour is so organised as to secure a considerable and steadily increasing amount of time for leisure, a new dynasty of technocrats will emerge, who will threaten to turn into a new despotism; and simultaneously the threat grows of increasing inactivity for the masses, with the transformation of their lives into a state of 'diversion', entertainment. The one threat is as great a spiritual danger as the other, and it is only on the spiritual level that they can be averted. The task is to educate the man who has been partially liberated from economic captivity, and who now faces the danger of spiritual repression in the wake of his liberation from the curse – which is also, though, just as much a blessing – of slavery to labour. Faced with a task like this, we may be tempted to protect ourselves by eschatological panic – the end is nigh, humanity is perishing in a universal deluge, except for those saved by the ark. Can one allow oneself such a logic of historical suicide, if it is not given us to know the time or the hour that the Father has fixed by his own authority [Acts 1.7]?

Not all these questions have already entered into our historical consciousness; but a growing restlessness and a new kind of questioning are emerging in contemporary humanity. *Es irrt der Mensch, solang er strebt*: 'man goes astray as long as he still strives'. But the Spirit of God living in the Church proclaims what is to come, and directs the Church towards that truth. It can only be sought for, as the Kingdom of God can only be sought for. But it is to this longed-for and sought-after social legacy – and also to all other human struggles towards justice – that the Lord's words apply: 'Seek and you will find; knock, and it will be opened to you' [Mt 7.7].

6

Social Teaching in Modern Russian Orthodox Theology (1934) and 'The Spirit of Prophecy' (1939)

INTRODUCTION

The Hale Memorial Sermon and the paper on prophecy[1] reproduced in this final section are at first sight very different documents. I have put them together here as examples of how Bulgakov addressed audiences that were neither Orthodox nor 'specialist' – but also because they put in very direct terms something of his vision of what Christian action within history meant. Both affirm in relatively simple terms the need for Christianity to recognise its continuing locatedness in history, while discerning and speaking what the prophecy paper calls the 'inner content' of history.

The Hale Sermon follows on very naturally from the preceding piece in this collection, especially in its (typical) candour

---

[1] 'The Spirit of Prophecy', published in *Sobornost'*, n. s., 19 (1939), pp. 3–7, is a digest of a paper Bulgakov was to have delivered to the Conference of the Fellowship of St Alban and St Sergius in 1939 (his health did not permit him to attend). His involvement with the Fellowship was arguably his most important single ecumenical contact; he was a regular speaker at its conferences and contributor to its journal, *Sobornost'*. He and Florovsky were for years the dominant Orthodox presences, exerting very differing kinds of influence. In 1933, Bulgakov proposed at a Fellowship Conference that intercommunion between Anglicans and Orthodox should be allowed on certain occasions and under carefully regulated conditions (see his article 'By Jacob's Well' in the *Journal of the Fellowship of St Alban and St Sergius*, 22 (1933), pp. 7–17). Florovsky denied vehemently that anyone had the right to absolve someone from the sin of schism to communicate on a single occasion and then return to schismatic worship. See Blane, *Georges Florovsky*, p. 65.

about the historical failures of the Church, not least the Eastern Church, in developing a vital theology of social transformation. It is notable that Bulgakov is singularly unembarrassed about admitting past deficiencies in Orthodox thinking; profoundly attached as he is to patristic and liturgical tradition, he clearly does not have to argue that all truth is already given there.[2] As in the earlier essay, his analysis focuses on the fact that in the wake of the collapse of organic-patriarchal society the Church finds itself strangely ill-equipped to combat the new mixture of collectivism and individualism. And because individualist ethics cannot cope with the new social forms of modernity, society is secularised.

Bulgakov's reference to Augustine as the ideologue of clericalism is odd (and he ascribes to Augustine the very un-Augustinian expression *civitas diabolica* for the profane world):[3] the blend of scepticism, interiority and pragmatism that characterises much of Bulgakov's own social vision is, in fact, very similar to the Augustine of the *City of God*. But Augustine is here little more than a cipher for what Bulgakov most dislikes in Roman Catholicism, the tendency to seek for ecclesiastical domination of the social order, contrasted with Protestantism's passive acceptance of a corner within the secular and pluralist marketplace. Orthodoxy has to do better than either, but it will do so only if it recovers its sense of the Church as the hidden energy of the world itself – and here Sophia is explicitly invoked, this time in close connection with the gift of the transforming spirit, manifest in prophecy as well as in the sacraments: i.e. presumably, in the discernment of tasks to be performed, the reading of the present world in terms of divine vocation. The Church must, again, transform from within; but the theological ground of that transformation is the most urgent task for a contemporary theology – a new doctrinal perspective, a new grasp of the meaning of the incarnation. Fyodorov is cited as a source for this new perspective, and the language of

---

[2] Likewise, he is surprisingly critical in *Uteshitel'* (see especially pp. 62–3) of what he describes as the relative underdevelopment of detailed theological work on the role of the Spirit in the Greek Fathers and the subsequent Eastern tradition.

[3] This antithesis is also found in 'Dusha sotsializma', though not ascribed to Augustine.

'Godmanhood' is proposed as the vehicle for expressing Christian hope. But also, congruently with Bulgakov's continuing work at this period on his treatise on the doctrine of the Holy Spirit, the concluding emphasis is on prophecy, conceived as a *social* fact – the concrete anticipation of God's future within the historical life of the Church.[4]

The short meditation on prophecy from 1939 spells out further what this may mean – particularly, and movingly, with reference to Bulgakov's recent experience of a near-fatal cancer. The approach to death is a 'prophetic' moment because it brings us closer to personal encounter with God; and it is in and from that relation that we learn the mystery of Pentecost – becoming open to new life, the active eros of the spirit towards God's fullness. Seen in this light, prophecy is something like the transparency of human speech and action to the divine, experienced as yearning and promise; and as such it is also the foundation of the theological enterprise, not as a means of acquiring new 'information' but as part of the whole process of being transformed by the reality revealed in the common life of Christ's Body. It is an appropriate coda to the whole of Bulgakov's own project.

Two major operations deprived him of his vocal cords, though he learned to celebrate the Liturgy in a whisper, and even to deliver lectures.[5] In 1944, however, he suffered a stroke on the night of the Monday after Pentecost (the liturgical anniversary of his priesting). He died forty days later, on 12 July. His friends and family kept continuous vigil at his bedside through a period of what was evidently great physical and mental pain for Bulgakov. On the fifth day of his illness, three witnesses report a transfiguration of his face like that described in the well-known testimony of Nikolai Motovilov concerning St Seraphim of Sarov;[6] other visitors confirmed this on several occasions in the weeks following. The transformation from

[4] Cf. *Uteshitel'* (*The Comforter*, Paris, 1936), pp. 327–38 on this concrete and social understanding of prophecy.
[5] For this and the information in the remainder of the paragraph, see 'The Final Days of Father Sergius Bulgakov: A Memoir by Sister Joanna Reitlinger', in *Sergius Bulgakov: Apocatastasis and Transfiguration*, ed. and trans. Boris Jakim (New Haven, 1995), pp. 31–53.
[6] Of which Bulgakov had first written in *Svet nevechernii* (*The Unfading Light*, Moscow, 1917), pp. 252–3.

within, of which he had written so often and so eloquently, the material world becoming translucent to the beauty of God's Wisdom, had never, for him, been just a theory.

Social Teaching in Modern Russian Orthodox Theology

The social question is now high on the spiritual horizon. It cannot be avoided – either in our thoughts or in our discussions. But it was not so from the beginning, in the primitive Church. We observe there rather a kind of social indifferentism and absence of attention to the social structure. In spite of evident sympathy with the destinies of the poor and their sufferings, we find here the preaching of humility and reconciliation, even with the bitter life of slaves,* and no question arises about social reorganisation. The Jerusalem community gave for all times an example of common life in love and in faith, but this practice has never been generalised as a doctrine. Labour was recognised in its dignity and still more in its ascetic significance, but we do not find any definite conclusion about the particular vocation and significance of the working class as the proletariat; for the Church recognised no difference of position 'neither slave nor free', only the soul in its relation to God. The chief reason for this indifference was that the primitive Church did not believe in the continuing existence of the world. On the contrary they were certain of the nearness of the end, of the Second Advent and did not realise that ahead would lie a very long, indefinitely long, history. It did not seem worth while to care about this world and its activities, because this world was soon to pass away. Social relationships were understood only from the individual point of view, as personal behaviour involving mercy and philanthropy. The primitive Church possessed a secret of

---

* 'Servants, be obedient unto them that are your masters according to the flesh, with fear and trembling, in singleness of your heart, as unto Christ ... as the servants of Christ doing the will of God from the heart' (Eph. 6. 5–6). And to masters is said, 'And ye masters, do the same things unto them, and forbear threatening: know that both their Master and yours is in heaven, and there is no respect of persons with him' (Eph. 6.9).

freedom from the world and all its activity, and particularly neglected the whole domain of economic and social life. In this respect it was eschatologically passive, conservative, quietistic. She despised wealth and ignored it, or even blessed poverty. Nevertheless, after two centuries Clement of Alexandria had to put the tempting question: *Quis dives salvetur?* And his first answer to it was not in the negative.

THE BYZANTINE CHURCH

The same tendency of ascetic neglect of the world is followed by the Fathers of the Church. The existence of the world and its continuance became obvious as a matter of fact. From the moment when the Emperor Constantine recognised the Church, the Church recognised in her turn the world and its activities, and gave her blessing to them; even more, she took responsibility for the world; the pagan state became a Christian one, although but slightly changed in its external worldliness and paganism. Christian morality and even canon law were recognised as leading principles in the whole life of the state, and even more, the Church in consecrating the Emperor for his throne proclaimed him the representative of God on earth in regard to the kingly ministry of Christ. The whole life of the world was recognised not only as having the right of existence but even as being sanctified by the Church. This tendency was quite opposite to the position of the primitive Church; this recognition was made too hastily and the change of mind was too superficial. Indeed, the state, as well as the whole of life, in a significant degree remained pagan, being only somewhat covered by the Christian garment; and the double moral standard received practical approbation as being in accord with both Christianity and the pagan world. The more scrupulous souls naturally were unable to agree with such double-entry bookkeeping. They preferred to preach the morality of radical asceticism, again denying the value of the world. This revival of primitive Christianity found expression in monasticism, which was in dialectic antithesis to the secularised Christianity of the age. This refutation of the world resulted in a freedom from the problems of the world and from any accommodation to it in questions relating to the social life. We find in the great Fathers of the Eastern as well as of the Western Churches, in St Basil the Great and St John Chrysostom, in St Augustine and Lactantius and others, very daring and radical convictions about the rich in their attitude to the poor, about private property, and so on. They preached a complete renunciation of property and complete equality, a community of life – but only for monks. The social problem remained an individualistic one, and was considered in the context of personal salvation.

The same problems and the same doctrine and practice were inherited by the Church both in the West and in the East during the centuries of the Middle Ages and even in the later period, particularly in Russia. After the fall of the Byzantine Empire, Russia considered herself its heir and the true centre of Orthodoxy. Russia became the Holy Empire and even the Third Rome. There were historical differences between Russia and Byzantium, but no differences in doctrine. Byzantium and Russia constitute a single epoch in the history of the Orthodox Church, the epoch of Constantine the Great. This epoch concluded with the Russian Revolution, and we are now at the beginning of a new epoch.

Development of Christian Sociology

It is to be noted that the Orthodox countries have belonged to the backward and stagnant parts of the world in the economic sense. They were principally agricultural countries with feebly developed industrial life. Natural and domestic economy prevailed. The slavery of the first centuries of our era gradually disappeared, partly through the influence of Christianity, but was followed by serfdom, which was severe enough even though mitigated by personal relations and customs, such as were described by Carlyle in *Past and Present* and by the Russian writers Turgenev and Tolstoy. Yet even in this torpid existence doubts arose about the justice and value of such a tenor of life, which seemed to be unchangeable. The attitude of the Church was ascetical and conservative, following the commandment of St Paul: 'Let every man abide in the same calling wherein he was called' (I Cor. 7.20), so that he might be a good slave for the sake of God, or a good lord for the sake of God. Peace and quietness of soul were esteemed more highly than any economic striving. It is quite characteristic that one of the most renowned bishops of the Russian Church in the first half of the nineteenth century was not favourable to the emancipation of peasants, although he later became the author of the text of the Tsar's manifesto granting such emancipation.

The asceticism of the first ages of Christianity has been the prevailing and even chief factor determining Christian social doctrine, or what we may call Christian sociology. Poor people have to endure their destinies for the sake of God and the rich people have a responsibility to use their wealth according to the teaching in the Parable of the Rich Man and Lazarus. Reconciliation with the existing social order, sometimes even of a worse kind, was a natural consequence of such a world-view; the communist hatred of religion which finds its expression in the phrase, 'Religion is the opiate of the people', is a practical sequel to this quietism, this social nihilism. Asceticism was of course a very great spiritual force which helped to stand the test of destiny, and it displayed great energy.

The early epoch of European history is under deep obligation to the moral force of asceticism for its potent strivings, expressed for example in the colonisation of new territories and in the first steps of industrial development (the original accumulation of capital, as described by Karl Marx). But as an unexpected result of these strivings and successes, the new economic and social world was developing its own force in quite opposite directions. We observe here an example of the dialectic of history which moves by contradictions: the ascetic denial of wealth leads to its accumulation. The simple and transparent structure of the natural household was changed into the complicated system of the national and international economies of capitalistic society, which in recent times has already become a partly socialistic society. A new world has arisen, a new organisation of life, in which every man feels himself to be only an insignificant part of the whole, a little screw in the big machine. Life is actually being socialised more and more. This aspect of life, which forced itself into the consciousness of all, became a subject of scientific observation, and the existence of the social organism, of the collective being, was put beyond doubt by social science and statistics. The dogmatic idea of the real unity of mankind in the one Adam, the old and the new, received unexpected confirmation from this conception. Social life was to be understood not only as an aggregate of personal acts but as a social organisation that was not sufficiently explained and exhausted by personal relations alone. These problems of social humanity were not to be fully comprehended by individualistic morality. It was obviously not sufficient for the new needs which simply had not been noticed or embraced by it. The individualistic point of view became not so much obsolete as insufficient for guidance in social life, which thus found itself beyond the conceptions of Church leadership, became secularised. The secularisation of life became a practical and unavoidable conclusion of such a state of things. The nature of spirit is that it does not sustain emptiness, and the vacuum created by absence of social leadership on the part of Christianity was filled in by a new paganism or by atheistic humanism.

Social life became paganised, and even this fact of paganisation itself put a new question before Christian doctrine, like the riddle of the Sphinx: Solve me or I shall devour you. Personal, individualistic Christianity remains in any case a necessary side of Christian doctrine and life inasmuch as Christianity is a religion of salvation which is a personal adoption of the redemption given by Christ, our Saviour and Lord. This redemption is given by Christ as the High Priest who gave himself as a sacrifice for the remission of sins. Each Christian soul has its own personal relation to Christ by the adoption of this forgiveness, its own way in the fight against sin. Each separate personality is a single reality from the point of view of redemption. But the question arises whether the whole reality of human life is exhausted by these separate personalities or whether there exists in addition humanity as a whole, as an organism? How are we to understand the life and history of the world and of mankind in this sense?

The Roman Catholic Church has answered by the doctrine of St Augustine about *Civitas Dei*, which is the Church as an organisation, and *Civitas diabolica*, the whole profane world, which has to be in obedience to the Church. According to this view, the world is to be clericalised, and this clericalisation is the only social form of Christianity. Protestantism neutralised the very question by its decisive separation of personal religious life from the life of the world. It recognised the right of existence for secular civilisation parallel with the Church, as two right but absolutely different ways. It reconciled itself with the separation of the Church from life – the state, culture and economics being included in the latter. But neither Roman obedience to the Pope nor Protestant compromise and reconciliation with paganism can settle the question and show the right way to the general salvation of mankind and of the world, God's creation. The Orthodox Church has preserved as an outstanding characteristic the asceticism of the primitive Church, supplemented partly by the conception of the Holy Empire. It may be said in a certain sense that the idea of social Christianity was included in this conception although not sufficiently explained. Here it is to be noted that this question became a central one for Russian religious thought in the nineteenth and twentieth centuries, and is now being seriously dealt with by our forward-looking theologians and philosophers. It is one of the chief problems in our studies. These doctrines are not yet formulated and recognised as dogmatic definitions or even as authoritative theological opinions (*theologoumena*). They are merely private opinions but yet are very significant.

Sociological Aspect of The Doctrine of The Church

The starting point for consideration of the problem is the doctrine of the Church. Is the Church merely a society or institution, having its beginning in time and place, consisting of different members, of the hierarchy and people, particularised by the sacraments? Or is it more than an institution, does it have its own eternal existence, existing in a certain sense before the creation of the world as its inward reason and purpose, its *entelecheia*? The existence of the Church in the world and history must be understood in the light of this leading idea. The Church is both created and uncreated, has its temporal and its eternal sides. In the latter sense she belongs to the life of the

Holy Trinity itself, and the creation of the world and of man is first of all the revelation of this pre-existing eternal principle. The Holy Trinity has one nature (*ousia*), one life, one self-revelation, which is achieved through three Persons, according to the personal properties of each of them, but in spite of this trinitarian character it is one. This self-revelation of God is not only a 'quality', it is an absolutely objective principle, divinity itself, which belongs to the Holy Triunity. That nature is not a fourth person, because it is not a person of God, but his divinity, God's revealed nature, his Wisdom and Glory, his own life, his own image. This Wisdom belongs to the Holy Trinity, is the content of its life, the eternal, divine and not created world in God himself. It is the ideal, divine principle of the creation of the world, which is created according to *paradeigmata* or *proorismoi*, to use the words of the Holy Fathers, or the ideas of Plato. God in the creation of the world has revealed his own Wisdom and reflected his own image given to it. Where is the fullness of this image concentrated? It is in man, who is created by God according to his own image and likeness. Man is not only the head of the whole world to whom the power in it is given by the creator himself, but he is the real centre of it, the microcosm, the world conceived as a unity, and he thus embraces the life of the world in himself. The Greek Fathers have called man 'a created god', 'a god by grace'. In him and through him God's image is to be realised in the world.

Man as having God's image is godlike, and God as having his image in man is manlike. There exists a positive relation between God and man, which may be defined as Godmanhood. This is the image of God in God himself or his Holy Wisdom (*Sophia*).

> The Lord possessed me in the beginning of his way,
>   Before his works of old.
> I was set up from everlasting, from the beginning.
>   Before the earth was.
> When there were no depths, I was brought forth,
>   When there were no fountains abounding with water,
>   Before the mountains were settled,
> Before the hills was I brought forth;
>   While as yet he had not made the earth, nor the fields,

> Nor the beginning of the dust of the world.
> When he established the heavens, I was there:
>> When he set a circle upon the face of the deep,
>> When he made firm the skies above,
>> When the fountains of the deep became strong,
>> When he gave to the sea its bound,
>> That the water should not transgress his commandment,
>> When he marked out the foundations of the earth;
> Then I was by him, as a master workman;
> And I was daily his delight,
>> Rejoicing always before him,
>> Rejoicing in his habitable earth;
> And my delight was with the sons of men.
>
> – Prov. 8.22–31.

This Wisdom has two kinds of revelation, being in God as his divine life and glory, and being the ground of the creation in man and through him in the world. This Wisdom which is, as we have said, the Godmanhood, is the true foundation for the incarnation of the Logos. Jesus Christ united two natures, divine and human, in his own person, not as two alien natures but as two kinds of existence of the same wisdom of God, of the uncreated and the created one. He is the true God-man, and manhood has its complete achievement in his holy humanity. This humanity was overshadowed by the Holy Spirit. The plenitude of the idea, the principles, of the world, its *logos*, was achieved through the plenitude of life in the Holy Spirit. The body of Christ became the temple of the Holy Spirit, which is the Church. The incarnation as well as Pentecost must be understood not only in the light of the redemption, as the restoration of fallen man and his salvation from original sin, but as the complete achievement of creation as well. Creation was raised to its perfection in the Godmanhood, and the realisation of this Godmanhood is the Church in the world.

The idea of the Church in this sense is applied to the whole world as its real foundation and aim, its *entelecheia*. The Church receives social, historical and even cosmic significance. Christ vanquished the world, which has, because of this, become his Church; the Holy Ghost descended upon this world in Pentecost and since then has remained in the world. The task of the Church includes not only ways of personal salvation but of the transfiguration of the world, it includes the whole history of mankind, which is the history of the Church. Pentecost, though accomplished as an historical event, is continued in the life of the Church, not only in the sacramental, mystical life, but in the prophetic spirit, as a call to new activity, to new tasks, to new achievements. And the general task for achievement is the realisation of the true Godmanhood, the appearance of the Church in her glory as of the wife clothed with the sun, as the bride who hath made herself ready for the marriage of the Lamb of God. The Apocalypse thus leads into eschatology, the fulness of history presumes its achievement. The mystical process is Godmanlike, it includes not only the action of God over man, but human action as well.

CREATIVE CHARACTER OF CHRISTIANITY

This general idea covering the apocalyptic and cosmic aspect of the Church involves necessarily the creative and social characteristics of Christianity. It includes not only personal ascetic and spiritual life, but also creativity in the world and in human society. The world belongs to man, who is its head; this basic principle is not altered, whether by original sin or by salvation from it through Jesus Christ. In a certain sense, in the incarnation of Christ the world itself became the body of Christ. It is glorified and transfigured in Christ through the Holy Ghost in his own life, but this life contains in itself the whole of humanity, which is to be glorified and transfigured. Here we find an analogy with personal salvation, which is given and accomplished through the sacrifice of Christ, yet has to be adopted by personal ascetic effort. And the salvation or the transfiguration of the world which is already achieved by Jesus Christ through the Holy Ghost has now to be accomplished from the human side by the sons of God. The road to salvation, and in this sense to the end of the world, must now be trod also by mankind, by the sons of God. The end of the world in this sense is not only the inscrutable will of God which is known neither to angels nor even to the Son of Man, but it is an end to be prepared and reached by human history as well. We may express this idea in the term 'Christian humanism', which is the opposite of the godless humanism of modern times. All these human creative efforts must be made in the name of Jesus Christ; being inspired by the Holy Ghost, Pentecost is continued.

Christian humanism, which presumes the development of all creative capacities of man, may be understood as a new comprehension, a new revelation of Christianity. It is no new Christianity, it is only its new comprehension. The various new dogmatic definitions given by the Church from time to time have been new comprehensions of the same Christianity. They were accepted as true answers to questions raised by the leaders of heresy. For instance, Arianism was such a question, and the Nicene Creed was the answer of the church. And now, false, atheistic humanism is a question put to the Church, and Christian humanism would be an answer. The leading idea of this creative apprehension of Christianity is that there exists in history, to use the expression of the Russian philosopher Fyodorov, a 'common work' for human brotherhood. This common work or task has no exterior limits, it embraces the whole world, it involves the overcoming of the blind forces of nature and the accommodation of them to human will and tasks as well as the appeasing of elementary social forces. Social life is to be organised according to the postulates of Christian love; so also the whole of political life. At present we have not only the separation of the church from the state – which means the freedom of the Church and is even favourable for her life – but the general secularisation of life, its paganisation. To meet this situation we must seek for a state of things in which the Church may penetrate as with inward power the whole of human life. The separation of the Church from life must at last be overcome, and all sides of the natural existence of men – certainly all except sin – are to be included in the grace-abounding life of the Church. This postulate of social Christianity or of Christian humanism is a new dogmatic generalisation or a new explanation of the incarnation. It is the general principle of the social philosophy which must be developed and applied to different sides of life.

The developing of this postulate I believe to be the chief outreach of modern Russian theological thought. As a doctrine it is not yet sufficiently developed, it is rather a dogmatic postulate than a completed programme of life, more prophecy than actuality. But it opens a new way for Christian life and for Christian history. It gives to it not only a negative but a positive sense, it includes the creativity of man in the means of his salvation. It does not deny Christian freedom from the world and the value of a spiritually ascetic way, or the fight against sin in the life of every man, but it calls all to work also for this world. It does not teach us to love this passing world, which is destined for the fire, but to love this world as the creation of God, who himself loves it. Particularly this Christian humanism contains the dream of all Christian youth, prophetically realised in the life of the community in Jerusalem, when all lived together in love and had all in common. This life of the Christian family, which has been called a Christian 'communism' or 'socialism', remains a guiding star on our horizon. The Christian life cannot be limited to an individualistic life; it is common or social, yet not violating the principle of Christian freedom. It must be unity in freedom and love. The glorified body of the Risen Christ was transparent for the spirit, was a spiritual body, being at the same time no spirit but a body which could be touched, and this transparence was its glorification and beauty.

The same ideal of the transfiguration of the inert and dark matter of the world, its obedience and transparence for the spirit of man, is the final task of the creativity of man, who is called by God to have dominion over the world. The world must become in this sense the subject of the art of man, who is the true artist. How may we define this greatest task of the participation of man in the work of God, who himself has called man to this participation? It is obvious that such last things are not to be defined other than symbolically.

Modern Russian Thought

We have a representative of our Russian religious thought who ventured to put the question, to give a name to the new spiritual birth. This was the Russian philosopher Fyodorov, who died in 1903. His chief writing is entitled *The Philosophy of Common*

Work and this common work or social Christianity is the centre of his doctrine.* Christianity must not be passive but active, and this activity has as its object the whole world, and its content is the regulation of nature, its subordination to man. Man has to do all that is given to him to do. Even his own body is to be made by human effort, earned by labour, for this is God's will for man. This dominion over nature must be achieved not for the luxury of a small part of society, which presupposes the poverty and exploitation of others, but for the common life of the whole of society. Mankind is a family which is connected by the relations of parentage. All are fathers or sons, brother or sisters, and we are all obligated for our very life to our own parents. All men are subject to the last and common enemy, to death, which was not created by God. And all have as their religious duty to fight against death, being helped by the Son of Man, who is the beloved Son of God, by Christ. All have to look for the resurrection of their fathers for the sake of love. Man has a call and a duty, the chief duty of children to their fathers, to share in their resurrection. This resurrection will take place in any case, according to Christ's promise. If men do not accomplish this duty to their fathers, they will be raised from the dead by God, but that will be rather the resurrection of wrath. This idea is the generalisation of all individual efforts, the last all-embracing aim of the regulation of nature. Of course this idea is ambiguous and its ambiguity is even dangerous. It may be understood in an atheistic and materialistic sense, and it was already so understood, particularly by some communists. It may become a fortress of atheism. But that would be a bad perversion of Fyodorov's philosophy. His true meaning was that this task of men has to be accomplished by man helped by

---

* Since the middle of the fourteenth century these ideas have been expressed in various ways, notably by the Slavophils, Khomyakov and Kireevsky, by the Archimandrite Fyodor Bukharev, by such well-known writers as Gogol and Dostoevsky, by the philosopher Vladimir Soloviev, by members of the so-called 'religious-philosophical societies' in Petrograd, Moscow and Kiev, in the works of present-day Russian thinkers, the Revd Pavel Florensky, N. Berdyaev, V. Zenkovsky and other professors of the Russian Orthodox Theological Academy in Paris. The outstanding work of N. F. Fyodorov, *The Philosophy of Common Work*, 2 vols., has appeared in two Russian editions (Moscow and Harbin). Of my own works the most important in this connection is *The Lamb of God* – or *On the Divine Humanity, Part I* (Paris, 1933; in Russian).

Christ and in his name, according to his will, by the true children of God, by the human family, in common parentage.

This task obviously presumes the change of the whole economic, social and industrial organisation of society. Instead of pleasing luxury, production becomes a serious and responsible way of laborious preservation and reconstruction of life, the common work of the whole of mankind. This main idea is developed by Fyodorov in many special points of religious and social philosophy. But the centre of the whole doctrine is the idea that Christianity must be social, must become common work. Fyodorov has few followers who share all his extremist views, but his philosophy is characteristic of tendencies in Russian thought. There exist at present two opposite streams of thought: atheistic humanism, which has its complete expression in materialistic socialism, particularly communism; and Christian humanism, which is of course more postulate and prophecy than the reality of contemporary Christianity.

Godmanhood

This series of ideas may be included and theologically explained in a still more general context, e.g. in connection with Christology and the doctrine of the Holy Spirit. There is a theological doctrine about the kingly ministry of Christ. What does this mean in its true sense? Is it already accomplished, as are his prophetic and high-priestly ministry? Or is it still continued in history, till the time when all things are subdued under his feet? 'Then shall the Son also himself be subject unto him ... that God may be all in all' (I Cor. 15.28). This subjection is to be accomplished by Christ as the God-man, that is, not only by his divinity but by his humanity as well, in their unity. Furthermore, the whole of mankind must participate in him and with him in this fight against his enemies and in his glorious victory. The Kingdom of Christ has to be won by common work, the creative effort of mankind as well as the creative work of God. Such is the true content of history as the revelation of Christ. The prophetic vision of this history, 'of things which must shortly come to pass' (Rev. 1.1), is given us in the Apocalypse. History as the Apocalypse must be understood as the way to the end or to the Second Advent of Christ. This end and this advent are not only the actions of God beyond the world, they are events in the life of the world. They prepare and in a certain sense they include the synthesis of history, its achievement. The common work of humanity finds in them its highest justification; as a movement toward the coming Christ, such is its inner content. 'And the Spirit and the Bride say, "Come". And let him that heareth say, "Come"' (Rev. 22.17). Social Christianity being understood apocalyptically leads to the eschatological end of this world and to its transfiguration into the new heaven and the new earth, to the heavenly Jerusalem, the Holy City, descending from heaven.

This ideology is not only a philosophy or science; it is a prophecy as well. The prophetic spirit is necessarily included in the Christian world-view. It was given to the Church in Pentecost, which was not only an event in history, but is continued in the life of the Church. It was promised then that 'your sons and your daughters shall prophesy, and your young men shall see visions, and your old men shall dream dreams' (Acts 2.17). This inspiration is given to the Church, and is the call to the Future. According to the promise of our Saviour, the Comforter 'will show you things to come' – *ta erchomena* (Jn 16.13). We are now standing before and participating in the great tragedy of history, the struggle of Antichrist, of anti-Christian forces against Christ. Through this tragedy and in it we have to reach complete historical ripeness and wisdom, to develop all kinds of human creativity, to discriminate definitely two poles of good and evil. The Christian Church has two sides, the eternal life and life in time. Yet this time is not an empty passage into eternity but is the Church's development and completion. It has necessarily its eternal content and its historical future so long as time exists, until the angel declares 'there shall be time no longer' (Rev. 10.6). This prophetic Future does not exist for personal and individualistic Christianity, but only for social Christianity, for the Church. Life in the Church always combines time and eternity, which are somehow practically identified in the soul of man.

The Spirit of Prophecy

I have been asked to give a brief summary of the main points of my paper. I can only do it in a most imperfect way. My chief contention is that prophecy is an act of religious life, a *personal* meeting with God, which does, may and ought to take place in the life of *everyone*, according to one's measure and capacity. For as Moses said to Israel, 'Would God that all the Lord's people were prophets, and that the Lord would put his spirit upon them!' (Num. 11.29).

Our life calls for a prophetic response to it. We may heed its call or not. It may ask great things of us or small, as the case may be. God calls his elect to receive his great revelation and declare his will, but it is given to those little ones too to feel the touch of his hand.

If I were capable of it at the present moment, my first task on returning to your midst would be to tell you of what I have lived through and what has been revealed to me during the terrible, and at the same time wonderful, days of my illness, on the brink of death. God in his mercy has brought me back to life in this world and given me new opportunities of meeting my brethren. To make my experiences a part of my life and thought, to declare unto others what God has shown me, will be a hard and responsible task for me in days to come. Such a task inevitably is one of the forms of prophetic revelation about life, whatever its content, and however powerless my stumbling words may be. Every one of us inevitably has to follow his own path to a prophetic revelation about life and death. Everyone is sooner or later bidden to receive the last revelation about death, and to meet his God – whether it be at the very end or in the pathways of life. I should like to tell you of the feeling of life and death opening out on either side of the dividing line between them – but that is unutterable.

But even on this side of the line, in our earthly life, we have sufficient evidence that man does meet God and hear his voice, and this is the basis of prophecy. Revelation itself tells us that this is so. Leaving aside the Old Testament I will confine myself to the New. In the New Testament, prophecy is not a general gift bestowed through the laying on of the apostles' hands. Like other gifts, it is something special, possessed by certain persons and not by others. 'Are all apostles? Are all prophets? Are all teachers?' (I Cor. 12.29). 'He gave some apostles; and some prophets, and some evangelists; and some pastors and teachers' (Heb. 4.11). Prophetic ministry is set apart as relating to the knowledge of the future (for instance Acts 11.28, 21.4, 11), especially to the *revelation* of 'things that must shortly come to pass' (Rev. 1.1), and also to special courage in preaching (e.g. turning to preach to the Gentiles in Acts 3.46), or in probing and inquiring as St Paul did, about the fate of Israel (Rom. 9.11). But alongside this special prophetic ministry Holy Writ mentions universal prophesying, concerning which it is said: 'Desire spiritual gifts, but rather that you may prophesy' (I Cor. 14.1; cp. v. 39). St Paul foresees the eventuality of all prophesying (v. 24) and says, 'Ye may all prophesy one by one, that all may learn, and all may be comforted' (v. 31).

Prophesying is thus made as it were a part of Church services, in the same way as the sermon of modern times, though evidently it is not connected with any special consecration but is a general charismatic gift in all its power and at the same time in all its vagueness. That gift is the power of Pentecost, according to the interpretation given by St Peter to the prophecy of Joel: 'And it shall come to pass in the last days I will pour out of my Spirit upon all flesh: and your sons and daughters shall prophesy and your young men shall see visions, and your old men shall dream dreams. And on my servants and on my handmaidens I will pour out in those days of my Spirit and they shall prophesy' (Acts 2.17–18; Joel 2.28–9). (The words of Moses quoted above – Num. 11.29 – may also be recalled in this connection.)

According to this text the gift of prophecy contains the very *power* of Pentecost. The reference is not to the particular gift of prophetic ministry alongside other gifts and ministries, but to the universal and essential gift of Pentecost. Those who received that gift appeared to the outsiders to be beside themselves or possessed: 'These men are full of new wine' (Acts 2.13). The gift of prophecy makes a man as it were a stranger to himself, living a life not his own and yet experiencing that life as though it were his own. It is both going out of oneself, being beside oneself, ecstasy, and receiving into oneself a new principle of life. In other words, prophecy is the *meeting* and the union of the human spirit with another principle, the divine. (There may also be false prophecy, or the meeting with the spirit of delusion, but anyway it is a meeting.)

Prophesying is therefore an *active* state of the spirit in which it reaches forward to meet a higher principle, so that it may identify itself with it and be fertilised by it. In this sense, it is the highest creative state of the spirit. It is what we call *inspiration*, its joy and delight. In the words of Pushkin, 'Without the divine, without inspiration life is sad and empty'. The subject or content of prophecy has no decisive significance for its nature; the Old Testament prophets prophesied about various matters. What is essential to prophecy is a creative and inspired attitude to life, a realisation of life's tasks and possibilities, spiritual activity and the recognition that the historical process is creative. The gift of prophecy as a Pentecostal gift means that the Christian man makes history through prophetic inspiration and is responsible for it. According to this interpretation, Pentecost is the universal consecration to prophecy for which everyone receives his special gift in the sacrament of confirmation – 'the seal of the gift of the Holy Spirit' – and in this sense no-one in the Church is deprived of the gracious gift. The gifts may differ but the prophetic spirit in them remains unchanged as a special *quality* of those gifts. And it is precisely in this *qualitative* sense that St Paul says: 'There are diversities of gifts but the same Spirit. And there are differences of administrations but the same Lord. And there are diversities of operations but it is the same God which worketh all in all' (I Cor. 12.4–6). In explanation of this general thought the apostle goes on to enumerate the different gifts: 'The manifestation of the Spirit is given to every man to profit withal; for to one is given by the Spirit the word of wisdom (philosophy), to another the word of knowledge (science) by the same Spirit; to another faith by the same Spirit; to another the gifts of healing by the same Spirit; to another the working of miracles; to another prophecy; to another discerning of spirits; to another diverse kinds of tongues; to another the interpretation of tongues; but all these worketh that one and the selfsame Spirit, dividing to every man severally as he will' (I Cor. 12.7–11). This passage indicates the multiplicity of the gifts of one and the same Spirit and his presence in every one of them. It is essential however to distinguish, and even to contrast, prophecy as the general gift of the Holy Spirit finding expression in the capacity to receive revelation, and prophecy as actual revelation itself. Prophecy means therefore the general spirit-bearing quality of Christian humanity after Pentecost, capable in its human inspiration as creatures to receive the gift of the Holy Spirit and be inspired by it. Human inspiration thus becomes *divinely human*. The difference of gifts indicates the many aspects of prophetic inspiration, among which prophetic ministry is singled out as a creative reaching out to the future: 'He will show you things to come' (Jn 16.3). It is the deification of the human spirit from within, through the union in it of the created and the uncreated elements. This must of course on no account be taken to mean that after Pentecost *all* human inspiration is, as a matter of course, prophetic and divinely human. Just the contrary! It is the highest and final *task* which is set before us, but at the same time the possibility of carrying it out is inwardly given us through Pentecost. In it the Holy Spirit descended upon men without depriving them of human freedom or of their own human inspiration. Prophecy in general is creativeness winged with daring and fired with inspiration. As such it is turned towards the future, not, however, apart from or without regard to the present, but *through* the present, which is pregnant with the future. Recall to what extent the thought of the Old Testament prophets is both turned towards their present environment and saturated with history; it cannot indeed be understood without a special historical commentary. It was essentially historical, but it started with a living sense of the needs and problems of their own day. In other words the true subject of prophecy is *history* understood in its inner content as *apocalypse* or even as *eschatology*, i.e., as something which lies beyond the limits of history. History as apocalypse is 'the last time', which is included in *supertime* in eschatology. That is the true object of prophetic contemplation, but the sands of time must not simply run out – there must be creative achievement.

The Spirit of Prophecy

It is of the nature of prophecy both to see into the future and to fathom divine things, to know God. Revelation about God was given through the prophets and crystallised into dogma – into doctrines about God. Dogmatic revelations were given to mankind both in the Old and in the New Testament through prophets – Moses, David, Solomon, the minor prophets, apostles and teachers, down to our own day. What is the common feature of their prophetic ministry? How is the divine truth revealed and announced to these elect of God? Are they merely a passive instrument, through which the divine words are, as it were, dictated? Or does the revelation preserve throughout its divinely human character, so that the human searching and questioning receives a divine answer: 'Seek and ye shall find'? [Mt. 7.7] Of course the last alternative is the true one. Revelation is given not to a cold heart and an unheeding intellect but to the fiery Elijah questioning God about the remnant of the righteous, to the fervent Paul tormented by the mystery of the rejection and the salvation of Israel, to the suffering Job crying before heaven of his torments. It is given to the seer Daniel, who made penitence for the sins of his people and with much lamentation questioned the Lord. If this was the case with great prophets and spiritual leaders, surely it must be the same with those little ones, even if in an immeasurably small degree? Insistent and searching thought invariably precedes the illumination of reason which contains the grain of revelation. This is prophecy as dogmatic creativeness and revelation.

But even this divine illumination of reason cannot and must not be the limit of prophetic knowledge. We are called upon to acquire a deeper and clearer understanding of the revelation that has been received in the past or given anew. In other words, prophecy includes – not for all, but for the chosen – the labour of expressing and formulating *theologically* that which has been revealed. That is to say, it also embraces theology, not so much as intellectual study but as intellectual intuition. This is how it was in Jewish theology, in the Talmud, and it remains so in our New Testament theology.

We must neither exaggerate nor belittle the prophetic element in theology. Without it theology loses its inspirational power and becomes abstract scholasticism. Of course, theology is not infallible, but even when it follows false issues it preserves its inspirational, and therefore prophetic, character. Old Testament piety knew of prophetic schools, 'a company of prophets', in union with whom a particular individual like Saul also prophesies and is 'turned into another man' (I Sam. 10.6). Are not our theological schools akin to these prophetic schools, in so far as they rise to the heights of their vocation? Should not they too seek that 'the Spirit of God should come upon them'? (I Sam. 10.10). And does not the same thing apply to the theological fellowship which at the present day takes place through various conferences so near to our hearts? Recall our liturgical fellowship, which has now become habitual to us, and is as it were taken by us for granted. Those mutual liturgical contacts during the conferences were to us like a fiery stream of unexpected revelations. And in the course of our work does not our theological fellowship prove to be a source of new inspirations, and indeed of revelations? Are not new prophetic schools arising before our eyes? They can have this character, however, on one condition only: they must breathe the spirit of inspiring quest and of believing love. To some people such communion appears doubtful and even dangerous, as a betrayal of the purity of one's own confession. They do not need *prophetic* schools but are content with self-sufficient scholasticism. But we who have breathed the air of gracious communion have need of the prophetic spirit which bloweth where it listeth. Religious experience precedes dogmatic formulation and prepares the ground for it. It calls us to a new understanding of the universal truth. It promises us not new dogmas but a new knowledge of them in which we shall be 'turned into another man', like King Saul in a company of prophets.

Appendix

Bulgakov and Anti-Semitism

One aspect of Bulgakov's thought that has attracted some attention recently is his attitude to Judaism. In 1991, a collection of his writings on 'Christianity and the Jewish Problem' was published,[1] containing extracts from published work and from private documents, and a lengthy and previously unpublished essay written in 1941–2 on 'Racism and Christianity'. The editor of this collection, Nikita Struve, had already summarised and discussed the material at a colloqium in 1988,[2] and the book was reviewed in English, by Jonathan Sutton, in 1992, in a special issue of the Keston College journal, *Religion, State and Society*,[3] mostly devoted to examining Christian–Jewish relations in the contemporary Eastern Christian context – not a very cheering theme, as a perusal of the essays will confirm. Since there is not a great deal in Bulgakov's published work to fill out his views on this, the collection has a very particular interest. Both Struve and Sutton provide a pretty benign reading of the material: Bulgakov is reacting to things that are indisputably problematic in the record of Russian Jewry; he shows great prescience in warning of the dangers of an anti-Semitic backlash among Christian Russians; he reflects a characteristically Russian interest in sketching the moral and spiritual destinies of peoples on a global or apocalyptic canvas; and so on.

There is no scope in a brief appendix to discuss in proper depth both Bulgakov's writings on this subject and the reactions of his interpreters; but it is impossible to ignore the subject. Struve and Sutton quite rightly point out the ferocity with which Bulgakov attacks the ideology of National Socialism: we

---

[1] *Khristianstvo i yevreiskii vopros* (Paris, 1991).
[2] 'S. Bulgakov et la question juive', *Le christianisme russe: entre millénarisme d'hier et soif spirituelle d'aujourd'hui* = CMRS, 29 (1988), pp. 533–42.
[3] *Religion, State and Society*, 20 (1992), pp. 61–7.

are left in no doubt that Christianity is incompatible, in his eyes, with any form of racism, any claims for natural supremacy on the part of one ethnic group. Bulgakov elaborates, in a manuscript of 1941–2 on 'Racism and Christianity', on the difference between a properly Christian account of the God-given *destinies* of the several nations and the Teutonic glorification of blood and soil, the quasi-biological distinctiveness of the Germanic races.[4] God has made 'of one blood' all nations (Acts 17.26), so that in terms of the ultimate spiritual foundations of the human race, there is a unity, which is concretely realised in the multiplicity of racial identities at the level of soul and body.[5] The Nazi doctrine of racial differentiation ignores this dimension of unity-in-multiplicity and represents a materialistic reduction of what constitutes human identity. Racial differentiation itself, Bulgakov suggests, has to be understood in relation to the biblical vision of the 'angels of the nations': and national identity is a divine thought and act, represented in the active force of the nation's guardian angel.[6] This links the whole doctrine of national identity with the themes of the sophiological vision; and Bulgakov accuses the National Socialist view of denying the feminine principle in national identity, as in the entire framework of reality. Identities constructed around the 'masculine' principles involved in the violent self-assertions of 'Germanism' are incapable of proper *mutual* relation. And in this sense, Russian Bolshevism, for all its purported internationalism, has much in common with the racist vision of Nazism, because its self-understanding is cast in terms of relentless expansionism and aggression.[7]

So far, so good: the themes are recognisable from elsewhere in Bulgakov's work, and the account of the need for plurality and mutuality, and for the overcoming of the spirit of 'masculine' self-assertion, links closely with the kenotic thrust of the sophiological scheme. But the section that follows in the 1941–2 essay, on 'Racism and Jewishness' (*yevreistvo*, incidentally, is the word consistently used for Jewish identity), moves into more dangerous waters. The assimilated Jew presents a

---

[4] *Khristianstvo i yevreiskii vopros*, pp. 38–45.
[5] Ibid., pp. 45–58, esp. pp. 56–7.
[6] Ibid., p. 58; cf. p. 43 on the identities of the nations as the 'thoughts' of God.
[7] Ibid., pp. 60–3.

cultural problem for a nation: lacking specific racial/national 'personality' (*litso*), he or she nonetheless preserves the ineradicable separateness of their race, and is therefore unwelcome in the host culture.[8] Some of the venom of anti-Semitism derives from the suspicion of a covertly hostile presence in the midst. But the whole situation is aggravated by the common refusal to consider the problem in its strictly *religious* dimension: Bulgakov here recapitulates some of what he says about the anti-Semitism of Marx, in the celebrated essay he had written many years earlier on Marx as a 'religious type' (part of which is also reprinted in the same volume on Judaism).[9] If you fail to see the question of Jewishness in religious terms, you are likely to end up, like Marx, with an ersatz eschatology, a secularised and trivialised version of religious, apocalyptic hope (again, a theme that recurs throughout Bulgakov's work). And, if this does not cash itself out in the language of Marxist internationalism, it is likely to encourage other nations to appropriate messianic rhetoric for their own self-construction.[10] At the end of the day, racism and anti-Semitism in particular are simply 'sublimated envy towards Judaism' – but an envy that results in the assimilation of the negative, not the positive, aspects of Jewishness.[11]

This is a nuanced but faintly disturbing position. The analysis, here as elsewhere, of the pseudo-religious character of radical political eschatologies is shrewd, as is the diagnosis of anti-Semitism as envy, and perhaps also resentment at the pre-emptive act of God in the election of a people: such designation as chosen or privileged must, in the framework of philosophical modernity, come from the human world alone. There is a good deal to ponder in this, not least the implication that without a religious account of national vocation, the way lies open to secularist messianisms that recognise no prescribed limits, and so slip into aggression and endemic conflict. But there is already a hint of that familiar strategy deployed against the dispossessed in all sorts of contexts that has been called 'blaming the victim'. The assimilated Jew is somehow responsible for those feelings

[8] Ibid., pp. 72ff.
[9] Ibid., pp. 165–8.
[10] Ibid., p. 81.
[11] Ibid., p. 83.

that provoke pogroms – even though such reaction is wholly deplorable from a Christian point of view; and it is Jewish messianism that generates its own persecutors, by providing the rhetoric for its enemies (fascist or Bolshevist). Bulgakov nowhere raises the question of whether Christian language *itself* contributes to the 'Jewish problem'. And this becomes painfully problematic in the last sections of the essay under review.

Russia and Germany are characterised as psychological antitypes: Russia is 'feminine', Germany 'masculine': that is, Germany is essentially (as we should say) 'proactive', Russia 'reactive', receptive, non-exclusive.[12] But this in turn implies that Russian Bolshevism is an alien importation, a Germanic distortion of what is properly Russian. Bulgakov is able to make some pungent and, in retrospect, accurate comments about the spiritual kinship between the Soviet state and the Third Reich. But the further connection follows, between Germanism and *yevreistvo*, Jewishness: Bolshevism is rooted in secularised Jewishness, both ideologically and as a matter of sociological fact, and this is the great 'sin' of *yevreistvo* against the true and sacred Israel, the real Jewish vocation.[13] There is a tragic distortion of the creativity and initiative of Israel into the violence of Soviet communism. But Russia needs Israel for the fulfilment of its own destiny, needs the properly masculine or voluntarist dimension that Israel offers. Russia thus has an interest in the *integrity* of religious Jewishness – though looking always to the conversion of Israel as the condition of this crucial symbiosis. Meanwhile, the involvement of Jews in the Bolshevist devastation of Russia can be described as a 'pogrom', for which corporate Jewish repentance is called.[14] The most tragic outcome would be if the history of Jewish 'persecution' of Holy Russia provoked a further and still bloodier reaction against the Jews (it is this that Struve considers uncomfortably prophetic).[15] But the possibilities are there for a 'new and creative epoch in history' if Russia and Israel can find how to live together: no other people is destined for religious creativity to the degree that Russia is, yet Israel remains the sole chosen race. In their

[12] Ibid., pp. 110ff.
[13] Ibid., p. 121.
[14] Ibid., pp. 136–8.
[15] Ibid., p. 139 and see Struve, 'S. Bulgakov et la question juive'.

symbiosis we may look for a new vision of Christ, and a recovery of the spiritual roots of Christianity.[16]

Struve and Sutton are quite right to stress that Bulgakov consistently denounces violence against the Jews; yet this final section of his essay must be regarded as profoundly troubling, written as it was in the early 1940s. It is true that few as yet knew fully about the death camps and the dimensions of the 'final solution'; we cannot read Bulgakov, or other theologians of that era, as if they are deliberately turning their backs on Auschwitz. Yet Bulgakov knew, at quite close quarters (through his involvement with the work of Mother Maria Skobtsova and her friends), something about Jewish refugees; and he cannot have been ignorant of the horrors of the thirties, from Kristallnacht onwards. His 1942 essay on the persecution of the Jews ('Goneniya na Izrail'', 'The Persecutions of Israel') is certainly full of anguish over the facts of persecution (which is clearly characterised as a persecution of Christ himself); yet it is curiously abstract in its analysis and conclusions. We find once again the comparison of Christian pogroms against the Jews with Jewish hostility or violence against Christians; the assertion of the necessary mutual involvement of the destinies of Judaism and Christianity; and, very insistently stated, the idea of the cross of Jesus as a definitive moment in the history of the Jewish people, a division of Israel into faithful and unfaithful halves. The sufferings predicted by Christ for Israel will therefore, for some, be a punishment for infidelity, and for others an opportunity to fulfil the perfect destiny of God's people, which is conformity to the cross itself and incorporation into its saving efficacy.[17] Symbolically speaking – and here Bulgakov picks up an image developed in a sermon for the Feast of the Dormition in 1941 – the sufferings of Israel can be seen as the participation of the Mother of God in the cross of her Son.[18]

None of this does anything to allay the anxieties raised by the slightly earlier and longer essay on racism. The general picture is clear: the real identity of Israel is constituted by its relation to the Church; the resolution of its historical 'tragedy' lies in the

---

[16] Ibid., pp. 139–40
[17] Ibid., pp. 155–9.
[18] Ibid., p. 160; the sermon ('The Destiny of Israel as the Cross of the Mother of God') is on pp. 13–18.

acceptance of its history as a vocation defined in Christian terms; and, most problematic of all, the corruption of Israel by secularisation and assimilation is one of the most significant roots of the attack on the Church by totalitarian modernity. It is true that Bulgakov consistently supported the idea of an independent Jewish homeland[19] (though he did not think it a matter of practical politics); but the whole tenor of his thinking implies that Jewish *self*-definition is effectively impossible or at any rate illegitimate from the point of view of Christian theology. To support the existence of the Jewish state because it satisfies the requirements of theology in which the Jewish people must be preserved in their distinctiveness is not necessarily the kind of support that is most welcome to Jews (we might think here of the widespread phenomenon of Christian fundamentalist support for the state of Israel). And to describe the Jewish people – as Bulgakov regularly does – as the axis of human history is, from a Christian theologian, potentially a poisoned chalice. Bulgakov in this respect stands very close to the kind of theological analysis developed by Karl Barth (another staunch supporter of the state of Israel); and the questionable areas are remarkably similar. Katherine Sonderegger, in a very thoughtful and sympathetic study of Barth's attitude to Judaism, sums up the position elegantly: 'The solidarity between Christian and Jew that Barth so vigorously advocates is based upon the quiet assumption that Judaism does not exist'.[20] At best, Judaism exists, not as a system or practice in its own right, but as the visible form of disobedience to God, as a parody of what should be. In Barth's brilliant exposition, this cannot and must not ever lead to Christian enmity towards the Jews, or to any attempt to enact God's judgement upon them: God has taken their judgement and their punishment, as he has taken on *all* judgement and punishment, on the cross, where he overturns all the efforts of disobedience and displays his freedom to disregard human achievement and human failure alike.[21] Although this differs significantly from Bulgakov's vision of a Jewish vocation to

---

[19] See the brief article on 'Zion', ibid., pp. 7–12, first published in 1915; cf. Struve, 'S. Bulgakov et la question juive', p. 534.
[20] Katherine Sonderegger, *That Christ was Born a Jew: Karl Barth's 'Doctrine of Israel'* (State College, Pa., 1992), p. 142.
[21] Ibid., p. 173.

share in the work of the cross, a notion that Barth would have found utterly inadmissible, the point in both writers is that what Judaism is always *about* is Christianity. And Stephen Haynes, in a recent and very searching monograph, notes the effects of a situation in which Christians 'use Jews to think with' (to adapt a phrase sometimes used of male theorising about women): 'Jews' become a collective signifier for Christians of the purposes of God (conceived in relation to the way Christians construct the world), and the connection between this signifying, mythical entity, 'Jews' or 'Jewish history' (or Bulgakov's *yevreistvo*), is never properly explored. Christians end up never talking to or about actual Jews, about Jewish identity or Jewish history as experienced by Jews.[22] As a diagnosis of Bulgakov's method, this is all too accurate: his call to corporate Jewish penitence for the Bolshevist 'pogrom' against the Church, his exposition of the potential meaning of persecution, his consistent refusal to see or discuss the massive imbalances of power in European history that make any equivalence between anti-Semitic violence and Jewish hostility to the Church a fundamentally nonsensical claim – all these things 'work' theologically only by an unbroken disregard for the interiority of Jewish practice and sensibility. In the context of 1941 and 1942, they cannot but read as crassly insensitive.

The comparison with Barth is a reminder that the best minds of Christendom shared the same insensitivity (and to turn to the work of Simone Weil at exactly the same time is to invite embarrassments just as great). However, as Sonderegger and Haynes agree, it will not do simply to describe positions like this as 'anti-Semitic' in any straightforward sense, or to claim that such views are – as it were – Nazism by another name. There has never been a theological case made for genocide, despite the horrifying record of popular violence against Jews in medieval and early modern Europe (and in Russia at the turn of the century). The theological tradition has in general insisted that the Jews are preserved by God's providence, for a variety of reasons, not least as 'reluctant witnesses' to God, to borrow the subtitle of Haynes's book. How far one can say that such a

---

[22] Stephen R. Haynes, *Jews and the Christian Imagination. Reluctant Witnesses* (London, 1995) pp. 8–10 and *passim*.

theological history made the 'final solution' easier or more attractive for the Third Reich is hard to say, and it is mere sloganising to say that Christian theological claims are the cause of the Shoah. We need, as many writers in their field acknowledge, a better typology of anti-Judaism; and, as Sonderegger argues with admirable clarity, we need a way of articulating the fact that Jews and Christians *disagree* without claiming that one is a corrupt and illegitimate version of the other. If we cannot find such a language, we are left with 'pious sentimentality or dogmatic certainty'[23] – or, we might add, crippling theological embarrassment and shame among Christians, afraid to sustain certain theological claims for fear of being accused of 'supersessionism', the belief that Christian revelation 'fulfils' Jewish history. As Sonderegger says, the important thing is to recognise that Judaism and Christianity are now separate religions, *both* claiming legitimate descent from the religion of biblical Israel. This at least saves us from the implicit or explicit claim that Judaism has no post-biblical history, from the ignorant assimilation of contemporary Judaism to the polemical targets of the New Testament rhetoric, and from the unbroken reading of Jewish experience in exhaustively alien categories determined by Christian needs and interests.[24]

It is not as easy as Struve and Sutton believe to acquit Bulgakov of a share in Christian 'tone-deafness' to Jewish reality, and it does not greatly help to note that he is not alone in this (Struve's comparison[25] between Bulgakov and the French poet and essayist Léon Bloy, a vastly influential figure in the background of the Catholic intellectual renaissance in early twentieth-century France, is a most apt and very interesting one, but, if anything, intensifies unease). On the positive side, it is important that Bulgakov is wholly serious about the Jewishness of Christianity (and, of course, his use of Jewish mystical and esoteric tradition in some of his theologico-philosophical work is remarkable; the connections between sophiology and Jewish mysticism, in Soloviev as well as Bulgakov, would be worth

---

[23] Sonderegger, *That Christ was Born a Jew*, p. 178.
[24] Ibid., pp. 177–9.
[25] Struve, in the record of the discussion following his paper, 'S. Bulgakov et la question juive', p. 542.

detailed exploration[26]); and the longing for a symbiosis of the Russian and the Jewish genius, even if only on Russian Christian terms, at least leaves the door a little way open for a dialogue whose outcome is not completely determined. The doctrine of national identity and vocation is tantalising, not least in its evocation of the 'feminine', sophianic principle in national identity: identity is, crucially, receptivity as well as self-definition or self-assertion. And, while Russia is unambiguously presented as a favoured child in the family of nations, this is in virtue of its sufferings, not its achievements or successes. Russia is, we could say, quintessentially the sophianic nation in Bulgakov's vision – for good and ill. Russia is never likely to see itself as a 'messianic' people on the basis of its moral and political excellences, and its corporate life is characterised by a level of passivity and vulnerability to outside forces that make it a natural victim for aggressive ideologies and policies from beyond its frontiers – all of which echoes themes in Bulgakov's earliest essays. But this can be apprehended as a vocation: Russian vulnerability means that Russia needs always to search for the right 'partner' and Bulgakov's account of Jewish destiny is an attempt to construct the perfect complement for Russia in God's chosen people. Whatever we make of this, it is not crude national messianism, to the extent that it names what Bulgakov considers a unique level of national weakness in civil society and public morality. That this is so plainly allied with the imagery of Russia as archetypally feminine presents, of course, another problem about the moral tenor of his language; but that is a question requiring a fuller discussion than is possible here.

Bulgakov's discussion of the 'Jewish problem' (even that designation tells us so much about a writer) has to be reckoned one of the most ambiguous and unsatisfactory areas of his thinking. But, as we have noted, he is not alone in this among major religious writers of the century. His thinking here focuses quite acutely some of the major problems besetting Christian understanding of Judaism, culturally and religiously, problems that have only relatively recently begun to be addressed at all

---

[26] Sutton, in the review article referred to (above, n. 3), has some very valuable material about Soloviev's general attitude to Judaism. The relation of his sophiological scheme to Kabbalistic writings is acknowledged in his own writings and is noted by several commentators, but has yet to be explored in full detail.

with any theological sophistication. In two respects at least, though, Bulgakov has a distinctive importance. In the first place, quite pragmatically, he helps the Western reader to grasp some of the sources of the complex response of contemporary Russian Christians to Judaism and Jewishness. The widespread interpretation of the Russian Revolution as a triumph of secularised *yevreistvo*, an interpretation that can be found in much dissident literature of the late Soviet period,[27] may appear to the Western liberal mind as an absurd and offensive caricature; to say that it needs to be heard and understood is not to say that it is other than a caricature. But the perception represented by Bulgakov obliges us to think through some of the difficulties posed, in a period of rapid and violent social transition, by the tensions between a powerful and resourceful local culture and a particular kind of radical universalism of the kind that will inevitably be attractive to groups who are dispossessed or rendered powerless by such a culture. And this brings Bulgakov's second contribution into focus. His doctrine of the distinctiveness of national vocation as resting on the 'sophianic' action of God through the angels of the nations may seem fanciful; but what it achieves is a model of theological thinking about national identity that builds in relationality

---

[27] Mikhail Agurskii summarises trends in this direction during the early seventies in 'The Intensification of Neo-Nazi Dangers in the Soviet Union', published in a very useful collection of materials, *The Political, Social and Religious Thought of Russian 'Samizdat': An Anthology*, ed. M. Meerson-Aksenov and B. Shragin (Belmont, Mass., 1977), pp. 414–19. The piece that follows ('A Letter to Solzhenitsyn' under the name of 'Ivan Samolvin', pp. 420–37) illustrates with alarming clarity the survival of the attitudes echoed in Bulgakov in connection with Jewish responsibility for the atrocities of Soviet totalitarianism. But it should be noted that 'Samolvin' is hostile to the state of Israel and exempts the early Bolsheviks from the taint of Jewish dominance. The whole tone of this piece is, of course, immeasurably more strident and vulgar than anything in Bulgakov, and as Agurskii himself notes, it is full of wild falsifications of history. But Agurskii also acknowledges that the percentage of persons of Jewish origin in the Soviet security police was disproportionally large. When Bulgakov writes in a journal entry for 1922, at the time of his sojourn in the Crimea and just before his expulsion, about the persecutory arrogance of Jews in the wake of the October Revolution (*Khristianstvo i yevreiskii vopros*, p. 169), he is reflecting a situation acknowledged with regret by some Jewish writers; unsurprisingly, at this time and later, the revolutionary forces provided some Jewish activists with a means of settling bitter scores. Even here, though, Bulgakov moves at once to a discussion of the spiritual calling of Israel, which he distinguishes from 'international Jewry'.

between national groupings as a constitutive part of national identity itself. The association of national self-assertion with models of masculine dominance is worth reflecting on; so too is the association of *both* racist and internationalist ideologies with displaced messianism. There is no denying that there is a serious political and intellectual agenda here, whatever the eccentricities and moral shadows of its expression.

Figures in Russian History or Literature Referred to by Bulgakov

BAKUNIN, Mikhail (1814–1876): influential revolutionary anarchist, hostile to Marx, apologist for direct terrorist activism.

BELINSKY, Vissarion (1811–1848): socialist and materialist philosopher, much influenced by Saint-Simon and Feuerbach in the search for a secular revolutionary creed with the same fervour and absolutism as religious faith.

BLACK HUNDREDS: popular name for groups of extreme right-wing activists in the 1890s and afterwards, responsible for anti-Semitic outrages.

BUKHAREV, Aleksei (1822–1871): monastic theologian who abandoned religious life to marry and wrote extensively on the poverty and self-humiliation of Christ. Influential for theologians concerned to emphasise the *kenosis* (self-emptying) of the incarnation.

CHERNYSHEVSKY, Nikolai (1822–1889): priest's son and ex-seminarian, materialist and socialist, exiled in Siberia for a lengthy period. One of the foremost heroes of the radical intelligentsia.

DECEMBRISTS: activists (including aristocratic radicals) responsible for an attempted *coup d'état* against Tsar Nicholas I in December 1825; the abortive rising was suppressed with great severity and cruelty.

DOBROLYUBOV, Nikolai (1836–1861): radical intellectual, associate of Chernyshevsky, and, like him, a prominent 'secular saint' in revolutionary circles.

Figures in Russian History or Literature

DONSKOI, Dmitrii (d. 1389): Muscovite prince whose campaigns against the Tatar rulers of European Russia (culminating in victory at Kulikovo in 1380 against Khan Mamai) signalled the beginnings of independence for the Russian principalities. Close associate of St Sergii of Radonezh (d. 1392), the greatest monastic saint of the Russian Middle Ages.

GARSHIN, Vsevolod (1855–1888): well-known writer of short stories concerned with the fate of the Russian peasantry.

HERZEN, Aleksandr (1812–1870): revolutionary, of aristocratic background and cosmopolitan education; less committed to materialism than other radicals of the period, interested in traditional Russian rural communes as a pattern of 'socialist' organisation.

KALASHNIKOV, Ivan (1797–1863): author of various widely read stories of Russian rural life.

LEONTIEV, Konstantin (1831–1891): conservative apologist, influenced by the Slavophils; enthusiast for the idea of 'Holy Russia', patriarchal, Orthodox, agrarian and impervious to Western corruptions.

MIKHAILOVSKY, Nikolai (1843–1904): journalist eager to propagate Western scientific ideas, but also enthusiastic for the Russian peasant commune; influential among the *Narodniki*, 'Populists', who looked to peasant society for the social idea.

NEKRASOV, Nikolai (1821–1878): poet sympathetic to Populism, author of influential poems on the pathos of Russian peasant life, often with a religious undertone.

PUGACHEV, Emelian (d. 1775): leader of a violent and bloody Cossack revolt against Catherine the Great.

RAZIN, Stenka (d. 1672): Cossack revolutionary.

RYLEEV, Konstantin (1795–1826): poet and revolutionary, involved in the Decembrist rising.

USPENSKY, Gleb (1843–1902): writer and journalist, supporter of the Populist school.

ZAPOROZHIAN COSSACKS (fl. early seventeenth century): mercenaries and freebooters living on islands in the Dnieper in southern Russian, noted for their savagery.

Some Background Reading

Major Works by Bulgakov

Ot marksizma k idealizmu (*From Marxism to Idealism*), St Petersburg, 1903.
Dva grada (*Two Cities*), 2 vols., Moscow, 1911.
Filosofiya khozyaistva (*Philosophy of Economic Activity*), Moscow, 1912.
Svet nevechernii (*The Unfading Light*), Moscow, 1917.
Drug zhenikha (*The Friend of the Bridegroom*), Paris, 1927.
Kupina neopalimaya (*The Burning Bush*), Paris, 1927.
Lestvitsa Yakovlya (*Jacob's Ladder*), Paris, 1929.
Ikona i ikonopochitanie (*The Icon and its Veneration*), Paris, 1931.
Agnets Bozhii: O bogochelovechestve (*The Lamb of God: On the Divine Humanity*), Paris, 1933.
Uteshitel': O bogochelovechestve, Chast' II (*The Comforter: On the Divine Humanity, Part II*), Paris, 1936.
Nevesta agntsa: O bogochelovechestve, Chast' III (*The Bride of the Lamb: On the Divine Humanity, Part III*), Paris, 1945.
Filosofiya imeni (*Philosophy of the Name*), Paris, 1953.
Khristianstvo i yevreiskii vopros (*Christianity and the Jewish Problem*), Paris, 1991.

In English

The Orthodox Church, London, 1935; new edn., St Vladimir's Seminary Press, Crestwood, NY, 1988. Translation revised, with introduction by Thomas Hopko.
The Wisdom of God: A Brief Summary of Sophiology, London, 1937; republished as *Sophia, the Wisdom of God: An Outline of Sophiology*, Hudson, NY, 1993.

A Bulgakov Anthology, ed. James Pain and Nicolas Zernov, London, 1976.
Karl Marx as a Religious Type, introd. Donald Treadgold, Belmont, Mass., 1979.

STUDIES OF BULGAKOV

Catherine Evtuhov, *The Cross and the Sickle: Sergei Bulgakov and the Fate of Russian Religious Philosophy, 1890–1920*, Ithaca, NY and London, 1997.
Charles Graves, *The Holy Spirit in the Theology of Sergius Bulgakov* (published privately for the World Council of Churches), Geneva, 1972.
Boris Jakim (ed.), *Sergius Bulgakov: Apocatastasis and Transfiguration*, New Haven, 1995.
Aidan Nichols, *Light from the East*, London, 1995, ch. 4.
Lev Zander, *Bog i mir* (*God and the World*) 2 vols., Paris, 1948.

GENERAL BACKGROUND

F. C. Copleston, *Russian Religious Philosophy: Selected Aspects*, London, 1988.
G. V. Florovsky, *The Ways of Russian Theology*, vol. 1, Belmont, Mass., 1979, vol. 2, Vaduz, Liechtenstein, 1987.
Judith Deutsch Kornblatt and Richard F. Gustafson (eds.), *Russian Religious Thought*, Madison, Wisc., 1996.
N. O. Lossky, *History of Russian Philosophy*, London, 1952.
Vladimir Lossky, *The Mystical Theology of the Eastern Church*, London, 1957.
Avril Pyman, *A History of Russian Symbolism*, Cambridge, 1994.
Marc Raeff, *Russia Abroad: A Cultural History of the Russian Emigration, 1919–1939*, Oxford, 1990.
Christopher Read, *Religion, Revolution and the Russian Intelligentsia, 1900–1912*, London, 1979.
Jutta Scherrer, *Die Petersbürger Religiös-Philosophischen Vereinigungen*, Berlin, 1973.

BULGAKOV

Donald Treadgold, *Lenin and his Rivals: The Struggle for Russia's Future, 1898–1906*, London, 1955.
Anthony Ugolnik, *The Illuminating Icon*, Grand Rapids, Mich., 1989.
Nicolas Zernov, *The Russian Religious Renaissance of the Twentieth Century*, London, 1963.

The above is only a sketchy bibliography; the notes to the General Introduction offer fuller references for literature on Bulgakov.

Index

Adorno, Theodor 67
aesthetics 18, 33, 128–30, 139–40, 145, 153–9, 178, 224–6
anti-Semitism 1 n. 1, 2, 233 n. 12, 293–303
arts in Russia 2, 8 (*see also* aesthetics; Symbolism, Russian)
Athos, Mount 8–12

Bakhtin, Mikhail 57
Bakunin, Mikhail 88
Balthasar, Hans Urs von 14, 172 n. 32, 179
Barth, Karl 169, 179, 298–9
Belinsky, Vissarion 76, 78, 100
Berdyaev, Nikolai 13, 14, 17 n. 67, 23, 62–3, 66, 231
Böhme, Jacob 113, 200
Bonhoeffer, Dietrich 68
Buddhism 35–8, 46, 217
Bulgakov, Aleksandra (née Azbukina) 4
Bulgakov, Elena (née Tomakova) 13 n. 48
Bulgakov, Mikhail 3 n. 7
Bulgakov, Sergii
  early years 3–4
  studies 4–6
  political involvement 6–7, 56–61
  return to Church 6ff.
  ordination 13, 163–4, 176, 271
  exile 13, 164
  life in Paris 14, 165ff., 230–1
  ecumenical activities 269 n. 1
  illness and death 271–2

Carlyle, Thomas 6 n. 22, 55, n. 4, 239, 275
Chernyshevsky, Nikolai 52, 74, 104
Chesterton, G. K. 58

Christian Brotherhood of Struggle 7, 56–8
Christology 171–2, 177, 205–8, 214, 260, 280, 281, 285–6
creation, doctrine of 137–40, 168–71, 183–227 *passim*, 279–80

Dobrolyubov, Nikolai 52, 74
Dostoyevsky, Fyodor 7 n. 25, 23, 52, 66, 72, 73, 77, 90, 94, 104, 105, 111, 128, 155, 161, 174, 179, 245
Duma, Second Russian 58–60, 63, 66, 70, 74

economics 4–6, 7, 23–53 *passim*, 57, 79, 120–4, 126–7, 128–30, 149–53, 160, 177–8, 240–3, 246, 274
Engels, Friedrich 56
Enlightenment 63–4, 71, 76, 79–81, 84, 92, 106

fall, doctrine of 213–27
Florensky, Pavel 7, 10, 17 n. 67, 19 n. 71, 56, 113 n. 1, 117–20, 121, 122, 124, 125–6, 127, 163, 165
Florovsky, Georges 14, 65 n. 33, 113 n. 1, 125 n. 51, 165, 173, 175, 179, 180, 269 n. 1
Frank, Semyon 14, 62 n. 27, 117 n. 11
Fyodorov, Nikolai xi, 126, 127 n. 57, 161, 242, 244, 245–6, 270, 282, 283–5

Georgievsky, Metropolitan Evlogii 172, 175, 230
Goethe 32
Gregory Palamas (Saint), Palamism 8, 11, 19 n. 71, 125, 165

309

Index

Habermas, Jürgen 67
Harnack, Adolf von 55
Hegel 19, 32, 41, 118, 121, 127, 143, 145, 169, 178, 179, 184, 200, 247, 249
Holy Spirit, doctrine of 25 n. 6, 136, 145, 177, 194, 195–6, 207–8, 221, 225, 252, 265, 271, 281–2, 285, 286, 288–92

Imyaslavtsy ('name worshippers') 9–13
intelligentsia, Russian 55–112 *passim*

Kadet (Constitutional Democratic) Party 7, 58, 62, 67, 85
Kant 121, 122, 125, 129, 188
kenosis (self-emptying) 16, 61, 177, 193–6, 200, 211, 216
Khomyakov, Aleksei 51, 174, 284
Khrapovitsky, Metropolitan Antonii 9–10
Kierkegaard 68, 180

Lenin 5, 6, 13, 58, n. 14, 61, 64, n. 31, 65, 67
Lossky, Vladimir 14, 18, 172, 174, 175, 176–80

MacKinnon, Donald 14
Marx, Marxism ix, 4–7, 15, 23–6, 29, 55 n. 4, 59, 61, 62, 63, 67, 101, 103, 121, 123, 127, 129, 150, 151, 164, 234, 235, 239, 240, 241, 242, 244–5, 248, 249, 265, 276, 294, 295, 296
Maximus, Saint 125
Men', Aleksandr 19
Morris, William 58

Nietzsche, Nietzscheanism 34, 62
Nicholas II, Tsar 60–1

Orthodox Action 230–1

Picasso 120
Plato, Platonism 134, 138–9, 144–5, 192, 212, 279
Plekhanov, G. V. 5–6

Plotinus 35, 128 n. 60, 146
Pobedonostsev, Konstantin 2 n. 2, 57, n. 10
Pushkin 52, 91, 94, 104, 249

Reformation 78–80, 108, 255
Ruskin, John 6 n. 22, 46, 55 n. 4

sacraments, doctrine of 142, 156–7
Schelling 121, 184
Schopenhauer 32, 38, 184, 217
Sergiev, Ioann 10
Skobtsova, Mother Maria 230–1, 236, 297
Slavophils 51, 69, 161, 176, 179, 284
socialism ix, 7, 17 n. 68, 23, 30, 56, 58, 79, 82, 85, 86, 90, 131 n. 69, 229–67 *passim*, 283
Soloviev, Vladimir xi, 7, 23, 34, 45, 52, 56, 77, 105, 114–17, 120, 121, 122, 123 n. 41, 126, 155, 161, 164, 174, 245, 284, 300
Sombart Werner 26, 31–5, 39, 46, 48, 51, 52
Sophia, sophiology 17 n. 69, 113–61, *passim*, 165–81, 183–227, *passim*, 279–81
Stragorodsky, Metropolitan Sergii 172–4
Struve, Pyotr 6, 58 n. 14, 62, 164, 165
Symbolism, Russian 12–13, 117, (*see also* aesthetics; arts in Russia)

Tolstoy, Lev 7 n. 25, 10 n. 39, 25, 29, 38, 50, 52, 77, 92, 161, 245, 275
Trinity, doctrine of 133–5, 146, 166–7, 168, 183, 187, 193, 194–6, 208, 211, 212, 279
Troeltsch, Ernst 55, 179
Trubetskoy, Evgenii 9–10, 56, 58–9, 117 n. 11
Trubetskoy, Sergei 58, n. 17, 77, 117 n. 11

Union for Christian Politics 58
Union of Liberation 7

Vekhi (*Landmarks*) 61–8 *passim*, 235